BEGINNINGS

Beginnings

Louis I. Kahn's Philosophy of Architecture

ALEXANDRA TYNG

A WILEY-INTERSCIENCE PUBLICATION
John Wiley & Sons
NEW YORK / CHICHESTER
BRISBANE / TORONTO / SINGAPORE

Library of Congress Cataloging in Publication Data

Tyng, Alexandra, 1954–
   Beginnings: Louis I. Kahn's philosophy of
architecture.

   "A Wiley-Interscience publication."
   Bibliography: p.
   Includes index.
   1. Kahn, Louis I., 1901–1974. 2. Architecture—
Philosophy. I. Title.
NA737.K32T96 1983   720′.92′4   83-6799
ISBN 0-471-86586-9

Printed in the United States of America

10 9 8 7 6 5 4 3 2 1

to my family

"You're not a philosopher by having read philosophy, not at all. I think you are a philosopher because you are just naturally one."

PREFACE

I can't remember my father without white hair. The image of Louis Kahn as a wise old man has become so strongly etched into my mind that sometimes I have difficulty imagining him as young and inexperienced, with most of his dreams and ambitions unfulfilled, lacking the mystique that enveloped him in later years. Hearing stories about him in his youth, looking through family photographs, and reading his old letters to my mother piqued my curiosity over the young Lou Kahn and the beginnings of his ideas that were to become so central to his life's work. Talking with my Kahn relatives produced more stories and many new insights that filled out my picture of my father as a total person. In this book I attempt to show how Kahn's potential was already present in the serious philosophical child and how later, his major ideas developed over a period of more than three productive decades.

The desire to write about my father's philosophy of architecture came over me several months after his death. For years I had half listened to him mull over his ideas in his office or at the dinner table, but I had paid little attention to what I considered to be his boring monologues. When I left home for college, and then especially after he died, I felt a need to know him as more than just a parent. In the fall of 1974, I decided to write my undergraduate thesis on his philosophy of architecture, and, despite the difficulty I had in forcing his flowing ideas into a strict academic format, I am glad now that my thesis provided an excellent excuse to devote months to exhaustive research that otherwise would never have been completed. As I probed more deeply into the material, I was amazed at the similarity of his thought processes to my own. Instinctively, I had always sensed that similarity existed, but for the first time, I had concrete proof. So in the process of writing the original version of this manuscript, not only did I learn about my father as a person, but I also learned more about myself at a crucial point in my identity-seeking process.

Discovering Lou Kahn's philosophy was also a way of making up for the gaps in communication that existed between us while he was alive. I saw my father less frequently than most children see their parents, yet when we did meet, a deep understanding passed between us. Perhaps our holistic way of thinking made ordinary conversation awkward. How could we exchange pleasantries when we were preoccupied with cosmic thoughts? I found it hard to confide in my father when I could tell by his expression that he read my emotions intuitively. Likewise, he seemed awed by the fact that my small person contained such great intensity of spirit. So while he was alive, we never managed to develop a relaxed relationship. Learning about his ideas brought him closer to me, and I felt for the first time that we were freely communicating about the things that most fascinated us.

When I began my project, I intended to concentrate purely on Kahn's philosophy and ignore his architecture, about which so much had already been said. But I quickly found that such a separation would have been artificial and, in fact, impossible. His theories and his buildings are unquestionably interdependent. Ideas led to designs, which led to new ideas, and thus developed a mutually influential relationship that lasted throughout his career. In this book, I have chosen to concentrate on those buildings that I believe represent key stages in the dialogue between ideas and architecture; however, I have by no means included all of Kahn's important designs. As I have said, my main purpose is to present a thorough developmental picture of his thought processes.

After much consideration, I decided the best way to examine my father's ideas would be to divide them into three major areas or themes. These themes are, in the order of their discussion: form, order, and design; city planning and urban renewal; and silence and light. While I realize that such a division is artificial, since Kahn's ideas are unavoidably interwoven, I felt that any in-depth exploration into his thoughts necessitated some rudimentary grouping, and so I have devoted a chapter to each of the three major concepts. At the ends of Chapters 2, 3, and 4 are collections of Kahn's speeches and writings on these three areas, arranged in chronological order so that the development of a particular theme can be easily traced from its source to its full maturity. Many of the quotations are excerpts of longer pieces covering much broader territory, and in this sense, my method of presentation falls short of providing an accurate picture of the fluidity of Kahn's thinking. My intent, however, is to provide a basis on which Kahn's words can be reread and perceived anew in their entirety.

Louis Kahn's philosophy seems complex and often confusing because it was not created for others' benefit, but for his own. It was his way of articulating his experience of the creative process. As his realizations reached an increasingly archetypal level, his language became more metaphoric and poetic—and even less easy to understand. Many of his admirers, usually young architects or students, have consciously or unconsciously tried to imitate him by speaking in an obscure, mysterious way. I cringe with embarrassment whenever I hear this happen. Kahn never tried to be obscure. He had a strong desire to simplify his language. But since he was doing this primarily for himself, the words often came out in a way that was hard to follow. When his admirers tried to converse with him in pseudo-Kahn language, he could sense the attempt at imitation almost before it began. He played along, though, by becoming exaggeratedly thoughtful and taking longer than ever to come out with exactly the right word, while his eyes twinkled impishly. Humor notwithstanding, he was also seriously engaged in the conversation. Kahn hated pretension and related to everyone with equal sincerity.

I believe, as I know he did, that everyone should be encouraged to develop his own way of thinking. Imitation is at best only an excellent copy. Imitators can easily come away with no better understanding of the original, unless they eventually go beyond it by creating their own original works. By demystifying Louis Kahn's ideas without destroying their poetic quality, I hope to provide a starting point for those who are brave enough to think for themselves.

Philadelphia
September 1983

Alexandra Tyng

ACKNOWLEDGMENTS

There are many people whose contributions have been essential to the writing of this book, but first I must thank Dr. Neil Levine, my thesis advisor at Harvard-Radcliffe University, who helped me with this project long before it became a book and without whom it might never have come about.

Special thanks go to my mother, Anne G. Tyng, for her constructive criticism and infinite patience and for sharing her storehouse of knowledge; Harriet Pattison, for reading over the rough drafts and filling in missing links of information; my brother, Nathaniel, for letting me use his terrific ideas; my sister, Sue, for supporting me in this undertaking; and Steven Kantor, for his proofreading and constant encouragement.

I would also like to acknowledge the contributions of other family members, and of Esther I. Kahn and Norman Rice, whose photographs, anecdotes, and other information helped me make this book as accurate as possible.

Lisa Sorensen and Dean G. Holmes Perkins, at the Louis I. Kahn Collection at the University of Pennsylvania, and Marshall Meyers, John Ebstel, George Pohl, Roy Vollmer, Nancy Crampton, and many others made it possible for me to include so many excellent photographs and drawings. I apologize to those photographers whose work I could not acknowledge because I was unable to trace it to the correct sources.

Funding for travel and my own photographs was provided by the Graham Foundation.

Kahn's words, quoted at the front of the book, were excerpted with permission from an interview with Patricia McLaughlin that appeared in the December, 1972, issue of *The Pennsylvania Gazette*, alumni magazine of the University of Pennsylvania. Copyright © 1972 by *The Pennsylvania Gazette*.

A.T.

CONTENTS

1
FOUNDATIONS

One learns constantly from the surrounding world, but the basis of one's inspiration comes from within.

The mental processes that characterize an individual, whether formed by heredity or environment or both, are evident from earliest childhood. In Louis Kahn, an introverted, philosophical nature, combined with deep convictions and an unusual degree of artistic talent, developed into a singularity of purpose. Through his architecture, he strove for the ideals he expressed in words.

Kahn, the eldest of three children, was born in 1901[1] to Jewish parents of mixed Slavic, German, Scandinavian, and Persian blood. The family immigrated to Philadelphia from the Baltic island of Ösel (now Saaremaa) a few years after his birth. Leopold, his father, had been a soldier in the Russian army when he met his future wife, Bertha Mendelsohn. In civilian life, Leopold was a copyist and a stained glass craftsman,[2] an extremely gifted man who nevertheless found no steady employment. "When he could work, there was a strike; and when the strike was over, he was sick," remembers Rosella Sherman, who lived for several years with the Kahn family after her marriage to Louis Kahn's brother. Leopold lived until 90, but his early years were difficult. After immigrating to the United States, he took a construction job, a humiliating situation for a man who took pride in his craft and would have been respected had it not been for the language barrier and his immigrant status. Soon he devel-

oped a chest problem that was mistakenly diagnosed as tuberculosis. At age 38, he was suspected of having a heart attack, but it is possible that Leopold's complaints were psychosomatic. During the years in Philadelphia, he tried several unsuccessful ventures, including running a candy store. Finally, he found some measure of satisfaction drawing patterns for stencils in a lace-making factory, but the company for which he worked was beset by strikes. Bertha, Louis's mother, kept elements of European culture alive in the home by reading Goethe and singing Schubert songs. She was an accomplished harpist but was forced by circumstances to work as a seamstress in a sweatshop to provide a regular family income. In spite of her unusual role as breadwinner, there was no antagonism between husband and wife. In fact, their marriage was exceptionally strong.

Louis Kahn was not the only one of the three children to inherit both artistic and musical talent from his parents. All three siblings taught themselves to play piano by ear because they could not afford music lessons. His sister, Sara, painted as a hobby. His brother, Oscar, whom Kahn claimed was much more gifted than he, was also the more outgoing and handsome of the two brothers. Oscar married early and became a businessman to support his own family, yet he maintained his involvement with art and music—drawing, writing songs, playing several instruments. Later in life, he went into the advertising business and introduced California radio listeners to the musical commercial jingle.

1

Leopold Kahn as a young man. (*left*)

Bertha Mendelsohn, at the time of her engagement to Leopold Kahn. (*Right*)

Louis Kahn, aged four, with sister, Sara.

Sara (*left*), Oscar, and Louis Kahn, c. 1908.

Even after Kahn chose his career, music and art remained side by side in importance to him, as was later expressed in his philosophy. When Kahn was in his teens, he earned much needed money by playing piano in a silent-movie house. During intermission, while the reels were being changed, he projected onto the screen slides of his own cartoon drawings, marked with captions telling the audience to "wait one minute, please." Later, the movie house installed an organ, and Kahn asked a local musician to teach him the basics of that instrument in a single afternoon so he could retain his job. The only thing missing from this quick lesson was how to regulate the volume. When the proprietor of the theater said, "That's fine, Lou, but it's too loud," Kahn thereafter played without pedals. This suited him fine because he had not quite mastered them, anyway. In this fashion, he supported himself through architectural school.

His parents provided the remaining support, both emotional and financial. Their energies focused on their eldest child, at some sacrifice to themselves and the rest of the family. For Kahn's sister, the sacrifice was willingly made. Because there was no question in her mind that her brother was a genius who would go far in the world, she gave up without a second thought any chances she might have had for a higher education and worked as a seamstress like her mother to supplement the family earnings. Oscar Kahn, however, was often resentful of the attention lavished on his older brother. Perhaps he felt that, if slightly more attention had been given to him, he would have developed a greater sense of purpose and direction at a younger age. Louis Kahn, on the other hand, envied Oscar for his good looks, social ease, and the casual confidence with which he mimicked such actors as Charlie Chaplin and mastered a variety of musical instruments. But the jealousy and rivalry between the brothers did not constitute a major part of their relationship, and the family remained a close, affectionate group.

Kahn's father wanted him to become an artist, but his mother had visions of his becoming a great musician. Kahn always felt emotionally closer to his mother. She was the one who prayed for his recovery after his face and hands were badly burned in a childhood accident. His father thought Kahn would be better off dead than disfigured, but she insisted that he would live and become a great man some day. Perhaps it was a mixture of her constant emotional support and her intuitive sense of her son's potential that saw Kahn through difficult times in his childhood and student years.

A tendency toward introspection was always a strong part of Kahn's personality, a trait that his parents fortunately did not try to discourage. In school his classmates called him "Scarface" because of his burns, making him self-conscious and socially withdrawn. His thought processes were profound and slow, and he did not respond well to teachers who demanded quick answers. At that time much of the material was learned by rote. Such subjects as arithmetic frustrated and alienated Kahn, who could not understand why 2 × 2 was not 2 if 1 × 1 was 1, because the *concept* of multiplication was never explained to him. However, a few understanding teachers called on him to explain how something was made or how it worked, and in this Kahn excelled. He also excelled in drawing. In retrospect, he believed that he got through school because of his drawing ability.

Kahn attended the Fleischer School of Art, a free institution for the children of Philadelphia. At age 12, he was encouraged by Fleischer's director to hold an informal drawing class at the zoo,

Leopold Kahn.

where he taught people older than he how to sketch animals. During his school years, he painted signs for grocery stores, earning a reputation as the neighborhood artist. The fluid, living quality of his line, which seemed to imbue inanimate objects with life, was apparent even then.

When he was a boy, Kahn loved to test his physical prowess, a habit that was influenced by his father, who could crack nuts and break apples in half with his bare hands. Near the three-story walk-up where he lived in Philadelphia, there was a narrow alleyway. Kahn used to jump across it from curb to curb without touching the street. One day he tried it with a bag full of groceries. He missed the opposite curb, slipped, and knocked himself unconscious. When he came to, he could not see. Frightened, he sat on the curb with his head in his hands, thinking about what he would do with his life. He had always wanted to be an artist when he grew up, but now he would have to face the fact that he was blind. So he decided to be a musician instead. Fortunately, for him and for the future of architecture, he regained his sight a few minutes later.

Kahn's parents shared a deep sense of spirituality in their love for each other, and this was communicated to their three children. During a time when Jewish immigrants were unerringly Orthodox, Kahn's parents cared more about inner religious beliefs than about the observance of the outer rituals of Judaism. Rather than keep kosher as did the rest of the Jewish community, they strove to live everyday life according to their ideals of human relationships. Their philosophy of life was so basic, so direct, it could not have failed to have been accepted without rebellion by their children. Kahn's nephew, Alan Kahn, reflects that in Kahn's philosophy he hears echoes of Kahn's parents' values rather than evidence of some mysterious mystical bent. Kahn's thoughts on realization, natural law, and the spirit in architecture are not the results of a formal religious training. On the contrary, they are indications of his profound grasp of religious experience.

A sense of humor and fun pervaded the Kahn household, softening the intensity of spirit that was passed from Leopold and Bertha Kahn to their children. The Kahn sense of humor can be described as a gentle self-mockery, a voice that says, "See, I'm fallible," almost managing to hide a penetrating inner light that belies mockery. It is exemplified by a joke that Leopold Kahn's father liked to tell on himself: While walking up a staircase in a public hall in Philadelphia, he encountered another man who was also just arriving on the landing, from a facing flight of stairs. Kahn's grandfather bowed and indicated with his hand that the distinguished gentleman should precede him up the next flight. At the same time, the stranger bowed to allow Kahn's grandfather to go first. Several times, the men bowed at each other simultaneously, until finally Kahn's grandfather realized he was seeing his own reflection in a full-length mirror. This comical sense of one's own fallibility was an integral part of Kahn's attitude. When he spoke, it appeared both in his anecdotes and in his moments of profound thought. By constantly reflecting on his self-image and on the image he projected to others, Kahn refrained from taking himself too seriously. Because his philosophy was not steeped in self-importance, it was able to extend beyond the personal realm to touch others.

Kahn's personality comprised elements of both his parents' natures. His father was a proud man with a volatile "artistic" temperament. Once he presented a finished stained glass window to a client. When the client voiced his suspicion that it was merely painted, Leopold Kahn broke the window in a fury to show him the glass was colored all the way through.

Leopold and Bertha Kahn in front of their Los Angeles home, c. 1938.

Louis and Leopold Kahn at the Museum of Modern Art, 1961.

"Don't you think it can be done, and very easy too, if you will send us tickets, but not by train by having such a distinguished son like Lou so by train won't be good enough, we must travel by air. Well by joking won't help us to fulfill our desire. So I'll close my letter with the heartiest gratitude and wishing you health & happiness." (*Reproduced, by permission, from a letter to Anne G. Tyng.*)

Kahn's mother was said to have been descended from the humanistic Jewish philosopher Moses Mendelssohn.[3] Of her parents, her mother was the more practical and outspoken; she occasionally acted as an unofficial representative for the Jewish community in settling disputes with the local government.[4] Bertha's father was more mystical in his orientation, and he had access to a family healing secret that he passed on to Bertha. (On her deathbed, Bertha, who considered herself unworthy of using the secret, intended to pass it on to her son Louis, but she died before Kahn could reach her.) Bertha Kahn was considered a "wise woman." People brought her their problems because of her nonjudgmental attitude and her calm acceptance of life's changes.

Both of Kahn's parents had an indefinable aura of specialness about them that caused friends and neighbors to gravitate toward them. Kahn inherited his grandmother's instinctual sense of justice and his mother's compassionate intuitive perception of human nature. From his father, Kahn received a stubborn pride and a loyalty to his belief system. Kahn's beliefs were based on feeling. He accepted others' differences and yet remained true to his own ideals. He commanded respect because, not only did he develop consistent principles, he also tried constantly to live and work by them.

Louis Kahn's philosophy of architecture was a direct outgrowth of his philosophy of life. His descriptions of the psyche, of wonder, of silence and light, when taken out of the context of architecture, become descriptions of his own existence. "Life to me is existence with a psyche; and death is existence without the psyche,"[5] Kahn said, and because the psyche to him was a prevalent soul that transcended the individuality of each human being, he was justified in searching within himself for principles common to all people, principles that could be expressed through architecture. By following the train of thought that eventually led him to the concept of silence and light, Kahn attempted to describe the origins of his own creativity. What he saw as the meeting point of the desire and the means to express represents his subjective understanding of inspiration, but it also applies to human creativity in general.

In Kahn's words, the creative person is

motivated by the sense that he has something in there, whether it is deep, deep in the silence, or whether it is already on the threshold of inspiration. . . . And he gets it also from another, beautiful source, and that is through the experience or the Odyssey of a life that goes through

the circumstances of living and what falls as important are not the dates or what happened, but in what way he discovered man through the circumstance.[6]

In a manner similar to that which he described, Kahn himself drew his inspiration from both internal and external sources. His philosophy is the combination of a quality deep within him and the moderating and articulating effects of life's experiences.

Contemporary discoveries are the tools, not the essence, of expression. Although individuals are always products of their time, they are victims of their time only to the extent that they let themselves fall into conventionality. Kahn's Beaux-Arts schooling and the International Style both had a deep effect on him, but only in that they either brought out, suppressed, or reshaped what was inherent in him. The ideas that were to spring from Kahn's personal form of creativity were not compatible with the architectural milieu that he entered after completing his training. Therefore, he had to wait until later in his life, when a more receptive climate encouraged him to voice his ideas.

The Ecole des Beaux-Arts was at its height in the last half of the nineteenth century, when it attracted such American architects as H. H. Richardson and Charles McKim. Beaux-Arts theory was steeped in the nineteenth-century conception of classical tradition: those qualities that had proved themselves consistent in architecture through the ages, overlayed with the rich and exuberant forms of Second Empire eclecticism. Into this setting fit Julien Guadet, professor of theory at the French Ecole. In the summary of his lectures, published in 1899 as the *Elements et Theorie de l'Architecture,* he insisted on the importance of composition in architecture but showed a complete lack of interest in style. "It was under his professorship that the Beaux-Arts training became almost completely focused on the elaboration of multi-axially symmetrical plan patterns of abstract, but unfunctional elegance."[7] *Plan, arrangement, composition, symmetry*—these words all evoke rigidity. The architect was given a predetermined vocabulary, one that had been tried and proven with time. Because it encouraged nothing new, it isolated itself from the architectural trends that marked the turn of the century.

In the fall of 1920, Kahn entered the University of Pennsylvania, the most successful Beaux-Arts institution in the United States. As a freshman, he was not entirely without a background in architecture, having already received an overview of architectural history from William F.

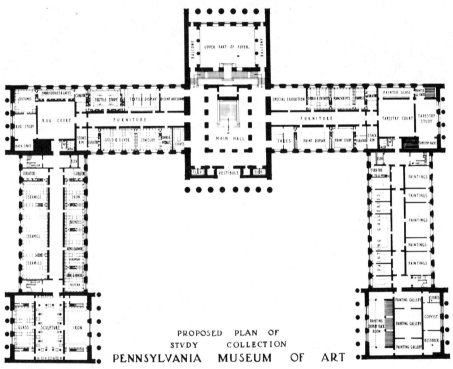

PROPOSED PLAN OF
STVDY COLLECTION
PENNSYLVANIA MUSEUM OF ART

The Philadelphia Museum of Art, a familiar example of Beaux-Arts symmetry.
Paul P. Cret helped design the Benjamin Franklin Parkway, in foreground.
(*Above*). East Side from Parkway and 23rd St. Philadelphia Museum of Art: Philadelphia Museum of Art.   (*Below*). Proposed plan of 1st floor, Study Collection, Philadelphia Museum of Art: Philadelphia Museum of Art.

Gray. Gray had been the architectural critic for the Philadelphia *Bulletin* before coming to teach at Central High School, where Kahn was a student. He strove to make his course interesting as well as informative, showing slides and requiring his pupils to make drawings of selected buildings every month. Kahn, who was proficient at drawing, made extra cash in an unorthodox way: He charged other less talented students a small sum for doing their drawings for them. To disguise his hand, he made mistakes and occasional blots. Gray, of course, saw through Kahn's scheme, but he good naturedly and wisely permitted him to continue "helping" other students as long as they did most of the drawing themselves. Gray's high school course was Kahn's favorite, and it

Portrait of Paul P. Cret by Carlo Ciampaglio. (*Reproduced by permission of the University of Pennsylvania.*)

Kahn's college yearbook picture, 1924.

sparked an interest that influenced him to change his career objective from painting to architecture.

In his first year at the University of Pennsylvania, Kahn was taught design by John Harbeson. Harbeson, later a partner in the firm Harbeson Hough Livingston and Larson, then practiced architecture with Paul P. Cret, who was also a professor at Penn. Both Harbeson and Cret had studied at the French Ecole des Beaux-Arts. According to Norman Rice, a long-time friend of Kahn who was a member of the same class at Penn, Harbeson was an excellent first-year teacher because he made his objective clear and gave constructive and helpful criticisms. Harbeson taught by his belief that an architect should be trained in the elements of design—the window, the door, the arch, the portico—before moving on to larger-scale projects. The first project that year was to design a garden niche![8]

In Kahn's senior year, his professor was Paul Cret, a neoclassicist who designed with an understanding of form that surpassed the merely correct use of classical vocabulary. Cret published an essay called "Modern Architecture" in

1923, in which he laid out his principles. Most striking was Cret's sense of the continuity of architecture. He believed that there were certain principles inherent in architecture that remained constant through its history, and he considered the permanence of ancient monuments praiseworthy. Speaking out against the popular criticism of the neoclassical style—that it lacked originality—he pointed out that all new forms were not copied from earlier ones but rather were inspired by their predecessors. Cret believed in what he called the "legacy of the past," that a seeming stylistic revolution was, in retrospect, only a slight change from what preceded it. Cret also adopted his views on design from the French Ecole. He described the architect's "program of construction" as the arrangement of the facilities at hand to meet the specific demands, conditions, and practical purposes of each building. He was speaking not of creating forms per se, because, to him, the elements with which the architect worked were preexistent.[9]

The relationship between Cret and Kahn was a positive one for both teacher and student. It was clear to Cret that Kahn, like other students with

ability, was benefiting by the studio experience, and Cret, in turn, was stimulated by his student's rapid absorption of what he had to teach. If Cret saw any special abilities in Kahn, he never acknowledged his recognition openly or showed any favoritism. Cret was the student advisor of the Architectural Society at Penn, a socially prestigious organization made up of the student crème de la crème. In 1924, even though Jews, like blacks, Italians, and other minorities were not fully accepted by the social establishment, Kahn was admitted into the society. Perhaps Cret had a hand in this decision because he saw some special potential in Kahn; perhaps not.[10] In fact, Kahn was not considered the most outstanding student. Although he worked hard, certain others consistently outshone him, a situation that caused him much frustration. At graduation he received the bronze Brooke Medal for distinguished architectural design; the gold and silver were awarded to others, as were the more prestigious prizes and fellowships.

Under Cret's instruction, Kahn absorbed attitudes toward architecture that he incorporated in his best work many years later. However, the Beaux-Arts school during the 1920s was far removed from the forefront of architectural thought. The first projects Kahn completed after

Three Penn graduates: (*above*), Louis Kahn, Herman Cunin, and Norman Rice. (*below*) (*Copyright Norman N. Rice.*)

Sketch by Kahn for the Philadelphia Sesquicentennial Exhibition, 1926, "pure Beaux-Arts Baroque." (*Reproduced from* **American Architect** *GXXX, 1926.*)

graduating from the University of Pennsylvania in 1924 show that he had adopted all the trappings of the traditional architecture of the time, as well as the more profound teachings of Paul Cret. Kahn's design for the Philadelphia Sesquicentennial Exhibition of 1926 was described by Vincent Scully as being "pure Beaux-Arts Baroque."[11] Yet in 1928, only two years later, Kahn met his future partner, Oskar Stonorov, who helped make him aware of the accomplishments of the Bauhaus school and its offshoots. In the same year, Kahn traveled to Europe, where he visited Norman Rice, who was then studying with Le Corbusier, the first American to do so. Kahn's exposure to the Modern Movement was a sudden awakening.

Two figures had headed the break from the art nouveau at the turn of the century: Tony Garnier and Auguste Perret. Both had been pupils of Guadet at the Ecole des Beaux-Arts, which was becoming quickly obsolete in France. Their architecture was aimed against academicism. Garnier wrote that "ancient architecture is an error. Truth alone is beautiful."[12] In search of this truth, buildings were rebelliously stripped of their surface ornament. This negative movement grew within a decade to a more positive ideological expression. After 1910, the work of Walter Gropius, Mies van der Rohe, and Le Corbusier began attracting attention. Gropius's Fagus Factory (1910–1914) utilizes the structural potential of industrially produced materials. Transparent volume is dominant over solid mass: Great sheets of window stand out from the narrow sup-

Kahn with family members and friend, c. 1929.

ports so that they are flush with the outermost wall plane. The absence of corner piers further denies the building's solidity. Le Corbusier produced similar effects in his projects for the Citrohan house from 1919 to 1922. In his second version, he elaborated on the mass-denying illusion by raising the house on stilts.

In the 1920s, the Modern Movement gained impetus through its association with the Bauhaus. This avant-garde school generated the belief that the twentieth century was characterized by technology and that the artist should apply himself to the improvement of the technological society. Beauty for its own sake was scorned. The word *functionalism* was coined to express the advocation of "the design of buildings . . . as direct fulfillments of material requirements."[13] This concept quickly gave rise to the popular assertion: "Form follows function." However, Gropius and his followers derived their particular type of aesthetic expression from just this rejection of the striving after beauty. Gropius's design for the Bauhaus headquarters in 1925–1926 includes a fully developed curtain wall. The glass skyscraper had already been introduced by Mies in 1920–1921 and again in 1922. These architects, along with Le Corbusier in his own way, emphasized that a building's surface was merely a thin membrane surrounding a volume. Inside, too, the traditional concept of the centralized plan divided into separate rooms had given way to a series of floating juxtaposed planes that stylistically resembled the contemporary work of Piet Mondrian. In general, space had become thin, fluid, uncaptured by nonexistent mass. Architects no longer built with permanence in mind, because they were adverse to any implications of tradition. The International Style, as it was called, was the negation of the solid, classical basis of the Beaux-Arts. It brought about a much needed revolution.

Walter Gropius and Adolf Meyer, *Fagus Factory.* 1910–14. Alfred, Germany. The great sheets of window and absence of corner piers deny the building's solidity. (*Collection, The Museum of Modern Art, New York.*)

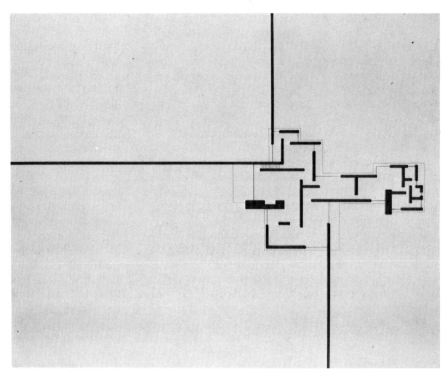

Ludwig Mies van der Rohe. *Brick Country House.* Project, 1923. Plan. Studio drawing, 1964. Ink on illustration board, 30 × 40″. The series of floating juxtaposed planes stylistically resembles the work of Piet Mondrian. (*Collection, The Museum of Modern Art, New York. Gift of Ludwig Mies van der Rohe.*)

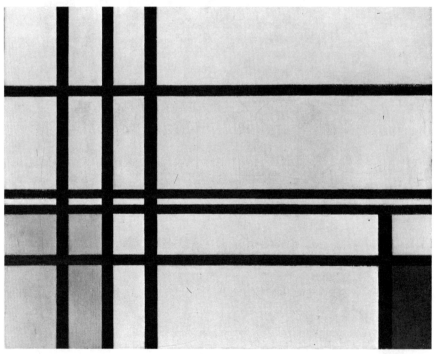

Piet Mondrian. **Opposition of Lines: Red and Yellow,** 1937. (*52-61-90 Philadelphia Museum of Art: A. E. Gallatin Collection.*)

At the end of the 1920s, while Kahn was becoming aware of Le Corbusier and his contemporaries, the International Style reached America with the works of Howe and Lescaze in Philadelphia and Neutra in California. In 1931, Kahn met George Howe, who was then in the process of designing the Philadelphia Savings Fund Society Building. Not only did Kahn respect Howe's professional achievements, but being of immigrant stock, he also envied Howe's blue-blooded American roots and corresponding worldliness and elegance. Howe responded with genuine warmth for the talented young architect. Kahn enjoyed telling the story of the time when he and Howe were riding in an elevator together. Kahn admired Howe's tie, and Howe took it off and gave it to him. The friendship that formed between the two men was one of the few truly equal exchanges that Kahn had with other people in his field; it led to a productive partnership in architectural ventures.

The Modern Movement was canonized in 1932 by an exhibit at the Museum of Modern Art in New York entitled "The International Style." Shortly thereafter, this style became truly universal. By the time Gropius and Mies settled in America in the late 1930s, Le Corbusier's work was achieving an international reputation. Kahn could not help but be drawn in by the pure force and enthusiasm of the movement. During these depression years, he worked for the Public Works Administration. In his capacity there, he was exposed to the living conditions of Philadelphia's poor—an abject poverty completely different from the kind he had known as a child. In 1932 he joined the Architectural Research Group, which gave him the opportunity to talk with other architects. Although the sociopolitical ideas they shared did not reach the center of Kahn's being, these verbal exchanges were jumping-off points for Kahn, who was experimenting for the first time with an architectural ideology and its relationship to the practical problems of the city. With Howe and Stonorov, he produced several projects in the 1940s for the Philadelphia Housing Authority. One of these was Carver Court, which contains dwelling units raised one story from the ground on parallel open walls that recall the pillars under Le Corbusier's high-rise towers and small-scale domestic architecture.

The International Style was Kahn's awakening. It freed him from the academic tradition that had dominated his training and earliest career. Through it, he became exposed to the new structural possibilities suggested by twentieth-century industrially produced materials.

For all his enthusiasm, however, Kahn had his moment of self-doubt. His designs of the 1930s

Howe and Lescaze. *Philadelphia Savings Fund Society Building.* Philadelphia, Pennsylvania, 1932. Kahn developed a friendship and professional partnership with George Howe during the designing of this building. (*Courtesy, the Museum of Modern Art, New York.*)

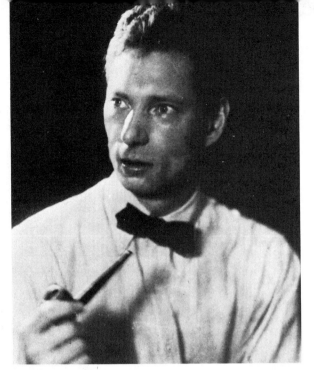

and 1940s certainly were not representative of his full potential, as was later to be proven. Such projects as Carver Court demonstrate his sensitivity to materials, but they lack distinction. Perhaps even more revealing, Kahn developed no characteristic philosophy during this period, though architects with pioneering ideologies, such as Gropius and Le Corbusier, had already set much admired examples. Kahn's essay "Monumentality," published in 1944, is typical of his thoughts of that decade. It alludes to ideas that later unfolded into his principles of form and commonality, but his language is stiff and halting in its attempt to stay within accepted bounds. The seeds of his originality were there, but they had not yet germinated. A major part of Kahn's potential, then, remained stubbornly undeveloped. Some factor in the contemporary climate that was not conducive to his expression led Kahn to suppress an important and profound aspect of his nature.

Louis Kahn, c. 1934. (*Photograph by Bachrach Studios.*)

Carver Court Housing Development, Coatesville, Pennsylvania. Houses are raised from the ground on parallel walls. The areas underneath are used as carports. (*Photograph by Gottscho-Schleisner. Reproduced from the Library of Congress.*)

(*Below left*). Kahn in his late thirties, c. 1939.

(*Below right*). Kahn at his office in the Bulletin Building in Philadelphia, while in partnership with Oskar Stonorov, c. 1946.

Kahn's first independent office was a single room at 1728 Spruce Street, Philadelphia, c. 1948. Half the room was occupied by engineers.

By 1950 the International Style in the United States was beginning to be conventional and denatured, as it had already become in Europe. The new inclination was toward the humanizing of the mechanistic approach. The later work of Le Corbusier led this change. As early as the 1930s, his architecture had begun to show sculptural tendencies. By 1950, with his design for the church at Ronchamp, he was expressing himself in a new way, creating solid forms with fluid contours, shaping an almost organic structure. Kahn, since his trip to Europe in 1928, had been a faithful admirer of Le Corbusier, but he did not read any of his books until 1947 or 1950.[14] In 1964 he expressed his feeling that this man, "even in the light of his marvelous revelation in architecture, is just beginning to create his greatest work."[15] Kahn went on to imagine a building Le Corbusier might make, describing it in terms of the castle and the Greek temple—historical references that would have been foreign to the Bauhaus mentality of the 1920s. The fact was that Kahn felt an admiration for the Modern Movement, but not an affinity. In 1950 the thought of the time was just beginning to move with him.

The growing appreciation of plasticity and three-dimensionality coincided with a reevaluation of Beaux-Arts theory. In 1952 Talbot Hamlin of the School of Architecture at Columbia University published his *Forms and Functions of Twentieth Century Architecture,* an attempt to rewrite Guadet's *Elements et Theorie de l'Architecture* in a

way that would be relevant to the architecture of his own time. The importance of Hamlin's work is confirmed by the reaction it produced. It was reviewed by Colin Rowe in the June 1953 issue of *Art Bulletin,* and in 1960 Reyner Banham included a complete reappraisal of the Beaux-Arts tradition as the basis of modern architecture in his *Theory and Design in the First Machine Age.* Hamlin searched into the underlying principles of Beaux-Arts theory, which had been disguised to a certain extent by nineteenth-century academicism. He cited three factors, originally named by Vitruvius in the first century BC, that he felt should be present simultaneously in the architect's mind during the process of design. The first was feasibility, or "*commodité,*" the consideration of the functional purposes of the building. The second factor was permanence. According to Hamlin, a true construction was not only one that stood up solidly for the duration for which it was designed but also one that gave a sense of its solidity. This idea was in direct opposition to the International Style notion of the temporary building that denied its mass. Hamlin cited beauty as the third requirement; great architecture had to have a coherent and meaningful pattern of forms that rendered it pleasing to the eye. He proposed that the abundance of surface ornamentation and "applied" style of the nineteenth century

caused the extreme reaction towards rationalism which characterized the birth of the so-called International Style . . . they have not denied the fact of architectural beauty, but they have considered it to be merely the by-product of good functional and structural design; they have claimed that a conscious search for beauty, by directing the architect's attention to "non-essentials," can lead only to sentimental or untrue design.[16]

Although Hamlin was protesting the International Style viewpoint per se, his conception of beauty as a quality inherent in the structure would have been impossible without functionalism.

The significant thing about Hamlin's theory is its remarkable similarity to the philosophy that Kahn was very soon to develop. Kahn was consistently striving toward beauty. Moreover, a synthesis of Beaux-Arts and functionalism is revealed in his belief that "joint-making is the beginning of ornament."[17] Just as Hamlin stated that beauty, as a visual experience, caused the building to transcend its function, Kahn said in 1969 that the "new architecture" was beyond functionalism because it was concerned with the psychological effect of the space. He also believed that the measurable design process in the end produced the unmeasurable[18] work of art. Hamlin's three factors of design, of which beauty was one, were to be conceived of simultaneously by the architect; similarly, Kahn maintained that the creative mind could not accept the separation of the various considerations of the design process.

The parallel does not end here, however. What is most abstract in Kahn's writing is also found in Hamlin's book. Hamlin, in line with his Beaux-Arts predecessors, described the plan of a building as an assemblage of rooms and spaces. These were available to the architect as is "alphabet," which he arranged in a meaningful pattern. In this context, he compared architecture to a musical composition. Beginning in 1960 and continuing until his death, Kahn made nearly identical comparisons between the plan and the sheet of music: "The architect fleetingly reads his composition as a structure of elements and spaces in their light," while "the musician reads, with the same overallness, his composition as a structure of inseparable elements and spaces in sound."[19]

Both Hamlin and Kahn distinguished between the plan's individual elements in much the same way. Hamlin divided building spaces into five types of "use elements." These included rooms for public use, rooms for private use, service areas, areas for mechanical equipment, and passages for horizontal and vertical circulation. The efficiency of the building, he stated, was dependent upon the proper organization of these pre-

determined elements. Clearly, he was acknowledging the need for separate rooms for the mechanics of the building, just as Kahn was to do within a few years by distinguishing the servant spaces from the spaces they serve. Unlike Kahn, Hamlin did not view the plan in terms of light. However, he did relate light to structure insofar as he believed that the exterior of a building was determined by variations of plane, color, and light: "Each one of these variations is due to the effects of light on the building materials employed, which have been placed in a designed relationship to fulfill certain purposes integral with the purposes of the building."[20] Hamlin's statement is similar to Kahn's observation of sunlight striking a wall, which figured in his concern for the wall's texture and articulation.

It must be kept in mind that, when Hamlin's work was published in 1952, Kahn had barely begun to develop either a philosophy or a distinctive style. What, then, does this parallel between his ideas and the Beaux-Arts reevaluation in the 1950s mean? Whether or not Kahn actually read Hamlin is irrelevant; the parallel is best explained by assuming that Kahn had absorbed the more profound aspects of his training that had lain dormant since his exposure to the International Style. His work during the 1930s and 1940s gives no positive evidence of this underlying current; it merely shows that he could not live up to his creative potential within the avant-garde mode of design. But the Modern Movement had had a cathartic effect on Kahn. It gave him a bold new medium with which to express his deeper-lying principles.

The 1950s were very important in establishing the direction of Kahn's subsequent thought. Because the mechanistic approach that characterized the International Style was being replaced by new, more humanistic ideologies, Kahn was no longer forced to design against his nature. He was beginning to open up, to discover other theorists who awakened aspects of his creativity of which he had not been aware. This decade, then, was a period of taking in and absorbing a great deal of material that would serve as inspiration. In 1948 Kahn became professor of architecture at Yale University. In 1947 he had opened an independent practice, and his office was receiving few commissions. Because he was both lecturing and relatively idle from the actual practice of architecture, Kahn was forced to give voice to his thoughts. Products of this introspective period were, at first, isolated fragments of ideas that appeared spontaneously between 1951 and 1953, when his Yale Art Gallery design was under construction.

Kahn in Rittenhouse Square, Philadelphia, c. 1952.

who advanced the Theory that there is a psychic order as well as a physical order. . . . The opposite end of the poles of Affective and Intellective is art and science. Somewhere in the middle lodges religion and philosophy. All these facets of our behavior or conduct are natural and inevitable and the cross insemination of these manifestations of the nature is what makes man a complex individual.[22]

That Kahn was directly influenced by this idea is evident in his later diagrams, in which he grouped religion with feeling and philosophy with thinking, and distinguished between physical and psychic order. In fact, Kunst's separation of affective and intellective was what prompted Kahn to distinguish between the measurable and unmeasurable, a distinction that was the basis of his view of creativity. It was unquestionably sources like these to which Kahn was referring when he wrote in 1954: "I must not forget . . . that the training I had in other relative fields made it possible to emerge from a thoroughly misguided start to one of a relatively realistic direction."[23] By this time Kahn was past 50, and understandably, he felt that he had had a late start in architecture.

When Kahn made the above acknowledgment, he was probably unaware of the extent to which his Beaux-Arts training had made an impression on him. Through Kahn's association with the International Style, the more profound implications of Beaux-Arts theory had been freed in his mind from their academic connotations. Kahn began to reveal, in his most expressive writings and in his best work, how he adapted this early influence to fit a context that was purely his own. His projects always started with rigid axial symmetry and gradually developed toward a sensitivity balanced asymmetry—but never to the intentionally picturesque haphazardness that characterizes Gropius's Bauhaus building. Kahn often developed his design from an original vision of rooms arranged around a central core, as exemplified by the First Unitarian Church in Rochester, New York; the Erdman Hall Dormito-

Many of these early ideas were reactions to the strict International Style ideology. The concept of thought and feeling, for example, began as a protest against the objective attitude toward design that so many of the architects of the time still advocated. Kahn himself was highly intuitive and feeling oriented, yet the influence of rational thinkers whom he knew and respected made him want to balance and enrich his own subjective thought. "Just think," he wrote in 1954, "if each doctor practiced his own way without regard for scientific understanding not as a hindrance but as the means of releasing the creative level possible in our time."[21]

In the same year, Kahn described his enthusiastic response to a lecturer, Kunst,

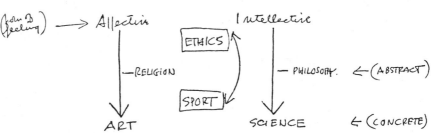
Kahn's impression of Kunst's theory, 1954. (*Reproduced by permission from Louis I. Kahn, Letter to Anne G. Tyng, April 25, 1954.*)

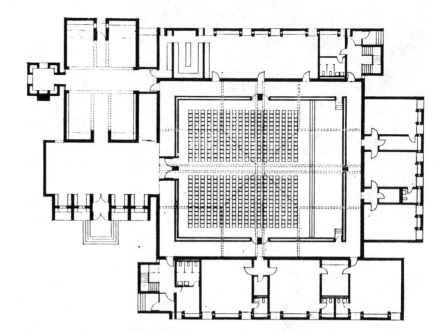

The floor plan for the First Unitarian Church, Rochester, New York, shows how the rooms are arranged around a central core.

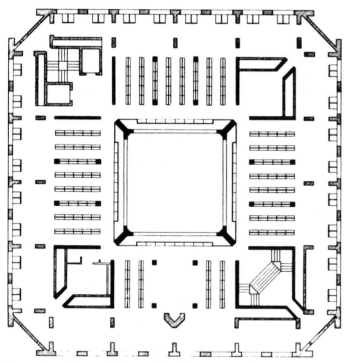

Floor plan of second floor of the library at Phillips Exeter Academy, Exeter, New Hampshire. As in the First Unitarian Church, the rooms are arranged around a central core. (*Copyright The Louis I. Kahn Collection, University of Pennsylvania and the Pennsylvania Historical and Museum Commission.*)

ries at Bryn Mawr College in Pennsylvania; and the library at Philips Exeter Academy in New Hampshire. The Choisyan belief that materials should be used as their properties indicate, revived by Frank Lloyd Wright earlier in the century, was made magical by Kahn, who spoke reverently of the "existence wills" of brick and concrete. Perhaps most significant, the Beaux-Arts vision of history as a whole helped articulate Kahn's feeling for the continuity of architecture, the validity of its present and future in terms of its past. But Kahn looked at the beginning in order to reevaluate the present. He believed that works of art created in the spirit of the first institutions transcended their useful functions, as do the greatest ruins.

Thus, two major currents, the Beaux-Arts and the Modern Movement, affected Kahn's early development. In the 1950s, he began to resolve these currents in his philosophy and, more slowly, in his architecture. Kahn at this time was receptive to influences from a wide variety of sources. A profusion of ideas was forming in his mind with great energy and force. After 1960 this large-scale receptivity tapered off and Kahn's philosophy became, if not closed to influence, remarkably self-contained. The energy remained, but it flowed from an inner source. Because it was more focused, it penetrated deeper into areas of central concern.

Kahn discovered theories that were in many respects parallel to his own, but only after drawing his own conclusions. Such was the case with the philosophy of Carl Jung, whose theory of the collective unconscious resembles Kahn's description of the psyche and whose archetypes of anima and animus are remarkably like Kahn's counterparts of creativity, silence and light. Kahn resisted psychology for many years because his nature rebelled against Freud's negativity and the behaviorists' objectification of the human mind. He mentally grouped Jungian thought with these unsympathetic philosophies without realizing the extent of its differences. Kahn finally became drawn to the Jungian approach to the human psyche because its acknowledgment of spirituality was unlike the attitudes of the psychologies he had known. In 1961 he read Jung's autobiography, *Memories, Dreams, Reflections,* and since the early 1960s, he owned *Man and His Symbols,* which he skimmed periodically. But by this time, he had already thought through his own definitions of the psyche and the tangible and intangible aspects of creativity.

Seeing the castles of Scotland was an experience that penetrated Kahn's philosophy only after he had discovered the parallel between fortress architecture and his own. Kahn had not fully recognized how the hollow walls of the castle contained rooms and stairways when he formulated the concept of servant and served spaces and when he designed the First Unitarian Church in Rochester, which has peripheral rooms opening off a central meeting space. While visiting Edinburgh in 1962, he was given a book on Scottish castles written by Stewart Cruden. At this time, he was at work on the Bryn Mawr dormitories. At first Kahn had been hesitant to enclose the major interior spaces on all four sides, but his visits to Scottish castles showed him that rooms at the core of the building could be made livable.[24] Kahn's description of the castle in various stages of its existence from conception to ruin prefigures his concept of silence and light.

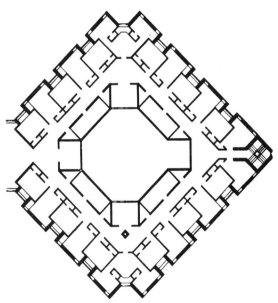

Portion of plan for Erdman Hall Dormitories, Bryn Mawr, Pennsylvania. The designs of Scottish castles showed Kahn that he could enclose the major interior spaces on all four sides and still make the rooms at the core of the building livable.

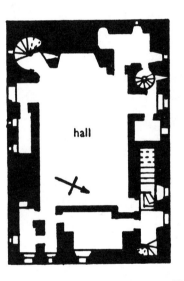

First floor plan of Elphinstone Tower, East Lothian, Scotland—a fifteenth-century castle. (*Reproduced, by permission, from Stewart Cruden,* **The Scottish Castle,** *Spurbooks, a division of Holmes McDougall Ltd., Edinburgh, 1962.*)

Other influences were not so direct, so traceable. On his trips to Europe, Kahn was fascinated by Hadrian's Villa, Italian hill towns such as San Gimignano and Siena, and the medieval walled city of Carcassonne. He felt a solidarity, a rightness about these places that led him to explore and sketch them. But he was annoyed by conjectures that the Salk Institute for Biological Studies in La Jolla, California, was directly influenced by Hadrian's Villa or that the towers of the Richards

Carcassonne was *not* the prototype for Kahn's urban renewal
proposal for Center City Philadelphia . . . And the pyramids
did not inspire the Yale Art
Gallery space frames!

Kahn and Tyng in discussion
with client at Weiss house site,
Norristown, Pennsylvania, c.
1949. (*Morton Weiss.*)

Medical Research Building at the University of
Pennsylvania were inspired by the towers of San
Gimignano. When the similarities were pointed
out to him, he was struck by them, but the idea
of direct influences was to him ridiculous. He
told the story of how, when one architectural
historian traced one of Kahn's buildings directly
to its ancient "prototype," another well-known
historian responded, "Why don't you ask Lou
Kahn—he's still alive and kicking!" To Kahn, his
favorite European architecture was symbolic of
certain qualities that he tried to evoke in his own
architecture.

The influence of Kahn's personal relationships
on his work was an important one that has so far
been ignored. Kahn's wife, Esther (Israeli), did
not contribute directly to the development of his
philosophy, but the values she and her family
represented to him were manifested in his work.
Esther Kahn's parents, unlike his, were not recent immigrants; they had received higher formal
educations and permitted only English to be spoken in their home. Kahn had been influenced by
his mother's faith in the United States as a country of unlimited possibilities, and he conceived a
deep admiration for the American way of life. To
him, his wife's family was fully American; what
they had intrinsically, he felt he had to acquire.
His involvement with city planning and redevelopment was based on a respect for American
ideals that came from having adopted the culture
rather than taking it for granted.

Kahn's relationship with his wife also led to a
crucial first step toward self-confidence. He was
married when he was 29, and although he had
exhibited his European sketches and was employed as a designer in Paul Cret's office, from a
personal standpoint, he was still very self-conscious about his scarred face. He always wore a
soft Italian hat pulled low over his ears, but on
the day of his marriage, he declared he would
never wear a hat again and threw it away. It is
doubtful that Kahn could have achieved the confidence that allowed him to project his ideas
compellingly and with humor if his personal
attributes had not been affirmed early in his career.

In 1945 Kahn developed a close personal and
working partnership with Anne G. Tyng. During
a time when Kahn was still unsure about expressing himself in words and in his architecture, Tyng recognized his creative potential. Not
only did she validate for him the originality of
his ideas, but she also encouraged him to set
down these ideas in tangible form. If during the
depression he had been known as a thinker
rather than a doer, now in these years of association with Tyng, he began to earn a reputation for
his accomplishments. He conceived the notion
that an idea was not an idea unless it worked.
His growing confidence was a major factor in his
subsequent break with Oskar Stonorov and his
formation of an independent practice in 1947.
Kahn worked in association with Tyng on the
projects that established a mature foundation for
his later work: urban renewal schemes for Center
City Philadelphia, Northeast Philadelphia, and
Mill Creek; the city tower project; numerous private homes; the Trenton Bath House; and the

Yale Art Gallery. The intense exchange of ideas between Kahn and Tyng tapered off around 1959 during the designing of the Bryn Mawr dormitories, when Tyng began forging her own creative direction; however, their working partnership, their friendship, and their mutual respect continued until Kahn's death.

Kahn's relationship with Harriet Pattison was a different kind of partnership. In 1959 Kahn and Pattison discovered a profound mental affinity, and although Pattison did not attempt to generate a cohesive philosophy the way Kahn did, she provided an intelligent and sympathetic response to his ideas. Pattison became informally involved in those projects that were under way in 1959—the U.S. Consulate in Luanda, Portuguese Angola; the Bryn Mawr dormitories; and the Salk Institute—contributing not from the point of view of architectural expertise but from an instinctive understanding of Kahn's direction. In a way, her lack of awareness of what was technically possible released Kahn to imagine things that were unimaginable. After Pattison received her degree in landscape architecture in 1967, her contribution to Kahn's work became more tangible, beginning with her design for the site and external features of the Kimbell Museum in Fort Worth, Texas (1966–1972). Her ability to understand and react to Kahn's thought and work continued to be a valuable part of his life.

In his relationships, Kahn sought an active, intelligent response rather than slavish devotion. Although he was an extremely private man who was discrete about his personal life, he did not, contrary to popular opinion, separate his relationships from his work. In his long-term intimate associations, Kahn's ideal was emotional and intellectual companionship.

At different points in his career, Kahn conceived an admiration for the work of other architects and people in the related fields of art and design. When Kahn's philosophy was first unfolding, and even before it began to take shape, these influential people included Le Corbusier, George Howe, and Anne Tyng, for her original use of geometry. In the early 1950s, Kahn became interested in the explorations of R. Buckminster Fuller while both men were teaching at Yale, and several years later he was impressed with Robert Le Ricolais's topology lectures. The friendship that developed between Kahn and Le Ricolais was valuable to Kahn because it was, like his friendship with George Howe, an exchange between men who had an equal amount to give to each other.

Later in his life, Kahn greatly admired the Mexican architect Luis Barragan, though he saw Bar-

ragan only two or three times. During the construction of the Salk Institute, Barragan was called in to advise him on how to treat the space between the two laboratory buildings; Kahn was delighted by and slightly envious of Barragan's suggestion that the space be left as a plaza, a "facade to the sky." In the late 1960s, Kahn visited Barragan in his house. His descriptions of the interior and gardens echo some of the strong magic that overpowered Kahn on his visit. His discussion with Barragan on tradition intensified the numinous quality of Kahn's experience there and prompted his thoughts on the "golden dust" of circumstance, which he incorporated into his already unfolding theory of silence and light.

An unusual figure in Kahn's life was Gabor, who styled himself as an architectural visionary and teacher. A tall, gaunt man who dressed in formal but slightly threadbare clothes, Gabor was rumored to have left Hungary during a revolution, but the details of his professional background were unknown to those who knew him at the University of Pennsylvania. Gabor was often seen in Kahn's masters studio and at students' juries, where he enjoyed philosophizing about specific projects and especially about architecture in general. Frequently, he would appear at Kahn's office late at night to discuss ideas that had just come to him, and Kahn would talk with him until two or three in the morning. Gabor's poetic and mysterious aura and his use of words as images were stimulating to Kahn's own way of thinking. Even if Gabor's train of thought seemed erroneous, it would inspire Kahn to think of the right word or expression. During one late night conversation, for instance, Gabor asked Kahn, "Is the interior of the column hope?" Kahn, feeling it was not hope, thought for a while before he decided that the interior of the column was "inspiration."

Kahn's ideas were not influenced by friends and associates in related fields only. His collaboration with Dr. Jonas Salk, for example, led to a sophisticated and joyous architectural expression, while confirming in Kahn's mind the belief that the scientist and the artist sought the same goals, although they did so by the methods appropriate to their separate disciplines. Kahn's interest in the wonder and mystery implicit in scientific discovery harked back to his schooldays, when he became fascinated by physics and only wished his teacher would ask him to *draw* physics instead of requiring him to sit through the traditional exam on the subject. Years later, Kahn was frequently found poring over his wife's physics books.[25]

In illustrating the theory of silence and light, Kahn used the example of the scientist and the

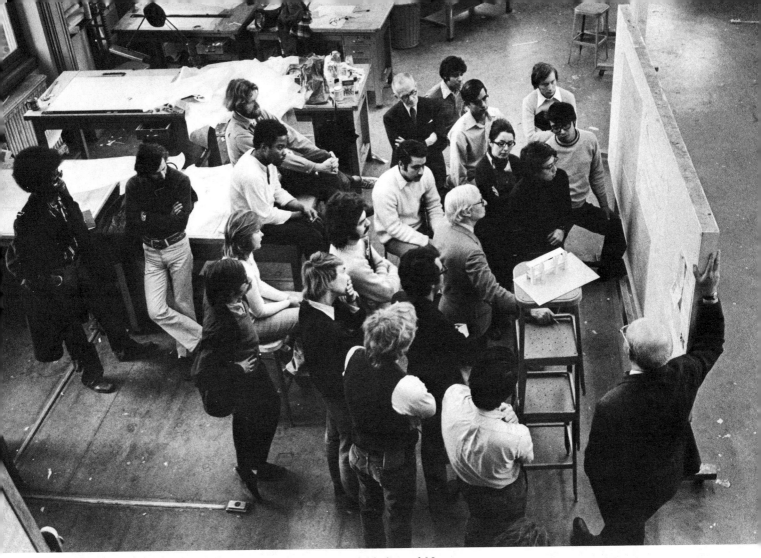

Louis Kahn, Robert Le Ricolais (behind Kahn, with arms folded), and Norman Rice (right foreground, hand on board) at masters studio jury, University of Pennsylvania. (© 1972 Nancy Crampton.)

poet traveling their different paths toward inspiration, and his description reflects his personal friendship with Salk, his conversations with other scientists during the design of the Salk laboratories, and his admiration for Albert Einstein, whom he considered to be more a poet than a scientist. Kahn had an insatiable desire to understand intuitively the workings of the universe, and his later writings and speeches indicate that he perceived a parallel between the creative processes within the mind and the physical structure of space.

The self-contained and yet all-encompassing nature of Kahn's thought processes was evident in the way he reacted to what he read in books. Some people absorb information like sponges and can expound on the theories of others with great facility and objectivity. Kahn, on the other

hand, was like a semipermeable membrane, absorbing selectively and rejecting the rest. For example, he used the concept of silence in Malraux's terms—or rather his interpretation of them:

By silence I don't mean quiet—but in the sense that Malraux calls his book "Silence" . . . he means only the feeling you get when you pass the pyramids, you feel that they want to tell you. . . . Not *how* they were made, but what made them *be*, which means what was the force that caused them to be made. . . . These are the voices of silence.[26]

Another example of Kahn's method of reading is his reaction to a poem by Wallace Stevens. Kahn was struck by a particular line, which he paraphrased as "What slice of the sun does your building have?" because to him it expressed the

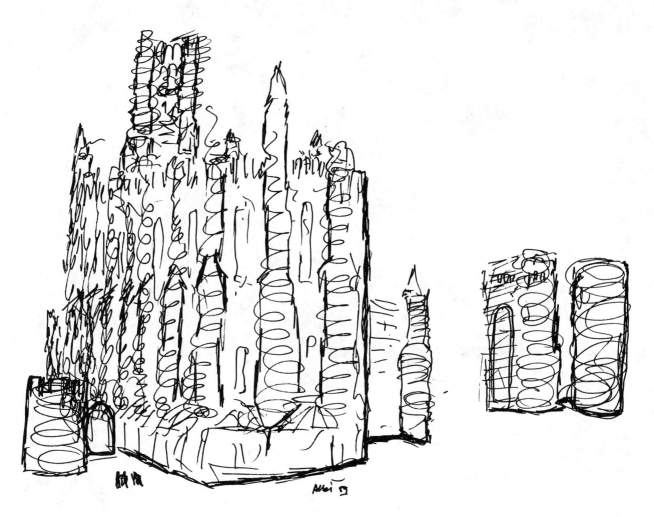

Kahn's sketch of St.-Cecile
Cathedral, Albi, France, 1959.

Kahn's sketch of Piazza del
Campo, Siena, Italy.

Kahn's sketch of the Acropolis, Athens, Greece.

way in which the structure of a room is defined by the light entering it. The image that Stevens's work inspired was much more important to him than the poet's actual intent. Kahn often admitted that if he were asked what a book were about, his explanation would not sound anything like the intended meaning of the book. Reading was a slow, laborious process for Kahn, and yet books were of such value to him that he could rarely pass a bookstore without buying one. He was possessive of them and kept his favorite volumes in his office, where he could open them whenever he liked. Kahn frequently studied the plans and drawings of ancient buildings and of the work of such modern architects as Le Corbusier, as well as drawings by Piranesi, Gustav Doré, and Cruikshank. Kahn treasured his books as sources of inspiration. When digesting information from the printed page, he distilled qualities he perceived in others' images for his own personal use and enlightenment.

Lecturing, teaching, writing, and talking with students and colleagues were his ways of articulating ideas as they formed. Much of his philosophy was speculation. He discussed what he was still searching for, what he had not yet explored thoroughly. A certain way of expressing a concept would catch his attention, and he would incorporate it into his own way of thinking. His need for a verbal understanding of architecture led him to add to his repertoire of expressions words that formed the basis for themes.[27] *Form, order, silence, light,* the *measurable* and the *unmeasurable, presence* and *existence,* the *psyche, commonality*—these all began as isolated words around which Kahn built his interrelated ideas.

Kahn used words that reflected the images he saw with great intensity in his mind. In his speeches and writings, he tried to impart something of his visions to others by using these words in a simple but unusual way that gave them special emphasis. The images Kahn symbolized with words were indicative of his sense of the archetypal quality of architecture. For this reason, he centered his vivid and unique observations around the great buildings in history. During his European travels of 1928, 1951, and 1959, he produced sketches of the Acropolis, Paestum, Carcassonne, and other monumental sites. His pen lines, which are simultaneously bold and sensitive, pick out the abstract form in a few well-chosen strokes. His color is sometimes so intense it becomes a distortion of nature. Both line and color speak of the visionary and personal quality of Kahn's experiences. The affinity Kahn felt for these buildings could not have been imbued in him by his Beaux-Arts training alone; it was a natural affinity. Throughout his writings are references to the Parthenon and the Pantheon, to the Greek column as a realization in light, and to the silence of the pyramids—indications of how indelibly the impression of his travels remained with him. When Kahn described these mental images, it was always with special words that he invented or pulled from his repertoire. Descriptions were thereby created from words that expressed the vivid nature of the pictures in Kahn's mind.

The tightly knit character of Kahn's thought is emphasized by the way in which he rejected concepts that superficially appeared to resemble his own ideas. The New Brutalism was such an ideology, generated in the 1950s by Alison and Peter Smithson. These two English architects believed "that the building should be an immediately apprehensible visual entity."[28] Buildings in this style exhibit their basic structures with a frankness approaching the primitive. Many critics saw in Kahn's Yale Art Gallery features that were reminiscent of the New Brutalism: uncompromising honesty in the use of materials, and the boldly exhibited space frame. However, a basic difference between the New Brutalism and Kahn's work is in the treatment of services. In the Smithsons' projects, "water and electricity do not come out of unexplained holes in the wall, but are delivered to the point of use by *visible pipes* and *manifest conduits*."[29] This treatment is contrary to Kahn's, because Kahn never let the servant space invade the served space. His reaction to the comparison was abrupt:

I do not like ducts; I do not like pipes. I hate them really thoroughly, but because I hate them so thoroughly, I feel that they have to be given their place. If I just hated them and took no care, I think they would invade the building and completely destroy it. I want to correct any notion you may have that I am in love with that kind of thing.[30]

The post-1960 influences gave breadth to Kahn's philosophy but did not change its orientation and inevitable direction. Even his Beaux-Arts training was not a source of Kahn's viewpoint toward architecture; rather it was what first appealed profoundly to tendencies in his own personality. In a 1972 interview, Kahn said that he was always conscious of thinking in the way he described as having "images in my mind, not fully examples either, not part of my experience, just a sense," and that his thinking about architectural spaces came out of this manner of thinking that was there from the beginning, not vice versa. Kahn went on to say, "I cannot absorb what is not part of me."[31] Kahn was describing the way he understood himself to be influenced by his environment. He learned only what was already potentially there, but in doing so enlarged himself and his realm of expression.

The things Kahn has said have been said before by others. As Kahn himself pointed out many times, although the way in which each individual expresses himself belongs to him, the expression per se wells up from universal urges somewhere deep within. But there is something so original about Kahn's way of expressing ideas—the result of his almost complete shunning of prescribed knowledge—which gives one's familiar surroundings, experiences, and emotions an aura as luminous as a freshly washed world after a storm. The joy of his discovery is contagious.

2
FORM, ORDER, DESIGN: THE INSPIRATION PROCESS

THEORY

How does a building come to be? How does the architect get in touch with his ideas and translate them from head to paper to the actual building?

Kahn first began to reflect on his own creative process in the late 1940s and early 1950s. His reaction against the International Style's dry, analytical approach to architecture prompted him to say that feeling was a more important process than thinking in the design of buildings. In making this statement, Kahn brought into the open his natural preference for feeling, which he had suppressed in his career up to that point. He ceased to follow the contemporary dictum and began forging a new way of approaching design, changing the direction of architecture in the process.

By *feeling*, Kahn meant the instinctual, intangible side of his mental processes. His writings are filled with the words *I sense*. Feeling is the way in which an idea comes to a person out of the blue; it is suddenly there, but its origin is inexpressible. Kahn's mind moved fluidly through time, exploring future possibilities in terms of their beginnings. The distinctions between past, present, and future were not important to him, because he considered any point in time as part of a greater timeless continuum. He often seemed to be far away, with his head in the clouds, making intuitive leaps among a series of images in his mind. Then suddenly he would

return to the here and now, having come to a realization without being able to articulate the process by which he had arrived at that point. Kahn tended to synthesize elements from a variety of sources into a cohesive whole rather than to focus on a detail of a particular problem. He would have failed a trivia quiz, because facts were to him needless clutter that he impatiently pushed aside to delve straight to the essence of the matter. When Kahn spoke of feeling, he was referring to his preferred mode of functioning.

Although Kahn considered feeling the source of all ideas, he had also learned the value of thinking rationally, of putting his ideas into cohesive order. Thinking was to Kahn an academic process useful for the disciplining of his creative drive. What Kahn called *thinking* is the ability to stand back from an idea and evaluate it objectively. Thinking also involves the rational step-by-step implementation of a theory, the testing of intuition in the world of fact to see if it proves valid. In 1953 Kahn initially envisioned thinking as an insignificant but necessary projection of feeling, like a ball that, when thrown from earth, falls back to the ground (see p. 64). Feeling, to Kahn, was like a great bottomless well full of creative ideas. Out of this well emerges thinking, which gains an objective perspective through its separation, then eventually returns to add greater impact to the original idea.[1] Kahn believed that the creative mind intuitively understood the design process as a whole but required the help of rational thought to direct the process by separating it into steps. Thinking acts as a tool with which to articulate feeling into express-ible shape. Those who do not acknowledge the importance of thinking become so inordinately fond of the intangibility of their ideas that they are unable or unwilling to realize them. The test of a great idea is its feasibility.

Feeling is the *desire* to create. It is the indefinable urge for self-expression that wells up from within. It is the feeling architects get when they see images in their minds that inspire them to design buildings. Thinking is the *means* to create. It involves the effort and discipline of picking up the pencil and committing the image to paper in a way that not only makes sense visually, struc-turally, and economically but also evokes some-thing of the original inspiration. Kahn recognized that thinking and feeling were both necessary in the creative process.

By 1959 Kahn envisioned thinking and feeling as functions that run parallel to each other in the mind of the architect. Gone was his earlier insis-tence that thinking was subordinate to feeling. Once he made the initial break from Interna-tional Style ideology, he gradually returned to a more moderate standpoint in which thinking and feeling were given equal importance (see Kahn's description of thought and feeling, p. 161).

Although Kahn felt that a fluid exploration of possibilities was the most joyous form of expres-sion, he was surprisingly as agile in the realm of logic and reason as he was disciplined about testing the validity of his ideas. Therefore, he put aside his preference for the feeling mode of functioning when he described the creative pro-cess in general. Both thought and feeling, said Kahn, have their moments of greatness; thought is capable of transcending into philosophy, and feeling is capable of transcending into religion.

Kahn chose the words *philosophy* and *religion* to express systems of thought and feeling that strike a common chord in all people.

When an idea reaches beyond one's personal experience, it becomes a collective experience understood by all human beings, regardless of cultural and environmental differences. The idea is then no longer one's own; it belongs to every-one. When both thought and feeling reach their universal forms, then they are able to join to-gether. At their point of fusion, a flash of insight occurs. This dramatic moment is often symbol-ized in cartoons by the light bulb going on in one's head: "I've got it!" Kahn called this mo-ment "realization."

The diagrams Kahn drew to show how thought and feeling relate to the form–design process are the results of a gradual synthesis of several ideas. In 1954 Kahn had not given special attention to the concept of form. To understand how form eventually became a central element in his view of the creative process, it is necessary to trace its evolution with respect to various related concepts.

At a meeting on education at Princeton Univer-sity in December 1953, Kahn advanced what he

Kahn's conception of his nature-of-the-space–order–design thesis in 1953. (*Reproduced by permission from Louis I. Kahn, Letter to Anne G. Tyng, December 18, 1953.*)

"This meets the approval of George Howe;" the design process as Kahn envisioned it in 1954. (*Reproduced by permission from Louis I. Kahn, Letter to Anne G. Tyng, 1954.*)

then termed his "order–design thesis," a representation of the design process involving a linear progression from the abstract to the concrete. In this earliest exploration of the inner mechanics of design, Kahn's description of order is halting, as if he were trying to express a thought that was as yet unarticulated. He tentatively defined order as the structural possibility, the seed that when planted grows into a living actuality—the building.[2]

Over the next few years, Kahn's idea of order shifted as it matured. In 1955 he could say with confidence that order *is*,[3] implying that order was the given, on which all possibilities of design might be based. When Kahn first wrote "Order is," he had been trying for some time to define order, making a long list of all the things order was. The effort left him so mentally exhausted that he finally threw out the definitions and kept the beginning of the sentence: "Order is." Amazingly, those simple words described order better than all the definitions put together. Suddenly he saw order in a new light. It was almost as if the word had begun to take on a life of its own. The image of order gained fullness and reality in Kahn's mind.

At this time, Kahn was still unsure of himself when it came to expressing his ideas verbally and in writing. He wondered whether the words he had just written sounded too radical—or worse, nonsensical. He read them aloud to Anne Tyng, with whom he had been working and whom he respected for her natural ability in the use of language. She confirmed the power of the words *order is.* After this incident, Kahn found a new freedom and confidence in the expression of his thoughts.

In the next seven years, Kahn was able to stand back sufficiently from the idea of order to give an objective and comprehensive picture of it—nonetheless keeping in mind that no description could equal the poetic force of "Order is." To Kahn, order was the basic, immutable law that governs the organization of natural structures. He believed that every element in existence from an atom to a galaxy was based on the same principle. Kahn's understanding of order was shared by Albert Einstein, who spent the last 30 years of his life searching unsuccessfully for a theory that would unify all the forces in nature. His quest stemmed from his conviction that everything in the universe was joined by a common underlying thread. Like Kahn, Einstein was a deeply religious man who intuitively rejected the idea that the universe included the element of chance. "I shall never believe that God plays dice with the world," he often said. Kahn also believed

that the order of nature was intrinsic, and not merely a product of the subjective human perspective.

Kahn stressed, however, that order did not imply beauty.[4] He used the contrasting examples of the dwarf and Adonis to illustrate that the same order produced results that seemed startlingly different. Nature, he said, constantly created variation after variation based on the same underlying order, and because it lacked awareness of what it made, nature did not intentionally create beauty or ugliness. And yet he believed there was a certain undeniable rightness or harmony in nature—thus, the word *order*—that was the basis for human understanding of beauty. Seen through the mind's eye, nature's inherent organization became the standard by which to judge one's own creations.

In architecture, the order of structure is the sense of the intrinsic capabilities of building materials (brick, concrete, stone, wood) and elements (joints, supports, openings, rooms) that fit together and form themselves into characteristic shapes. Materials and elements do not, of course, simply fall into place by themselves. Kahn believed it was the task of the architect to facilitate this process by treating the materials and elements of a building as if they were alive, with wills of their own. What does concrete want to do? Would it rather form joints or span long distances? Does the reception area want to be next to the kitchen? How would these rooms arrange themselves if they could? Architects must understand the natural order of structure so they can be faithful to it.

The year 1959 was the turning point for Kahn's conception of the design process as a whole. This turning point hinged on his introduction of the idea of form. In the early 1950s, Kahn had often used the word *form* casually, without attaching any special significance to it. By 1955 the word had begun to intrigue him. He felt that form somehow played a part in the design process, but in order to incorporate the new concept that was developing in his mind, he would have to rethink his "nature of the space–order–design" sequence. Kahn was becoming dissatisfied with the way he had so far described the design process, and *form* evoked an image that appealed to him emotionally.

Kahn did not simply replace existing terms with this new one, although a comparison of his 1960s' writings with earlier writings gives the impression that he did. In a few passages where he previously used the word *order*, he now substituted the word *form*.[5] He was actually narrowing down his previous definition of order and making room for form. Another early term, *the nature of the space*, disappeared as it was incorporated by the idea of form. To Kahn, form had come to mean the essence created by a certain relationship of elements in a whole. The form Chair, for instance, is a piece of furniture designed to accommodate one sitting person. It consists of a seat, a back rest, and a support system that elevates it from the floor. Regardless of whether the chair is made of plastic, wood, or metal, it is still recognizable as a chair as long as the seat, back rest, and legs remain in a certain relationship to one another.

Kahn's understanding of form closely resembles Jung's definition of archetypes.[6] Archetypes are psychological structures originating at the deepest level of unconsciousness. All human beings, regardless of differences in race, culture, and conscious personal experience, are born with the same tendency to perceive life's experiences and relationships in terms of these same meaningful structures. Archetypes themselves are so primitive they cannot be described, but they underlie

more tangible images. Such archetypal images as the Wise Old Man (Merlin, Moses), the Great Mother (Isis, Kwan-Yin, the Virgin Mary), the Eternal Child (Peter Pan, the Little Prince), and the Hero (Christ, Hercules, Superman) appear in the myths and folklore of all cultures from the very primitive to the highly sophisticated.

Using these archetypal structures as guidelines, one adds a symbolic dimension to one's interactions with real people. For example, one may project a hero archetype onto a political leader or see qualities of the Great Mother in one's own mother. Archetypes also take abstract visual forms, such as the circle, the cross, and the triangle. Artists have always used the circle to symbolize a state of psychic wholeness or a need for self-protection in times of illness or stress. Kahn was familiar with Jung's use of the word *archetype* and was aware of its similarity to his own idea. He chose to discard what he considered to be complicated psychological jargon for the simpler word, *form*.

The process by which the transcendent forms of thinking and feeling produce the realization of form, as understood by Kahn in 1960. (*Reprinted from the April 1961 issue of* **Progressive Architecture**, *copyright 1961, Reinhold Publishing.*)

Form implies a certain order of elements. Whereas the form of a chair is its inherent chairness, the order of a chair is its particular relationship of back to seat to support. In the construction of a chair, one must understand and be faithful to its order because, by changing the relationship between its parts, one might arrive at a different form—that of a stool or couch, perhaps. In establishing the final meanings of form and order, Kahn showed that the two were tightly intertwined, but never identical.

Form is conceived when philosophy (the greatest moment of thinking) and religion (the greatest moment in feeling) come together to spark a flash of realization. The conception of form is not unlike human conception, when the disparate yet complementary elements of egg and sperm fuse to initiate the growth of a new and unique life. The form stage of architecture is the stage at which a given arrangement of elements is envisioned abstractly rather than in a specific shape or size. The form of a building is timeless; it is unaffected by the changing architectural styles. Form is intangible. Design, on the other hand, is completely tangible. By the time the original idea has gone through the long gestation process, it can emerge as a particular building with dimensions, style, and structure. It is now part of physical reality. In order to arrive at the final design, the original form is tailored to fit circumstantial requirements. Order acts as a catalyst to help the form archetype become a design reality.

When a building is being built it must conform to practical restrictions: It must be built from the ground up; it should be able to support its own weight; and it must be constructed with appropriate materials. But Kahn felt that a building should not become a *mere* design, so much a victim of circumstance that it loses the impact of its original inspiration. In order for it to be a great work of architecture, it must retain as much of its archetypal form quality as possible. After the scaffolding is taken down and the workers leave the site, it is possible to forget the building had to be built by machinery and human hands. It seems to take on a life, a personality of its own, as if it grew from the ground before time began and has been there ever since. The final product of design, the most important product, is the expression of the building's original form essence.

PRACTICE

Order: Servant and Served

From his understanding of how the trunk and branches of a tree carry nourishment to the leaves and how the heart pumps a life-sustaining supply of oxygen through the arteries to every cell in the body, Kahn conceived the idea that a building should have separate space for the mechanical system that provides ventilation, electricity, and plumbing to every room. His perception of the order inherent in living forms inspired his idea of the order of servant and served spaces.

The idea evolved from Kahn's realization that architects had continued to think in antiquated terms of constructing buildings with solid walls, although technology had produced materials, such as concrete and steel, that made the use of heavy supports unnecessary. The traditional solid construction left no room for mechanical facilities, which then intruded on those spaces intended for living and working. As these solid walls were made thinner, ducts and wires were stuffed between interior and exterior finished walls or hidden between ceilings and floors. Holes for pipes were drilled through structural members. Kahn suggested that, if walls were opened up and made hollow, they could become actual rooms for the accommodation of ducts, pipes, and wires, thus providing services to living spaces without invading them. In this way, buildings could be divided into servant spaces and the spaces they serve. Because the servant and served concept introduced a revolutionary method of spatial organization, it was one of the most influential contributions to contemporary architecture.

The idea of servant and served space had its roots in Kahn's earliest commissions. Much of his work during the 1930s and early 1940s consisted of housing projects for the Philadelphia City Planning Commission. The abundance of these projects reflected the widespread need for low-cost housing caused by the depression. Strict financial limitations forced Kahn and other architects of the time to design primarily in terms of economy. Kahn therefore began to arrange the plan around a central utility core.

Other commissions of the 1940s included private homes. His Weiss house of 1948–1949, in Norristown, Pennsylvania, is an example of the way in which Kahn extended the techniques he used in low-cost housing to the single detached dwelling. Like the strictly economical plan, the Weiss house radiates from a functional core consisting of kitchen and utility room. Kahn was not yet thinking of designing in terms of served space around a servant core. Not having developed a cohesive ideology, he was merely following the dictates of economy and logic.

While the first stirrings of the order–design thesis were occurring to Kahn, the Yale University

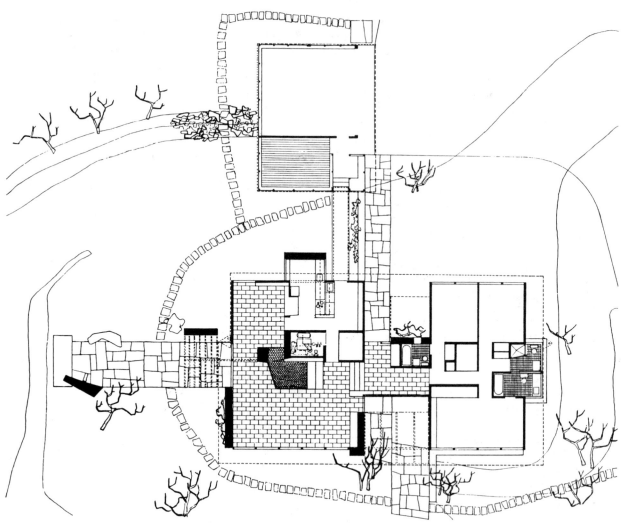

Plan of Weiss house. An L-shaped service core consisting of bath, kitchen, and utility room runs through the center of the house.

Art Gallery (1951–1953) was under way. The simultaneity of the two is significant because the Yale Art Gallery is commonly considered to be Kahn's first mature work. The gallery required flexible interior spaces that could be easily subdivided in a variety of ways. Exhibits were to be displayed on movable panels. Kahn was therefore faced with the task of designing spaces that were as large and unbroken as possible.[7] Because of its great strength, a concrete space frame composed of tetrahedral units was proposed by associate architect Anne Tyng for the spanning of these large unsupported areas. The mechanical facilities were grouped in a central shaft that also included a unique triangular stairway set within a circular well.

By chance, it was discovered that the arrangement of tetrahedral units in the space frames was such that pipes, ventilation ducts, and electrical lines could be run out horizontally from the central service core along hollows within the frames. Kahn called the space frame a "breathing ceiling," after a "breathing wall" idea he had used earlier in a low-cost housing project.[8] The mechanical equipment had found its own place in the voids made by the structure. Because it provided the first, accidental discovery of the possibility of reserving a separate space for the services, the Yale Art Gallery was crucial in determining the direction of Kahn's subsequent thought concerning the separation of servant and served spaces.

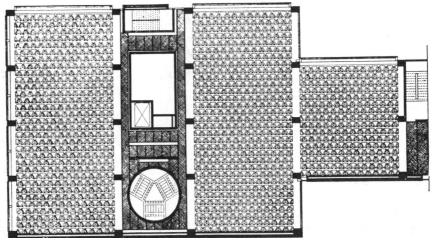

Yale Art Gallery plan, showing tetrahedral space frame, and service core containing triangular stairway. (*Copyright The Louis I. Kahn Collection, University of Pennsylvania and the Pennsylvania Historical and Museum Commission.*)

First-floor of Yale Art Gallery. The tetrahedral space frame spans large areas without support. (*Balthazar Korab.*)

Yale Art Gallery space frames during pouring of concrete. (*Copyright The Louis I. Kahn Collection, University of Pennsylvania and the Pennsylvania Historical and Museum Commission.*)

Triangular stairway set within a circular well, Yale Art Gallery. (© *John Ebstel.*)

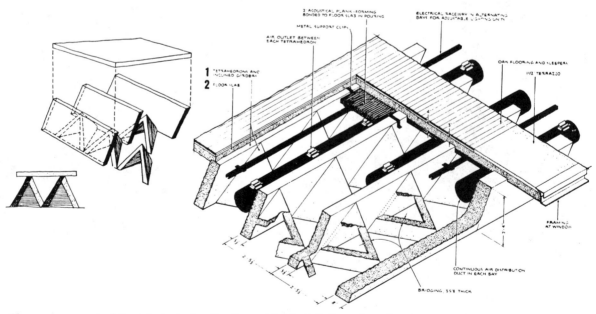

The arrangement of the tetrahedral units allowed for installation of services in the space frames of the Yale Art Gallery.

From 1952 to 1953, Kahn and Tyng designed a triangulated city tower as part of a proposed urban scheme for Philadelphia. Although it was never built, it represented a conceptual advance over the Yale Art Gallery in that the entire structure, not just the ceiling–floor spans, was composed of a tetrahedral space frame. The design was published in *Perspecta* 2 in 1953, along with a statement of an idea that had been influenced by the development of the space frame. In this statement, Kahn indicated that he considered the use of voids an acknowledgment of an order inherent in the character of spaces created with modern building materials. In other words, since architects no longer needed to build massive support systems, the use of hollow walls was a natural outgrowth of the capabilities of concrete and steel. Furthermore, building with voids, or "hollow stones," cooperates with the service needs of these spaces: plumbing, electricity, heat, and air conditioning. Rather than continuing to imitate "solid stone" construction by hiding services behind false walls and dropped ceilings, the architect should find a new way to organize spaces in keeping with modern materials and needs.

In the 1950s, Kahn began to explore the possibilities of the column. He felt that the column no longer need be merely a support; if it were hollowed out, it could become a shaft for carrying mechanical facilities. The area of its support would carry electricity and ventilation, as a living artery transports oxygen and energy to each part of its system.

The idea of the hollow column was contemporary with Kahn's work on the Adath Jeshurun Synagogue in Elkins Park, Pennsylvania, the DeVore house project in Springfield Township, Pennsylvania, and the Adler house project in Philadelphia, Pennsylvania, all in 1954. Kahn's correspondence with Tyng at this time indicates that he consciously applied his newly developed concept of the hollow column to these projects. The Adath Jeshurun Synagogue's triangular plan stemmed from Kahn's feeling that the Yale Art Gallery should have been triangular rather than rectangular. In each corner, clusters of columns surround the stairwell and support a tetrahedral space frame. In the DeVore and Adler houses, Kahn designed each space as an independent system of spans and supports. The columns that held up the structure also enclosed mechanical facilities.

In the Trenton Bath House (1955–1956), Kahn employed a more sophisticated form of this concept. The cinder block walls become square columns at the corners of each unit to provide

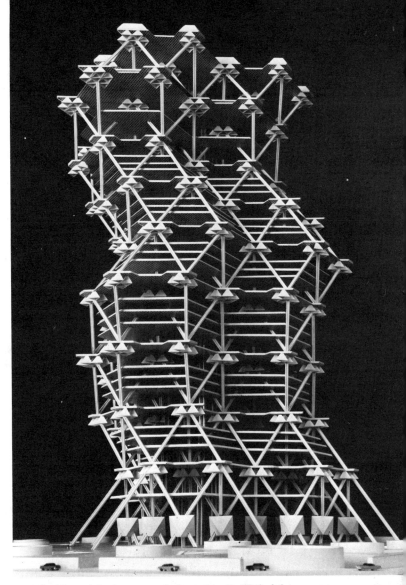

Structural model of proposed city tower in Philadelphia. The entire structure was composed of a tetrahedral space frame. (*Photograph by Damora.*)

support for the pyramidal roofs. The columns were made hollow, taking advantage of the strength of the building material. The spaces within—entrances to dressing rooms and small rooms for plumbing and storage—open off the large central spaces. In the Trenton Bath House, the hollow column had already begun to be a room. Kahn later said that his realization of the hollow column was the beginning of his realization of servant and served spaces. The Trenton Bath House contained the clue to this new idea, but the clue was not perceived as such until Kahn became involved in subsequent projects.[9]

The hollow wall, ceiling, and column were destined to become facets of a single objective. In 1957 Kahn articulated these ideas, adding the important observation that the spaces designed

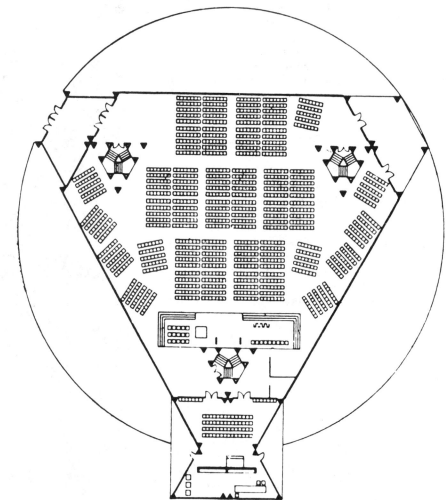

(*Right*). Second-floor plan for Adath Jeshurun Synagogue. The triangular shape stemmed from Kahn's feeling that the Yale Art Gallery's plan should have been triangular rather than rectangular.

(*Below*) Model for Adath Jeshurun Synagogue. In each corner, hollow columns surround the stairwell and support a tetrahedral space frame. (*Copyright The Louis I. Kahn Collection, University of Pennsylvania and the Pennsylvania Historical and Museum Commission.*)

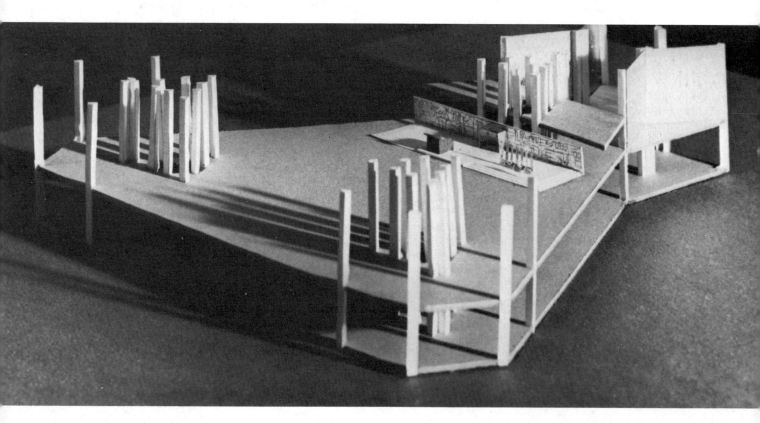

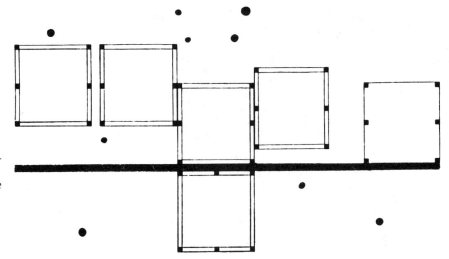

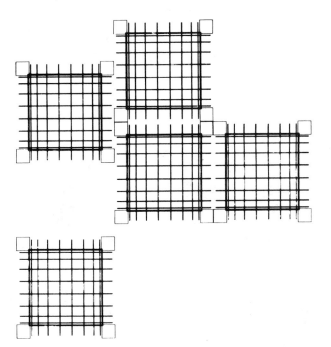

Schematic plans for DeVore (*right*) and Adler houses, showing clusters of independently supported spaces. (Adler house plan, *Copyright The Louis I. Kahn Collection, University of Pennsylvania and the Pennsylvania Historical and Museum Commission.*)

to hold the services should not be thought of as voids, but as rooms, equal in importance to the living spaces. Kahn believed that if the services were not given their own place they would invade the building. He suggested that the architect should plan ahead, leaving extra space for the inventions of the future.

Out of these thoughts came the design for the Alfred Newton Richards Medical Research Building at the University of Pennsylvania, begun in 1957. The Richards Building consists of three laboratory towers clustered around a central building that houses the fresh air intake system and other services. Kahn surrounded each labo-

ratory tower with its own cluster of hollow service columns for the removal of exhaust fumes. He discovered that the separation of the laboratories from the mechanical systems was a recognition of the building's natural order: The rooms inhabited by working people should not be mixed up with the fresh air and exhaust system, just as our brains are not next to our lungs, and our food intake and elimination points are not side by side. The central building around which the towers are located has evolved from the earlier concept of the utility core to a fully enclosed entity. It is in itself a large hollow column. Above each laboratory ceiling, a crawl space high enough for a seated worker is incorporated into the structure as a separate room. These spaces carry pipes, air ducts, and electrical lines out to each laboratory from the central utility shaft.

In the Richards Building, however, Kahn's expression of servant and served spaces had not reached the same degree of sophistication as the concept he so clearly put forth in words. Pipes and ducts hang in profusion from the laboratory ceilings, where they gather dust and pollute the controlled environment. Some laboratories that should be private rooms are merely spaces or alcoves. Not all the existing problems are due to the building's overcrowded conditions. But even with its imperfections, the Richards Building is remarkable for its time. Other architects were not even remotely concerned with the nature of servant and served spaces, and thus the usual laboratory building was, and still is, an uninspired maze of long corridors and look-alike rooms. The Richards Building emerged as unique because it was the only laboratory building in which each kind of space was given distinctive treatment.

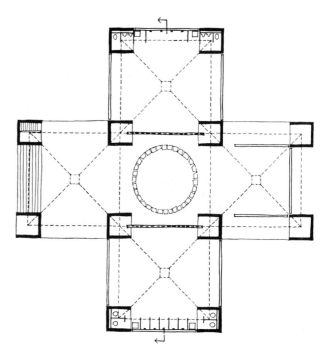

Court of the Trenton Bath House. The entrances to dressing rooms and plumbing and storage areas open off the large central spaces. (© *John Ebstel*.)

Floor plan of the Trenton Bath House. The cinder block walls become hollow square columns at the corners of each unit to support the pyramidal roofs.

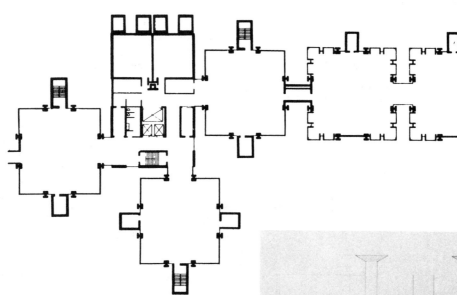

Second-floor plan of the Richards Medical Research Building. Three laboratory towers (and two additional biology towers to right) are clustered around a central service tower. Each tower has its own smaller exhaust subtowers. (*Copyright The Louis I. Kahn Collection, University of Pennsylvania and the Pennsylvania Historical and Museum Commission.*)

Early scheme for the Richards Building, in which the exhaust subtowers resemble smokestacks. (*Copyright The Louis I. Kahn Collection, University of Pennsylvania and the Pennsylvania Historical and Museum Commission.*)

Richards Building exterior. Kahn surrounded each laboratory tower with its own cluster of hollow columns for the removal of exhaust fumes (*Malcolm Smith.*)

Laboratory interior of the Richards Building, showing exposed services above the level of lights and window mullion. (*Photograph by Alexandra Tyng.*)

Kahn next concentrated on the process of perfecting in practice what he had realized philosophically. His Tribune Review Publishing Company Building (1958–1961) in Greensburg, Pennsylvania, consists of three different sections: two two-story blocks with a four-story service core sandwiched between them. Here, servant and served spaces are clearly defined, but as a result, the building tends to be experienced as three separate sections rather than as an expression of the interdependency of the two orders. It was not until Kahn began work on the Salk Institute for Biological Studies in 1959 that he came to grips with the relationship between servant and served spaces.

The fact that the Salk Institute was Kahn's second laboratory building gave him a chance to improve on his translation of the laboratory form into a feasible, well-organized design. The major difference in requirements was the nature of the site: Kahn adapted his Salk Institute scheme to the broad, canyoned terrain along the southern California coast, and thus it is laid out horizontally rather than vertically. Otherwise, the requirements for the laboratories and their mechanical needs were virtually identical for both the Richards and Salk buildings. In the Salk laboratories, however, the distinction between servant and served spaces has been clarified. The spaces for mechanical equipment between floors are not merely crawl spaces but nine-foot-high rooms that Kahn called "pipe laboratories." Also in the Salk Institute, Kahn had the opportunity to rectify the mistake he had made in the Richards Building of failing to create definitive served spaces.

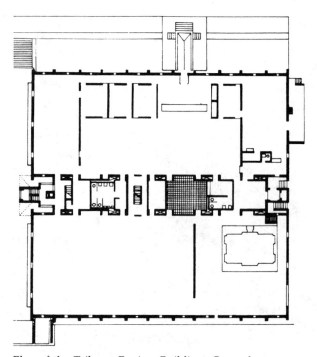

Plan of the Tribune Review Building, Greensburg, Pennsylvania. Kahn sandwiched a narrow service area between larger served areas.

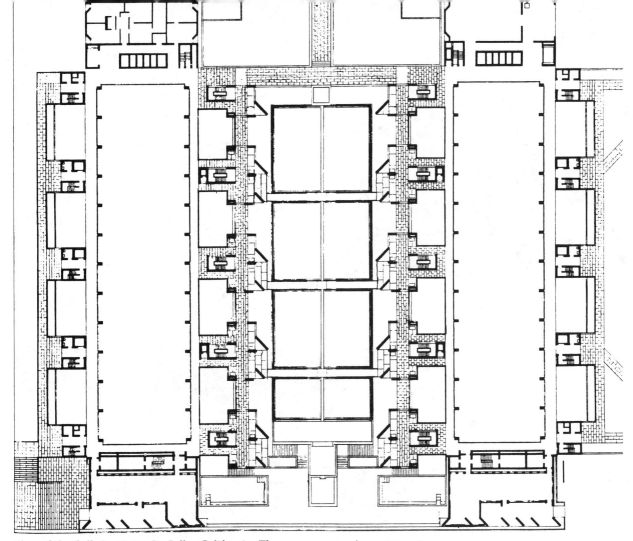

Plan of the Salk Institute, La Jolla, California. The program requirements were similar to those of the Richards Building, but the servant-served relationship between laboratories, studies, and areas for mechanical facilities has been clarified.

Salk Institute, site model. The buildings' horizontal layout suits the broad, canyoned terrain of the California coast. (*George Pohl*.)

View of the Salk laboratories from the shore of the Pacific Ocean (*Photograph by Alexandra Tyng.*)

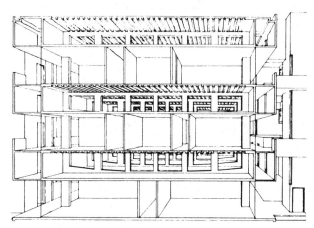

Perspective section of the Salk Institute showing "pipe laboratories" sandwiched between "people laboratories."

Interior of a Salk Institute laboratory. (*Photograph by Alexandra Tyng.*)

Dr. Salk's study. The intimate space and wood detailing provide a contrast with the large, utilitarian space of the laboratories. (*Photograph by Alexandra Tyng.*)

Jonas Salk's belief that medical research belongs not only to medicine but to humanity in general[10] led Kahn to a new realization that a laboratory building need not be for experiments only. Kahn and Salk had many long talks in which they explored the idea that the scientist needed a place to study alone and a place to relax, talk with others, reachieve the sense of wholeness that is often lost during long hours of concentration. Whenever Kahn strayed from his intention to provide such places for the scientist and to separate them physically from the work areas, Salk reminded him of their joint aspirations, filling Kahn with renewed enthusiasm and determination.

As a result, in the Salk Institute the study is distinguished from the laboratory, as it is not in the Richards Building, and each type of space has its own character. The laboratories are long, utilitarian rooms arranged for the maximum efficiency of controlled experiments. The studies, on the other hand, are intimate enclosures designed for comfort and personal expression. Simple oak details give these rooms warmth and livability. Windows look out to the central terrace and the ocean beyond. The difference between working and living spaces is clear in the Salk Institute. Obviously, the unusual partnership between architect and client was what produced an extraordinary building that went way beyond its utilitarian function.

The fact that the servant and served concept is part of a larger hierarchy of spaces in the Salk Institute indicates Kahn's mastery of his concept in practice. Self-confident experimentation characterizes his later efforts along the same lines. The Olivetti-Underwood Factory (1966–1970) in Harrisburg, Pennsylvania, has overhead servant spaces. Although they are not visually isolated from the space they serve, an uncompromising boundary line between them is formed by the level of the suspended grid to which the lighting fixtures are attached. Serving the work areas are skylights, air intake and exhaust units, and electricity and water supply lines. The servant space

above the cafeteria, containing huge twisting ducts, is especially exciting visually.

All Kahn's buildings after the Salk Institute show a true mastery of the servant–served relationship, an understanding that this is not merely a relationship between two kinds of rooms but a connection between many types of spaces, each serving and being served by another in different ways. Kahn's application of the servant–served idea to each design was not contrived or self-conscious. Rather it was intuitive, because it was derived from a realization of the natural order of the spaces involved.

Form to Design

Form is an abstract idea; design is its material application. In Kahn's writing of 1959, the idea of form took on its decisive meaning as the beginning step of the design process. Simultaneously, Kahn began to conceive of individual buildings in terms of their evolution from archetypal essence to finished product.

The full impact of his newly synthesized form–design idea was concentrated in the First Unitarian Church in Rochester, New York, commissioned in 1959. The central room is the church proper, which is surrounded on all four sides by a corridor. Clustered asymmetrically around the outside of the corridor are classrooms, offices, and meeting rooms.

Aerial view of the Olivetti-Underwood Factory, Harrisburg, Pennsylvania. Skylights in the roof illuminate the working area below an overhead servant space. (*Copyright The Louis I. Kahn Collection, University of Pennsylvania and the Pennsylvania Historical and Museum Commission.*)

First Unitarian Church, Rochester. The church proper is surrounded by a corridor. Clustered asymmetrically around the outside of the corridor are classrooms, offices, and meeting rooms. (*Copyright The Louis I. Kahn Collection, University of Pennsylvania and the Pennsylvania Historical and Museum Commission.*)

When he began to design the church, Kahn became familiar with the Unitarian philosophy of questioning as a means of maintaining a constantly evolving belief system. He envisioned the church as a large question mark around which learning and spiritual growth would radiate. His first sketches expressed this basic realization of the ideal Unitarian church. He began with the focal center, the sanctuary of the church itself. Around the sanctuary was an ambulatory where one could walk without entering the sanctuary. Encircling the ambulatory was an outer corridor belonging to the outermost circle, the school.

What followed the original form conception was a gradual adjusting to the circumstantial that Kahn called design. The needs of the church committee were discussed, with resulting changes in the plan. In the end, it was found that the scheme that best served the clients' needs closely resembled the original idea. Throughout the design process, the form remained manifest. The arrangement of spaces seems to have grown naturally out of the requirements of feasibility and economy, yet it is also true to the original realization of Unitarian activity.

In 1960 Kahn was given the commission to design a dormitory for Bryn Mawr College in Pennsylvania. When he began the commission, Kahn had the feeling that the spaces where group activities took place were inherently separate in nature from the sleeping quarters, so he originally placed the two kinds of rooms in separate buildings. But then he realized that combining them within a single structure would give the dormitory the feeling of a house. The structure as it stands is arranged with the large, skylit communal spaces as the cores of each of the three square units. Bedrooms are strung around the peripheries of the squares. Kitchens and bathrooms on four sides of each square make smaller clusters of rooms where students can meet. Kahn believed that this arrangement was an expression of the form, or essence, of Dormitory. The successful realization of form in this particular project led him to a deeper understanding of the term, which he described in great detail in a paper delivered at the International Design Conference in Aspen, Colorado, in 1964.

Kahn's insight into the process of communicating abstract ideas through the program's limitations affected his later projects. His intense search for the correct expression of form, often necessitating frequent last-minute changes, had by now become his characteristic method of dealing with the process of design. As a result of the deeper insight that came with experience, the projects Kahn began in 1962 and 1963—the capitol Shere-Banglanagar at Dacca, Bangladesh, and the Indian Institute of Management at Ahmedabad—are bolder, simpler, and more directly expressive of their form ideas.

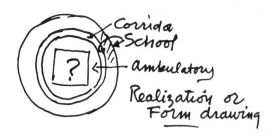

Corrida

School

Ambulatory

Realization or Form drawing

NO!

Test of the validity of Form

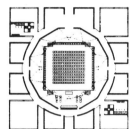

FIRST DESIGN close translation of realization in Form

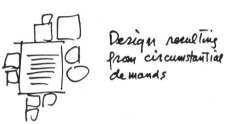

Design resulting from circumstantial demands

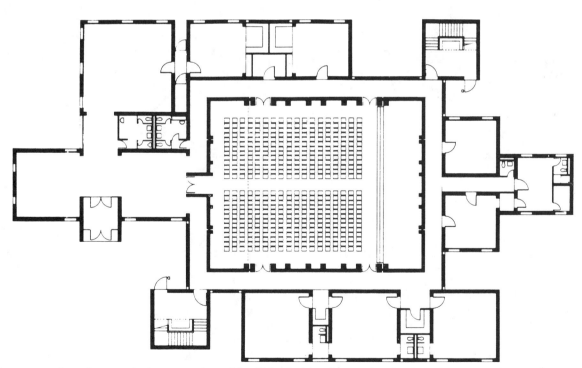

The process from form to design, experienced by Kahn in his schemes for the First Unitarian Church. Kahn's initial realization of a question mark surrounded by a circle evolved into his final design. (*Reprinted from the April 1961 issue of* **Progressive Architecture,** *copyright 1961, Reinhold Publishing.*)

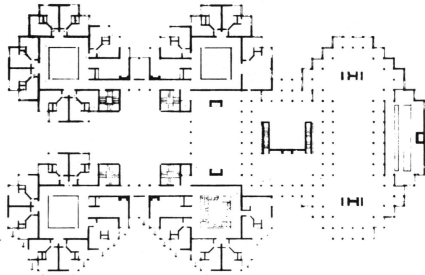

Early scheme for Erdman Hall Dormitories, Bryn Mawr, Pennsylvania. Spaces for group activities are separate from sleeping quarters.

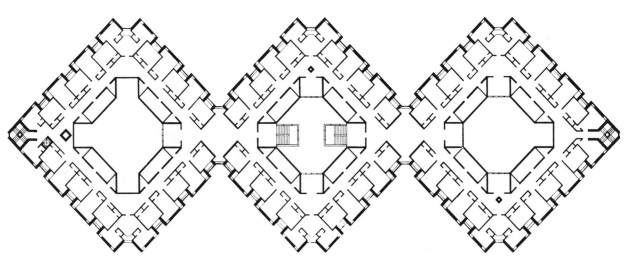

Final scheme for Erdman Hall Dormitories. Kahn achieved the feeling of a house by surrounding the communal spaces in each unit with sleeping quarters.

The buildings at Dacca comprise the legislative center of Bangladesh. The National Assembly itself is cylindrical. According to Kahn, its shape was derived from the idea of expanding the hollow column to create a monumental served space. The hollow column as a carrier of light and air is at Dacca a court in which the vital energy of the community gathers. Thus, it expresses the form nature of the word *assembly*. One of the entrances to the assembly is through the adjacent prayer hall. Because Kahn originally hoped to convince his clients to build an entire mosque, his design aspires to transform the mere hall or room into an independent structure. In

trying to find a shape to express the nature of the prayer hall, Kahn first thought of the traditional mosque symbolism of four minarets. Later he considered a pyramidal shape, crowned by a single minaret. The prayer hall finally evolved into a central space, cornered by four hollow columns. Rather than copy obvious traditional motifs, Kahn chose to dig deeper and find the basic form essence of the Religious Place. The resulting design is not a copy of any other historical building or style. Kahn found his own pure expression of the form Mosque, the same form that also prompted the design of other religious sanctuaries in different cultures and times.

Bryn Mawr dormitories, seen from campus side. (*Photograph by Alexandra Tyng.*)

Detail of concrete frame and slate infill, Bryn Mawr dormitories. (*Photograph by Alexandra Tyng.*)

Student lounge, Bryn Mawr dormitories. (*Photograph by Alexandra Tyng.*)

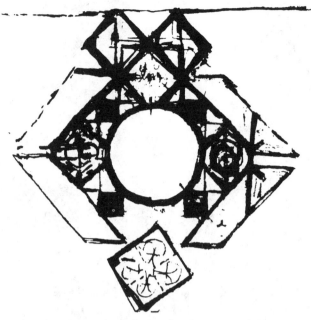 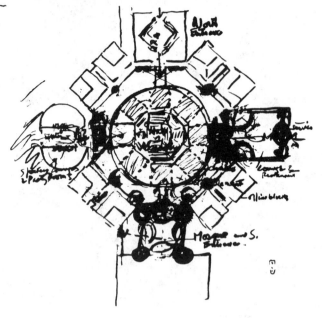

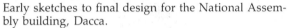

Early sketches to final design for the National Assembly building, Dacca.

(*Above and right*). *Copyright The Louis I. Kahn Collection, University of Pennsylvania and the Pennsylvania Historical and Museum Commission.*)

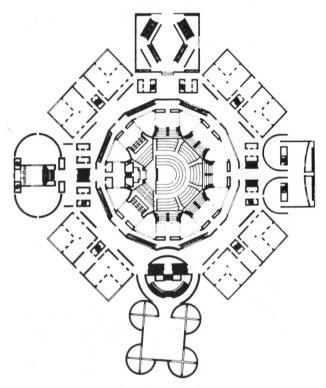

Early scheme for mosque or prayer hall, Dacca. Kahn considered a pyramidal shape, crowned by a single minaret.

(*Right*). Prayer hall as built at Dacca. Central space is created within the meeting of four hollow columns. (*Reproduced by permission of Henry Wilcots.*)

(*Far right*). Lounge–dining building for government officials, Dacca. (*Reproduced by permission of Henry Wilcots.*)

Arches under Presidential Square, Dacca, show the dramatic contrast between the massive expanses of wall and the cutout openings. (*Reproduced by permission of Roy Vollmer.*)

From the boldly aggressive quality of Dacca, there is a distinct change to the greater serenity of Ahmedabad. At Dacca, the contrast between the massive expanses of wall and the cutout openings is perhaps too dramatic. At Ahmedabad, Kahn created more modest facades, with transitional zones of shadow between the walls and fenestration. The dormitories, with their tree-trunk-like profiles, seem to have grown naturally from the ground. And the graduated increase in scale from the smaller, more intimate residential buildings to the moderate dormitories to the larger communal structures is clearly differentiated.

The facades of the residential quarters at Ahmedabad are more modest than those at Dacca, with transitional zones of shadow between the walls and fenestration. (*Photograph by P. M. Dalwadi. © National Institute of Design, Ahmedabad.*)

The dormitories at Ahmedabad have a tree-trunk-like strength. (*Photograph by P. M. Dalwadi and Renée Doring. © National Institute of Design, Ahmedabad.*)

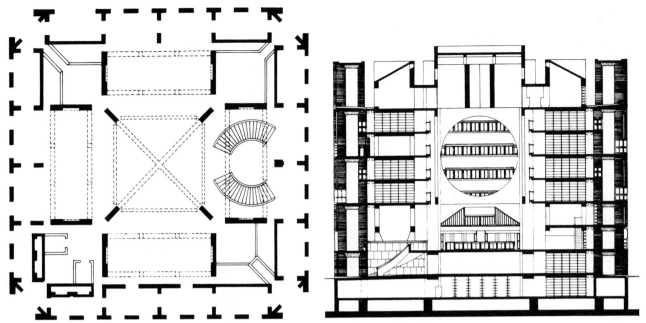

Plan and section of Exeter Library, Exeter, New Hampshire. Concentric doughnuts of brick and concrete create three layers of space: a reading room around
the periphery, library stacks within, and entrance space in the center. (*Plan
copyright The Louis I. Kahn Collection, University of Pennsylvania and the Pennsylvania Historical and Museum Commission.*)

Kahn's expression of form was maturing, becoming more refined. His last major buildings are
quiet but direct translations from form to design.
Most significant, each is strikingly unique. The
Exeter Library in Exeter, New Hampshire (1967–
1972), the Kimbell Museum in Fort Worth, Texas
(1966–1972), and the Mellon Center for British
Art and Studies in New Haven, Connecticut
(1969–1974) are expressive of the fact that each
performs a different function and sprung from a
unique form realization.

The plan of the Exeter Library is similar to those
of the Bryn Mawr dormitories and the First Unitarian Church in Rochester in that it consists of
an inner core ringed by an outer shell. But even
more than the earlier buildings, the Exeter
Library is expressive of the form nature of the
function it serves. According to Kahn, the library
was conceived as two concentric doughnuts. The
outer, brick doughnut was intended as a reading
room near the light, discovered in the leftover
spaces between the support system just as the
rooms for services were discovered earlier in
Kahn's career. Kahn saw the inner, concrete
doughnut as a place where books could be
shelved away from the harmful effects of direct
sunlight. The central entrance space is the "hole"
inside both doughnuts. Each kind of room serves

and is served by the others; there is a constant
flow between the concentric doughnuts. In this
building, Kahn's use of the servant–served concept ceased to be merely a recognition and expression of the building's mechanical needs. The
relationship between lobby, stacks, and reading
rooms is also a recognition of the form essence of
Library.

The corner entrance in the simple brick facade
leads directly to the five-story concrete core, a
space overwhelming in its strength and scale.
Equally impressive is the simplicity of the structural members overhead, their joints as precise
as those in a Chinese puzzle. Stairways in each
corner lead to stacks, carrels, and reading alcoves. The last two spaces, occupying the outer
doughnut, receive light from plate glass windows. The warm color combination of brick walls
and wood paneling gives these spaces a cozy,
inviting atmosphere. Each concentric doughnut
is separate in spirit, yet they are visually joined
because one can see directly through to the
study nooks from the large circular openings in
the walls of the concrete core.

The Kimbell Museum is a series of cycloid vaults
that form long interior galleries interspersed with
open-air courts. The scale of the building, personal rather than monumental, provides an ideal

Reading alcoves, Exeter Library. (*Photograph by Joseph Molitor. Billboard Publications, Inc., 1515 Broadway, New York, New York 10036.*)

Kimbell Museum, Ft. Worth, Texas. A series of cycloid vaults form long interior galleries. (*Photograph by Alexandra Tyng.*)

(*Left*). Arcade in three-dimensional brick facade leads to corner entrance of the Exeter Library. (*Photograph by Joseph Molitor. Billboard Publications, Inc., 1515 Broadway, New York, New York 10036.*)

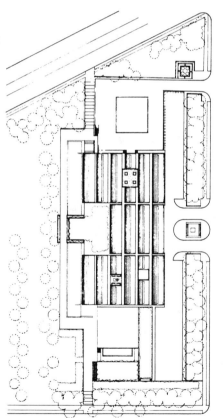

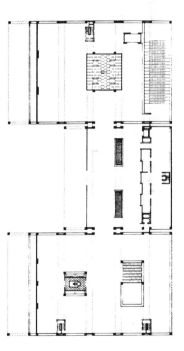

(*Left*). Center space, Exeter Library, with view of stacks through circular openings. (© *John Ebstel.*)

Kimbell Museum, plan and site plan. The lengths of the six parallel vaults are varied by the placement of entrance plaza and open-air courts.

View across vaults, Kimbell Museum. (*Photograph by Marshall D. Meyers, © 1972.*)

Interior of Kimbell Museum. Lower spaces between vaults serve arched spaces by carrying ducts and wires in ceilings. The distinction between served and servant areas is emphasized by the use of different floor materials. (*Photograph by Alexandra Tyng.*)

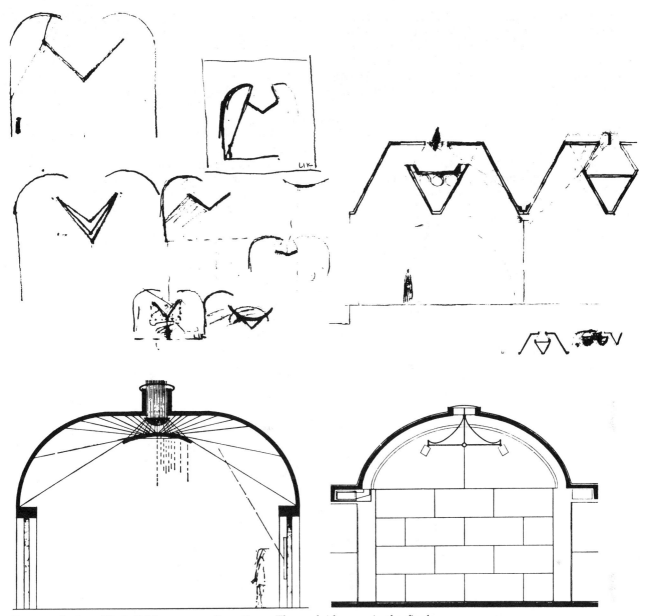

Form to design, Kimbell Museum vault sections. The cycloid curve in the final design resembles the intuitively drawn curve in the first sketches. (*Copyright The Louis I. Kahn Collection, University of Pennsylvania and the Pennsylvania Historical and Museum Commission.*)

condition for viewing a small collection of paintings and sculptures. The varying lengths of the rooms and the opening of each vault into contiguous vaults make natural distinctions between areas. The flow from interior to exterior spaces spreads the focus laterally, so that one does not have the usual tedious museum experience of walking down echoing, never-ending corridors. The spaces lack the self-consciousness of rooms constructed for one purpose only. The walls seem to have grown together in such a way that the works of art find natural places to stay. The Kimbell's final design so successfully evokes the quintessential museum spirit that it appears to have always existed, never having gone through the laborious process of being built. It represents the point in Kahn's work at which he was able to create spaces whose form spirit completely transcends the mechanics of design. For this reason, the Kimbell Museum is one of the few truly magical buildings in the world.

After such a climax, one would almost expect the Mellon Center (1969–1974) to be a disappointment. In fact, it serenely holds to the same degree of excellence. The Mellon Center is significant not only as Kahn's last building—completed after his death by Marshall Meyers and Anthony Pellecchia—but also as his third museum and therefore his third design expression of a particular form essence. A student once asked Kahn whether he kept preformulated designs in his mind for each form: School, Church, or Museum. Kahn answered no, that he started anew with each commission, letting the design develop naturally from the form according to the requirements of site and budget and, more importantly, according to his intuitive response to the nature of that particular building. Even compared to the Yale Art Gallery across the street, the Mellon Center is strikingly unique. Many have been intrigued by the comparison, because the Yale Art Gallery is considered to be Kahn's first mature work, whereas the Mellon Center is his last. The raw energy of the Yale Art Gallery space frames, like so many strong arms thrusting in all directions, seems radical next to the containment of energy in the Mellon Center. The Yale Art Gallery's tetrahedral motif expresses tension; the Mellon Center's rectilinearity symbolizes stability. Kahn acknowledged the connection between the two buildings by repeating the circular stairwell, but in the Mellon Center the stairway in this circle is square, like the structure as a whole.

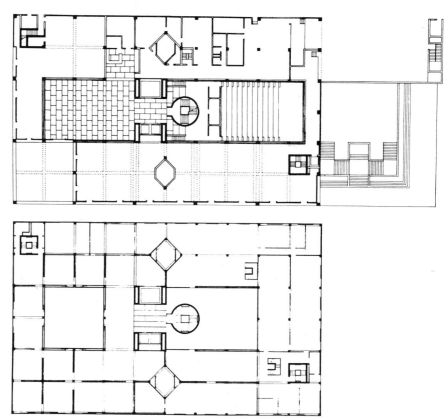

First- (top) and third-floor plans for the Mellon Center for British Art and Studies, New Haven, Connecticut. The basic rectilinear structure allows for varying degrees of subdivision of gallery spaces. (*Third-floor plan copyright The Louis I. Kahn Collection, University of Pennsylvania and the Pennsylvania Historical and Museum Commission.*)

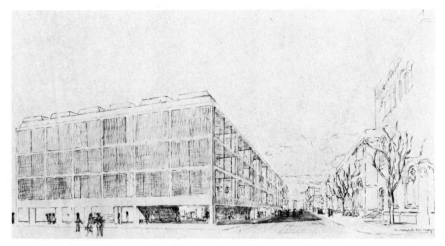

Kahn's drawing of the Mellon Center, viewed from Chapel Street. Ground-floor shops and restaurants reflect the street's commercial quality. (*Copyright The Louis I. Kahn Collection, University of Pennsylvania and the Pennsylvania Historical and Museum Commission.*)

Both the Yale Art Gallery and the Mellon Center have circular stairwells, but the stairway in the Mellon Center is square in plan, like the structure as a whole. (*Mellon Center stairway, left: Photograph by Marshall D. Meyers, © 1977; Yale Art Gallery stairway, right: Copyright The Louis I. Kahn Collection, University of Pennsylvania and the Pennsylvania Historical and Museum Commission.*)

Fourth-floor gallery, Mellon Center. The restricted flow between interlocking spaces creates an intimate atmosphere. (*Photograph by Marshall D. Meyers,* © *1977.*)

Entrance gallery, Mellon Center. The gallery spaces are arranged vertically as a concession to the museum's urban location. (*Photograph by Marshall D. Meyers,* © *1976.*)

In Kahn's last building, the pattern of interlocking spaces allows just enough flow from one space to the next, while maintaining the room quality of each. The organization of space is dictated by the structure itself, which is in turn dictated by the translation of form into design. This particular museum houses a permanent, relatively homogeneous collection of small drawings and paintings. The nature of this collection requires an intimate atmosphere in which close inspection of the work is possible. Here, there is no need for the large, unbroken spaces and movable panels of the Yale Art Gallery. In the Mellon Center, each wall is meant to enhance the personal quality of the work that hangs on it.

Compared to the Kimbell Museum, which was also designed for a small personal art collection, the Mellon Center holds its own equally well as a unique design. Its urban location is expressed by its vertical arrangement of gallery spaces, by the incorporation of shops into its facade as a concession to the commercial character of the street, and by the conformity of its external proportions to the surrounding buildings.

Although Kahn felt he would never finish expressing the possibilities in his mind, the balance and restraint with which the Mellon Center expresses the form idea of Museum is a sensitive, if arbitrary, last statement.

Kahn

Monumentality in architecture may be defined as a quality, a spiritual quality inherent in a structure which conveys the feeling of its eternity, that it cannot be added to or changed. We feel that quality in the Parthenon, the recognized symbol of Greek civilization. . . .

Science has given to the architect its explorations into new combinations of materials capable of great resistance to the forces of gravity and wind.

Recent experimenters and philosophers of painting, sculpture and architecture have instilled new courage and spirit in the work of their fellow artists.

Monumentality is enigmatic. It cannot be intentionally created. Neither the finest material nor the most advanced technology need enter a work of monumental character for the same reason that the finest ink was not required to draw up the Magna Charta.

However, our architectural monuments indicate a striving for structural perfection which has contributed in great part to their impressiveness, clarity of form and logical scale.

Stimulated and guided by knowledge we shall go far to develop the forms indigenous to our new materials and methods. . . .

No architect can rebuild a cathedral of another epoch embodying the desires, the aspirations, the love and hate of the people whose heritage it became. Therefore the images we have before us of monumental structures of the past cannot live again with the same intensity and meaning. Their faithful duplication is unreconcilable. But we dare not discard the lessons these buildings teach for they have the common characteristics of greatness upon which the buildings of our future must, in one sense or another, rely.[11] (1944)

In Gothic times, architects built in solid stones. Now we can build with hollow stones. The spaces defined by the members of a structure are as important as the members. These spaces range in scale from the voids of an insulation panel, voids for air, lighting and heat to circulate, to spaces big enough to walk through or live in.

The desire to express voids positively in the design of structure is evidenced by the growing interest and work in the development of space frames. The forms being experimented with come from a closer knowledge of nature and the outgrowth of the constant search for order. Design habits leading to the concealment of structure have no place in this implied order. Such habits retard the development of art. I believe that in architecture, as in all art, the artist instinctively keeps the marks which reveal how a thing was done. The feeling that our present-day architecture needs embellishment stems in part from our tendency to fair joints out of sight, to conceal how parts are put together. Structures should be devised which can harbor the mechanical needs of rooms and spaces. Ceilings with structure furred in tend to erase scale. If we were to train ourselves to draw as we build, from the bottom up, when we do, stopping our pencil to make a mark at the joints of pouring or erecting, ornament would grow out of our love for the expression of method. It follows that it would become intolerable to hide the source of lighting and unwanted ducts, conduits and pipe lines by pasting acoustical material over structure. The sense of structure of the building and how the spaces are served would be lost. The desire to express how it is done would filter through the entire society of building, to architect, engineer, builder and craftsman.

Proposed City Hall Building

The requirements of generous public areas, meeting rooms and exhibit spaces which could be located in an area not requiring natural light, suggested a building of large floor area. . . .

The space frame tower was developed to satisfy a desire to express one of the endless potentialities of three dimensional construction and to make such choices as would integrate structure with the programmed space needed for working and for the harboring of the mechanical requirements. It is an exploration of the resultant forms of extending a triangular space frame system in a vertical direction. The floor plans are not directly over each other, shifting in a triangular relationship with each other as a result of the geometry of the structure. The entire building is trussed by the cross framing and intersecting of the column system.

. . . In the octohedron spaces of the floor structure are exposed the conditioned air ducts and wiring conduits. The floor slab over the tetrahedrons is poured on insulation panels which absorb the sound. The ceiling pattern itself tends to break up sound. The air ducts are round pipes spaced 3' apart and follow the structural module and are installed at the pouring of the ceiling structure. Their openings point upward to the ceiling, with the air filtering down after striking the slab. This continuous mechanical system provides a complete flexibility of space division. Such a system is now being used for the Art Gallery Building at Yale University.[12] (1953)

Last week end 11-12-13th was the Princeton meeting on education. I believe I already wrote you who was there. Everybody appeared. I discussed my "order-design" thesis but added another area of design influence — the nature of the space. This latter as you will see I believe keeps the picture a lot. This is how the "nature of the space" came about. — I am giving a problem at Yale Theatre we called in (to talk to us) people acquainted with the various sides of its activity

1. A Theatre layout man — he told us about acoustical lines, sight lines, lobby requirements, the house itself, the stage, the stage house etc.

2. An actor — he told us of the problems of reaching the audience but what was more important that many plays fare badly because of the limitation of the proscenium. The actor is framed the people are outside looking in etc etc.

3. An Author — the same story here as the actor

4. An electrical planner: He wanted to be able to change the atmosphere of the stage by electrical devices. Suddenly the place must become red or black until a pin point of light on a man (Hamlet) a blaze of light, a star like pins of over all sight etc

5. The mechanical planner: The Renaissance welcomed like welcomed the best and all of the machinery we can now build. The Theatre was then alive with creative impulses and means of illusion

This man also reminded us that Television is producing a new crop of actors with also the T.V. stage. He predicts and shows the basis that acting is back to stay but once more room to work in.

I realized by all these unsatisfied desires ideas and pent up energies that the present Theatre is dead. That the students now (relying the instructions of to just concur out and just modifying known shapes enough to save ones self respect. Enumerable architects, some from best, are still just modifying while has long lost is life. The nature of the space of the Renaissance Theatre no longer can ~~quite~~ induce the exchange between the actor and the author because the illusion has changed is character. Startling exploits of man in flying thru space claims the flying carpet, Arabian Tales, the legend hardly appeals as much. We need a new kind of acting space one a different nature one that will come to life again to give birth to much wanted expressions which the author will feed the actor and the actor the author. External shapes must wait until 'the nature of the space' unfolds. and before 'order' can be evolved or created.

Now that is the reason why I had difficulty explaining order to you. The basis from which order could be derived was absent.

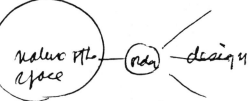

The genius works without separation but he must in those times of so many unsolved problems use separation. And the student and the teacher who must understand the student can profitably make the separation. And also I believe that the puzzle of who is who is not a designer can maybe be discovered and all unified project consequently.

Now order

Order I believe is mostly the structure. The structure idea backening embodying the needs of air, light, quiet, noise, it is not walks the structure grow into a life of fibers enveloping the space so that its nature can be felt just the seed the integration from which Design can work

and design

is the arranging adjusting (choosing?) (throwing away?) to maybe order? meet circumstantial conditions.

Though the creative mind combines design with order and its space, but the separation happens less obviously

it is akin to what happens in feeling and Thinking

Feeling is our great well of consciousness. Thinking is a satellite, a meteor, meant not to be shot from feeling and never to return. It must return to the field of feeling to take meaning in depth. But some people always separate feeling from thinking and build their solution around Thinking only.

[Handwritten note in box, upper right:] feeling will *always* remain the source made effective for creativity by the adventures of Thinking brought home again.

[Handwritten text:] That is why the creative mind cannot accept the separation categorically of the nature space – order – design and rightfully so, because feeling embraces all at once intuitively, BUT the intuitive needs help to activate and direct is [illegible] to a single objective at times (To build a building) We must know – Therefore we must separate – in order to feel with greater creative effect.

Last weekend 11–12–13th was the Princeton meeting on education. I believe I already wrote you who was there. Everybody appeared. I advanced my "order–design" thesis but added another area of design influence—"the nature of the space." This latter as you will see I believe helps the picture a lot. This is how the "nature of the space" came about.—I am giving a problem at Yale *A Theatre*. We called in (to talk to us) people acquainted with the various sides of its activity

1. A theatre layout man—he told us about acoustical lines, sight lines, lobby requirements, the house itself, the stage, the stage house etc.
2. An actor—he told us of the problems of reaching the audience, but what was more important, that many plays fare badly because of the limitation of the [word illegible]. The actor is framed, the people are outside looking in etc., etc.
3. An author—the same story here as the actor.
4. An electrical planner: he wanted to be able to change the atmosphere of the house by electrical devices. Suddenly the place need become red or black with a pinpoint of light on a man (Hamlet), a blaze of light, a star like pins of overall light etc.
5. The mechanical planner: The Renaissance would like welcomed the best and all of the machinery we can now build. The Theatre was then alive with creative impulses and means of illusion. . . .

I realized by all these unsatisfied desires, ideas and pent up energies that the present Theatre is dead. That the students were following the instruction of the first consultant and just *modifying* known shapes enough to save one's self-respect. Innumerable architects, some of our best, are still just modifying what has long lost its life. The nature of the space of the Renaissance Theatre no longer can induce the exchange between the actor and the author. Demands in illusion has changed its character. Startling exploits of man in flying thru space dims the flying carpet, Arabian Tales; the legend hardly appeals as much. We need a new kind of acting space, one a different nature, one that will come to life

Before the trip to the site [of the Vincent Kling "lift slab" job] I gave a little talk to Samuely and the others on some of (my/our) latest theories. He was completely taken by them. My latest idea is that the area of support of each column is the area for the control of light and air so that we can say that we have evolved from the Greek completely. The order of [diagram] is no more but it is the proof of a magnificence of its order since it has persisted so long. *Now* the column *must* be hollow like the stem of a leaf or the trunk of a tree. The flow of [diagram] is umbrella like in form—the logical one for the space he described to-day. The columns need not be the same size because in a very large area of more than 4 columns the air conditions are different and the column would change in size. The traditional structural rhythm is not necessarily the answer. I showed him also the idea for a office building with a bell bottom and how the columns near the ground *grew* larger from [diagram] to [diagram] to [diagram].

These columns also were hollow and allowed the air and light to pass them.[14] (1954)

Order is
Design is form-making in order
Form emerges out of a system of construction
Growth is a construction
In order is creative force
In design is the means—where with what when with how much
The nature of space reflects what it wants to be
    Is the auditorium a Stradivarius
      or is it an ear
    Is the auditorium a creative instrument
      keyed to Bach or Bartok
      played by the conductor
      or is it a convention hall
In the nature of space is the spirit and the will to exist a certain
    way
    Design must closely follow that will
    Therefore a stripe painted horse is not a zebra.
    Before a railroad station is a building
    it wants to be a street
    it grows out of the needs of street
      out of the order of movement
    A meeting of contours englazed.
Thru the nature—why
Thru the order—what
Thru design—how
A Form emerges from the structural elements inherent in the
    form.
A dome is not conceived when questions arise how to build it.
    Nervi grows an arch
    Fuller grows a dome

Mozart's compositions are designs
    They are exercises of order—intuitive
    Design encourages more designs
    Designs derive their imagery from order
    Imagery is the memory—the Form
    Style is an adopted order
The same order created the elephant and created man
    They are different designs
    Begun from different aspirations
    Shaped from different circumstances
Order does not imply Beauty
    The same order created the dwarf and Adonis
Design is not making Beauty
    Beauty emerges from selection
        affinities
        integration
        love
Art is a form making life in order—psychic
Order is intangible
    It is a level of creative consciousness
    forever becoming higher in level
    The higher the order the more diversity in design
Order supports integration
From what the space wants to be the unfamiliar may be revealed
to the architect.
From order he will derive creative force and power of
self-criticism
to give form to this unfamiliar.
Beauty will evolve[15] (1955)

Order is not repetition. It is a central idea. An architect's sense of order is like a composer's sense of music; it has nothing to do with counterpoint or orchestration. It is something underneath and beyond the elements of style. It is something beyond *design*. The elephant and man are different designs. But the same order created them. . . .

A building is like a human. An architect almost has the opportunity of creating life. It's like a human body—like your hand. The way the knuckles and joints come together makes each hand interesting and beautiful. In a building these details should not be put in a mitten and hidden. You should make the most of them.[16] (1957)

I do not like ducts; I do not like pipes. I hate them really thoroughly, but because I hate them so thoroughly, I feel they have to be given their place. If I just hated them and took no care, I think they would invade the building and completely destroy it. I want to correct any notion you may have that I am in love with that kind of thing.[17] (c. 1959)

The plan expresses the limits of Form. Form, then, as a harmony of systems, is the generator of the chosen design. The plan is the revelation of the Form.[18] (c. 1959)

To begin is the time of belief in form.
Design is the maker that serves this belief.
To build is action from a sense of order.
When the work is completed the beginning must be felt.
Form is the realization of inseparable characteristics.
Form has no existence in material, shape or dimension.
A design is but a single spark out of form;
It is of material and has shape and dimension.
It is hard to talk about a work when it is done.
You feel its incompleteness.
I recall the beginning as Belief.
It is the time of realization of Form
It is feeling as religion, and thought as philosophy.
Then there is no material no shape no dimension.
And then I recall the adventure of design when dream-inspired
Form must answer to the laws of order so as to be.
One feels the work of another in transcendence—in an aura
of commonness and in the Belief.[19] (1959)

I want to talk a bit about realization. I like to think that the transcendence of thought in the individual is philosophy, and the transcendence of feeling of an individual is love or religion. Realization is the combining of these transcendencies. It is not the individual thought; it is not the individual feeling. It is a kind of fact of both.

Realization stems from this. Realization may be said to be a harmony of systems that lead you to a feeling of form rather than design.

Form doesn't have shape or dimension. It simply has a kind of existence will.

Design is the means by which you bring into being that which form seems to indicate. In form you might say the spoon has to have a container and an arm. You bring it into existence by designing it as deep, or shallow, or long, or short, or made of gold, silver or wood.[20] (1960)

A young architect came to ask a question. "I dream of spaces full of wonder. Spaces that rise and envelop flowingly without beginning, without end, of a jointless material white and gold. When I place the first line on paper to capture this dream, the dream becomes less."

This is a good question. I once learned that a good question is greater than the most brilliant answer.

This is a question of the unmeasurable and the measurable. Nature, physical nature, is measurable.

Feeling and dream has no measure, has no language, and everyone's dream is singular.

It is the role of design to adjust to the circumstantial. At one stage of discussion with the members of the church committee a few insisted that the sanctuary be separated entirely from the school. I said fine, let's put it that way and then I put the auditorium in one place and connected it up with a very neat little connector to the school. Soon everyone realized that the coffee hour after the ceremony brought several related rooms next to the sanctuary, which when alone were too awkwardly self-satisfying and caused the duplication of these rooms in the separated school block. Also, the schoolrooms by separation lost their power to evoke their use for religious and intellectual purposes and, like a stream, they all came back around the sanctuary.

The final design does not correspond to the first design though the form held.

I want to talk about the difference between form and design, about realization, about the measurable and the unmeasurable aspects of our work and about the limits of our work.

Giotto was a great painter because he painted the skies black for the daytime and he painted birds that couldn't fly and dogs that couldn't run and he made men bigger than doorways because he was a painter. A painter has this prerogative. He doesn't have to answer to the problems of gravity, nor to the images as we know them in real life. As a painter he expresses a reaction to nature and he teaches us through his eyes and his reactions to the nature of man. A sculptor is one who modifies space with the objects expressive again of his reactions to nature. He does not create space. He modifies space. An architect creates space.

Architecture has limits.

When we touch the invisible walls of its limits then we know more about what is contained in them. A painter can paint square wheels on a cannon to express the futility of war. A sculptor can carve the same square wheels. But an architect must use round wheels. Though painting and sculpture play a beautiful role in the realm of architecture as architecture plays a beautiful role in the realms of painting and sculpture, one does not have the same discipline as the other.

One may say that architecture is the thoughtful making of spaces. It is, note, the filling of areas prescribed by the client. It is the creating of spaces that evoke a feeling of appropriate use. . . .

A great building, in my opinion, must begin with the unmeasurable, must go through measurable means when it is being designed and in the end must be unmeasurable. The design, the making of things is a measurable act. In fact at that point, you are like physical nature itself because in physical nature everything is measurable, even that which is yet unmeasured, like the most distant stars which we can assume will be eventually measured.

But what is unmeasurable is the psychic spirit. The psyche is expressed by feeling and also thought and I believe will always be unmeasurable. I sense that the psychic Existence Will calls on nature to make it what it wants to be. I think a rose wants to be a rose. Existence Will, *man*, becomes existence, through nature's law and evolution. The results are always less than the spirit of existence.

In the same way a building has to start in the unmeasurable aura and go through the measurable to be accomplished. It is the only way you can build, the only way you can get it into being is through the measurable. You must follow the laws but in the end when the building becomes part of living it evokes measurable qualities. The design involving quantities of brick, method of construction, engineering is over and the spirit of its existence takes over. . . .

I am designing a unique research laboratory in San Diego, California.

This is how the programme started.

The director, a famous man, heard me speak in Pittsburgh. He came to Philadelphia to see the building I had designed for the University of Pennsylvania. We went out together on a rainy day. He said "How nice, a beautiful building. I didn't know a building that went up in the air could be nice. How many square feet do you have in this building?" I said, "One hundred and nine thousand square feet." He said, "That's about what we need."

That was the beginning of the programme of areas. But there was something else he said which became the Key to the entire space environment. Namely that Medical Research does not belong entirely to medicine or the physical sciences. It belongs to Population. He meant that anyone with a mind in the humanities, in science, or in art could contribute to the mental environment of research leading to discoveries in science. Without the restriction of a dictatorial programme it became a rewarding experience to participate in the projection of an evolving programme of spaces without precedence. This is only possible because the director is a man of unique sense of environment as an inspiring thing, and he could sense the existence will and its realization in form which the spaces I provided had.

The simple beginning requirement of the laboratories and their services expanded to cloistered gardens and Studies over arcades and to spaces for meeting and relaxation interwoven with unnamed spaces for the glory of the fuller environment.

The laboratories may be characterized as the architecture of air cleanliness and area adjustability. The architecture of the oak table and the rug is that of the Studies.

The Medical Research Building at the University of Pennsylvania is conceived in recognition of the realizations that science laboratories are studies and that the air to breathe should be away from the air to throw away.

The normal plan of laboratories which places the work areas off one side of a public corridor and the other side provided with the stairs, elevators, animal quarters, ducts and other services. This corridor is the vehicle of the exhaust of dangerous air and also the supply of the air you breathe, all next to each other. The only distinction between one man's spaces of work from the other is the difference of the numbers on the doors.

I designed three studio towers for the University where a man may work in his bailiwick and each studio has its own escape *stairway sub tower* and *exhaust sub tower* for isotope air, germ-infected air and noxious gas.

A central building to which the three major towers cluster takes the place of the area for services which are on the other side of the normal corridor plan. This central building has nostrils for intake of fresh air away from *exhaust sub towers* of vitiated air.

This design, an outcome of the consideration of the unique use of its spaces and how they are served, characterizes what it is for. . . .

From all I have said I do not mean to imply a system of thought and work leading to realization from Form to Design.

Designs could just as well lead to realizations in Form.

This interplay is the constant excitement of Architecture.[21] (1960)

Realization is really realization in form, not in design. Realization has no shape or dimension. It is simply a coming to a deep, revealing understanding in which the sense of order and the sense of dream, of religion, becomes the transference of I into thou. A man does not have a philosophy—he lives what he lives; but he gives philosophy as though it didn't belong to him, because he can't live the philosophy that he senses. From this sense of order and sense of dream come realization. Realization in form. Now form, in my opinion, has no shape or dimension; form is merely a realization of the difference between one thing and another—that which has its own characteristic. A circle is not a triangle, though tautologically it may be the same thing. It isn't the same thing in form. It has characteristics or rather inseparable parts. If you take one thing away, the form is destroyed. Each part must be accountable to the other. This is realization in form. . . .

In a dormitory I'm doing for Bryn Mawr College, I had a feeling that the dining room, living room, reception rooms and entrance were different, in every respect, from the sleeping quarters. And I kept the sleeping quarters apart from these rooms, believing that I was expressing that one was different from another. But I discovered my mistake. I realized that a person sleeping in a room felt well about his house if he knew the dining room was downstairs. The same way with the entrance to the building. The sense of hospitality, or reception, of getting together must be part of the fabric of the house itself. I changed, much to my delight, the whole conception, and I made these spaces part of the fabric of the other spaces. To me, this is realization in form.

Now if I had just looked at it as design, as I did before, I would have been led to something which may look well, but which had no power to convey one very wonderful thing about architecture. Because architecture really is a world within a world.[22] (1964)

The original concept of the three parts which expresses the form of the Salk Institute—the laboratory, the meeting place, the living place—has remained. The acceptance of the separation has made Dr. Salk my most trusted critic.

Two major changes from our collaboration: the two laboratory gardens and four laboratory buildings have become a single garden flanked by two laboratory buildings; the distinction in the construction of the spaces of the laboratories from the spaces for the pipes has become greatly clarified to the point where a far more interesting construction, intended in the beginning to serve this distinction, has given way to a system of construction far less exciting but one that serves more characteristically the intended use.

I realized that two gardens did not combine in the intended meaning. One garden is greater than two because it becomes a place in relation to the laboratories and their studies. Two gardens were just a convenience. But one is really a place; you put meaning into it; you feel loyalty to it.

The laboratories, now under construction, are conceived of as work levels and service levels. Each of the three work levels is related to a garden or to a view of a garden. The space above each laboratory is, in reality, a pipe laboratory, nine feet clear, where service men can install equipment relative to experiments and make changes to ducts and piping. This dismisses the apprehension of needing the room to satisfy the mechanical means for experimentation. In the laboratories at Pennsylvania, the vertical services and the expulsion of all unwanted air had its undeniably right position. The horizontal services were in the spaces of the Vierendeel truss and exposed. This answered in one way only: the pipes are visible and accessible but they do gather dust and, in biological studies, this could be a disadvantage. So, in the first scheme for the Salk laboratory, crawl space was provided in a generously deep folded plate construction. This gave an awkward but possible accessibility as well as integral enclosure. Dr. Salk, when his belief in what must constitute the nature of a laboratory space was fully realized, could not turn back to something that was less than what we finally accepted, even though it meant drastic change. I felt the loss of the folded plate construction. My structural engineer was not for change. The mechanical engineer still believes that the folded plate could work. Yet study and new architectural potentialities finally gave rise to everyone's belief in the validity of the last choice.[23] (1965)

I think of Form as the realization of a nature, made up of inseparable elements. Form has no presence. Its existence is in the mind. If one of its elements were removed its form would have to change. There are those who believe the machine will eventually take the place of the mind. There would have to be as many machines as there are individuals. Form preceeds Design. It guides its direction for it holds the relation of its elements. Design gives the elements their shape, taking them from their existence in the mind to their tangible presence. In composing, I feel that the elements of the form are always intact, though they may be constantly undergoing the trials of design in giving each its most sympathetic shape. Form is not concluded in presence, for its existence is of psychological nature. Each composer interprets Form singularly. Form, when realized, does not belong to its realizer. Only its interpretation belongs to the artist. Form is like order. Oxygen does not belong to its discoverer.[24] (1967)

The orders which you think about when you are, in a sense, determining the elements of design—that is to say, the elements, and how you are considering them in design to be perfected. There is in the design the consideration of the difference between the order of structure and the order of construction. They're two different things. There is an order to construction which brings in the orders of time. They're very much married to each other. The order of structure can make conscious the crane. The crane that can lift twenty-five tons should appear in a specification of present-day architecture which does not appear now. The architect says "Oh! They're using a crane on my building. Isn't that nice—so they can pick it up more easily," never realizing that the crane is a designer; that you can make something that's twenty-five tons coming to something that's twenty-five tons, and you can make a joint that's so magnificent, because that joint is no little thing. In fact, if you'd put gold into it, you wouldn't be spending too much money, because it's so big. So the realization that joint-making, which is the beginning of ornament—because I do believe that the joint is the beginning of ornament—comes into being again, you see. What you can lift as one thing should be something that motivates the whole idea of making a single thing which comes together with another single thing. So in the order of structure you make this decision like I did in Ahmedabad when I said that a beam needs a column. A beam needs a column; a column needs a beam. There is no such thing as a beam on a wall. And if you make the decision which I made, saying that the beam of brick is an arch, therefore, since I did not want to use any concrete beams, and since I was not going to use any columns, it became so natural to use an arch, because it was only part of the wall construction which is characteristic of brick, and I placed everything supported under arches, and invented many things about arches, like big arches which stretch as much as twenty feet, let us say, with a very low thing using restraining members in concrete like this to take the thrust away, bringing the wall very close together, giving a space with that much opening because I made a composite order in which the concrete and the brick will work together. This is a composite order. A sort of sense of structure, a sense of the order of brick, sense of the order of structure, which made this possible. The design goes on and on; speculation of the ways you can do this thing in the most characteristic fantastic ways, because you recognize that structure has an order; that the material has an order; that the construction has an order; the space has an order in the way of the servant spaces and the spaces served; that the light has an order because it has an order in the sense that it is given by structure, and that the consciousness of the orders be felt.[25] (1967)

I have no method of work, I only have principle around which I work, there is no method, there is no system. There is nothing systematic about the servant space and the space it serves, because it is only a realization of a kind of nature that is the realization of what I think is true of Architecture.[26] (1973)

The greatest offering, the greatest work, the greatest *part*, the most *wonderful* part of an artist's work does not really belong to him. He is a catalyst of this eternal quality, and he can only claim the way he himself interprets it.

Picasso opened new avenues. His paintings belong to him, but the new avenues do not. In that way you explain the catalyst—he was just there, he senses it . . . it is these qualities which the next painter—or the painter next to him, put it this way—recognizes as an opening to his *own* talent. That's why Picasso has many followers. But if they imitate him, they're no one—you see? To write like Mozart is meaningless, right? To be influenced by Mozart's eternal quality—*eternal quality*—is the seed which stimulates the true artist.[27] (1972)

3
RENEWAL: SEARCH FOR THE BEGINNING

THEORY

Louis Kahn's proposals for urban renewal and the reevaluation of the city's institutions have been considered purely poetic by many critics. In truth, his schemes are highly functional. His language is visionary because it arises from an understanding far more profound than the practical aspects of the problems he considered.

Kahn applied his form–design concept to the city as a whole and to its various institutions. The search for beginnings was considered essential by Kahn, who sought to imbue the present city with the sense of inspiration that prompted its origin. His schemes for urban redevelopment are feasible in a way no others are, because they are rooted in an instinctive perception of the city's nature. He believed that only with such an unclouded perception could the architect contribute to the solving of the problems of the modern metropolis.

Taking the revitalization of the city literally, Kahn treated the urban configuration as a living organism whose vitality was dependent on its full and healthy expression. If the expression of the city's natural function and purpose became obscured with time, it would begin to die. Kahn believed that, if given the chance, the city could work through its own problems and thereby revitalize itself; its ability to act in its own best interest was an indication of its life. However, when he spoke of "letting" the city solve its own problems, Kahn was not implying that the architect should take a passive attitude toward redevelopment. Expedient solutions, he said, contributed to the thwarting of the city's true nature by allowing undesirable changes to gradually build one upon another. Kahn's goal was to block out the layers of interference so he could listen to the true voice of the city and thereby discover how to help it live again.

Kahn's concern with redevelopment began before midcentury when Philadelphia's downtown area had fallen into decay as a result of the depression and large-scale decentralization. Beginning in 1949, Kahn developed a hierarchical concept of movement by which the flow of intercity traffic could be directed and sorted. His idea was to discriminate between traffic of varying speed and intention. He felt that the pedestrian, the car, the bus, and the trolley each had its own nature that should be given its own relative place on the streets. In describing the concept he used metaphors—river, harbor, canal, and dock—for roads and parking facilities.[1] The imagery of flowing water brought to his mind nourishment and growth, reinforcing the picture of the city as a living entity. According to Kahn, traffic should flow along life-giving channels that would irrigate every section of the city. It is clear that he thought of Philadelphia's city center as a dead or dying part of an organism that, given sufficient circulation, could be brought back to useful life.

As Kahn's concept of order emerged around 1950, he began to speak of his hierarchical traffic proposal as an "order of movement"[2] or "or-

Expressways are like **RIVERS**

These **RIVERS** *frame the area to be served*

RIVERS *have* **HARBORS**

HARBORS *are the municipal parking towers*

from the **HARBORS** *branch a system of* **CANALS** *that serve the interior*

the **CANALS** *are the go streets*

from the **CANALS** *branch cul-de-sac* **DOCKS**

the **DOCKS** *serve as entrance halls to the buildings*

Kahn's hierarchical system of sorting traffic, 1953. (*Reprinted by permission from Louis I. Kahn, "Toward a Plan for Midtown Philadelphia,"* **Perspecta 2: The Yale Architectural Journal,** *1953, p. 11.*)

The "cathedral of the city"; sketch of Center City Philadelphia.

derly discrimination."[3] It became part of his total understanding of order as it figured in his nature-of-the-space–order–design thesis, also evolving at that time. In the late 1950s, Kahn was articulating his sense of order, and he felt that only through this hierarchical way of directing and sorting traffic could a city renew itself. Kahn advocated the consolidation of all institutions into a single area in the center of the city, toward which the orderly movement of traffic would flow. He described the city center as the "cathedral of the city,"[4] recalling the focal point of the Gothic town, the center of its spiritual presence, around which bustling commercial and cultural activity took place. Such a concentration of all activities into a central area Kahn believed would strengthen surrounding areas as well as stimulate interest in the city center as a usable place.

The street, to Kahn, was never just an empty space between buildings. He began in the late 1940s and early 1950s to suggest that the buildings lining each street be zoned according to the nature of the traffic that flowed along that street.

He expressed the unconventional view that garages were not buildings but parts of the street and should be treated as such. He also considered parking towers—"harbors"—to be wound-up extensions of the street. Even at this early stage of his city planning experience, he obviously believed that the character of the city began with its streets rather than with its buildings. By 1955 his thoughts on the subject had progressed to the point at which he declared that the street "wants to be" a building. He was implying that the street was not a void, but a solid with its own character and life.

As stated in Chapter 2, Kahn's nature-of-the-space–order–design thesis remained constant through the 1950s but reached a turning point in 1959 when he developed a clear idea of form and gave it a decisive place in the design process. In the same year, Kahn concluded that the expression of the city's natural order of movement, accomplished by the sorting of traffic, would clarify the form of the city. In the Voice of America *Forum* Lecture Series, Kahn presented a new concept, viaduct architecture, which incorporated his earlier plan for street movement. Kahn's initial realization of the viaduct occurred in relation to his vision of the form, City. He saw as a symbol of the city center a water tower from which aqueducts radiated in all directions. Around the aqueducts, buildings grouped themselves according to their relative functions. This starlike form represented the source of urban life, just as the heart with its system of veins and arteries is the source of human life. The integration of earlier water metaphors into this archetypal vision clearly coincides with Kahn's first use of the word *form.*

Viaduct literally means a "carrying street." Kahn extended its original Roman meaning to signify a complex consisting of levels for pedestrian traffic, automobile traffic, mass transportation systems, and rooms under the street for piped services, which could then be repaired without interruption of traffic. The viaduct is actually a hollow column turned on its side, channeling the energy flow of the city. The proposal of the viaduct system realized the street's desire to be a building by connecting enclosed spaces for traffic with parking towers and ground-floor shops.

Kahn described the viaduct as a method of separating the avenues for automobile traffic from the pathways used by pedestrians. He considered this discrimination necessary because each part of urban architecture had its own speed, its own sense of space relative to that speed, and, thus, its own nature. Kahn observed that it was the car that upset the original order of the city, causing its form to be obscured and consequently destroying the life of the city's center. He implied that before the car was invented the city was oriented toward only one architecture, that of human activity, because it was completely pedestrian. The subsequent introduction of the car became an invasion because it was not dealt with wisely. Kahn's viaduct proposal gives the car a place of its own in which it does not interfere with human activity. The viaduct concept is an adaptation of the order of servant and served spaces to urban scale.

The city is composed of institutions: schools, libraries, churches, and hospitals, to name a few. Once Kahn had established the relationship of form to design, he thought in terms of comparing present-day institutions with their form essences. Kahn believed that existing institutions were functioning with no relevance to the true needs of the people. By forgetting for a moment the condition of these institutions, he said, the architect could let his mind go back to their beginnings and sense the resourcefulness and energy that determined their original purposes. With a sense of the inspiration of these begin-

ning moments, the architect could create spaces that would more effectively serve the needs of the population. In the context of renewal, Kahn contrasted the terms *need* and *desire.* Need, he said, denoted what was necessary, whereas desire was a noble emotion resulting from human creative instinct and origin. He objected to design based on the rationale "but that's what the people need!" because present needs may be based on a shaky foundation of random circumstances. By building from desire, however, the architect can offer the population new standards on which to base new, healthier needs. Kahn predicted that these inspired spaces would transcend their functional values and emanate the qualities inherent in their form natures.

In 1972 Kahn began using the word *availabilities* in place of *institutions.* He spent much time teaching and lecturing to students and was sensitive to the negative connotations that the word *institutions* had for the radical generation of the 1960s. Because Kahn cared deeply that his ideas were communicated accurately to others, he felt that the word *availabilities* better expressed the unlimited possibilities that the city's organizations could offer if they became fully expressive of their intentions. Kahn thought a city should be a place where a small boy could sense what he wanted to be when he grew up by just walking along the city's streets. To Kahn, the city's potential for growth was unlimited, provided its institutions were redefined.

The school was the institution, or availability, about which Kahn spoke most often. He considered the school of great importance because he saw learning as a process that continued throughout life and was central to it but that did not occur often enough in the existing educational system. In 1960 he described the institution of school as beginning with a man under a tree discussing his realizations with others. Teaching and learning were at that moment spontaneous, unself-conscious acts. The school as it exists today, Kahn pointed out, does not adequately serve its function because it has strayed so far from the eager, willing exchange that initiated the first school.

In order to convey the essence of School in the final design, the architect must translate the required program of square footage into spaces that not only serve their practical function but also recreate the inspiration inherent in the first school. Kahn felt that a variety of classroom shapes and sizes, plenty of natural light, and the transformation of long hallways into rooms with alcoves were important ingredients of his personal form realization of School. Such spaces would better reflect the individuality of each

The City from a simple settlement became the place of the assembled Institutions

Before the Institution was natural agreement — The sense of commonality. The constant play of circumstances, from moment to moment unpredictable distort Inspiring beginnings of natural agreement.

The measure of the greatness of a place to live must come from the character of its Institutions sanctioned thru how sensitive they are to renewed. and Desire for new Agreement

student. They would also inspire a continual reevaluation of the curriculum and the meaning of the institution, leading to better student–teacher relationships.[5] Kahn sensed in older architecture some of the magical quality of beginnings; he often said he would love to have his office in a deserted school building, because the large, high-ceilinged rooms flooded with natural light were especially conducive to inspiration.

Whatever institution Kahn designed, he always emphasized the importance of finding its archetypal significance. He pointed out, however, that a single building in a city is never an isolated entity. The form nature of each organized human activity is expressed not only by its own transcendent quality but also by its relationship to other organizations in the city. The school, the boys' club, the residential section, the govern-

ment offices give direction to the city because they create the need for traffic systems connecting important urban focal points. In 1969, for example, Kahn described how finding the most appropriate relationship between the marketplace and the university would strengthen the expression of both their natures. The archetypal university is represented by persons striving toward their chosen avenues of creativity. The archetypal marketplace refers to the practicalities of life, the way each person earns a living. Kahn pointed out that the practical problems of the marketplace are irrelevant to the aspirations of the university, but that the university is not in a position to disdain the marketplace because it is supported by financial concerns. Kahn believed that all cities must have commercial centers that are physically separate from the centers of learning and self-expression so that the marketplace and the university could respect each other without encroaching on each other's territory. If such a relationship could be established, the true meanings of the marketplace and the university would be mutually supported.

Kahn's descriptions of institutions, like those of the city as a whole, are evocative of life. The institution originates as an archetype whose urge toward consciousness prompts its continual change and growth. The unlimited directions for this growth are implied in Kahn's later use of the word *availabilities*. Like the city as a whole, each of its parts will revitalize itself if given the chance. It is the architect's responsibility to listen to each building as though it had the voice to tell how it began and what it strives to become.

By 1971 Kahn's thoughts on the city had reached a highly symbolic level. In his talk "The Room, the Street and Human Agreement" he used words as symbols without scale, thus freeing them from their conventional meanings. One scale then becomes a metaphor for another. The room–street–plan hierarchy can be taken literally or as a metaphor for the institution–viaduct–city hierarchy.

The room is the simplest unit on which all architecture is based. Kahn described the room as a living entity created by people. Because it is alive, it is sensitive to what goes on inside it. The form idea of each room should be so clearly stated that the room automatically implies its use. One's own room is a personal space in which one can be alone to think, whereas a large

room is a space for collective events, for communication between people. Moreover, since the room is alive, it can adjust itself to the moment. Kahn suggested that, if a personal conversation took place inside a large room, the walls would move inward to form a more intimate space.

But how can a room suggest its use and also change to fit its use? The adaptability of the room does not actually contradict Kahn's idea of form as an archetype composed of a specific, unalterable order of parts. An established form can be experienced differently by each individual who walks into a room, just as an unlimited number of designs can be extracted from one form. The room is like the institution in that the activity itself is established through the collective agreement of all city residents, yet every individual's participation in the established activity is unique.

In the plan, each element assumes a specific place so that the entire arrangement becomes a tightly woven, meaningful whole. Like the buildings of a city, the rooms of a plan will naturally arrange themselves in a pattern appropriate to their functions. And just as institutions should be placed in relative positions that allow for their mutual support, rooms should be grouped so as to strengthen the uniqueness of each.[6] If the relationship of the elements is right, the whole works. Kahn compared the plan to the musical composition, which is heard as a single image rather than as a collection of distinct parts. All the elements in the plan have a desire to create a greater unity possessing its own form quality.

A conceptual sketch by Kahn, showing the room as the basic unit of architecture, c. 1971. (*Copyright The Louis I. Kahn Collection, University of Pennsylvania and the Pennsylvania Historical and Museum Commission.*)

The Street is a Room by agreement A community
Room the walls of which belong to the donors ......
Its ceiling is the sky ...... from the stree. must have come
the Meeting House who is place by agreement

Kahn used metaphor in his 1971 talk to show the relationship between the elements of connection in a plan and the avenues of connection in a city. For more than a decade, he had pointed out how the stair, the landing, and the corridor, which were usually considered subordinate to the rooms of a plan, had equally strong desires to proclaim their significance. Kahn stressed that these elements were not voids but spaces in their own right.[7] Likewise, he viewed the city's streets and parks as more than just voids between buildings. Kahn believed these open spaces should be treated as parts of a separate "architecture of connection" that is vital to the city's life.[8] In "The Room, the Street and Human Agreement" the parallel between these two scales becomes clear.

Kahn saw the street as a room, with buildings as walls and the sky as its ceiling. Such an outdoor room could be low-ceilinged and cozy or high-ceilinged and grand, residential or commercial, depending on the height and character of the buildings on either side. The street was to him a "room of agreement," specifically because it served the community. It was where people met, where children played, where vendors displayed their wares. The long street of many blocks was like a string of rooms imbued at the corners with the characters of intersecting streets.

By speaking of the street as a room, Kahn was referring to the inspiration of its beginning rather than to the street as it exists today. He pointed out that major traffic arteries have lost their precious room qualities since the advent of motor vehicles. As traffic speeds carelessly by, adjacent pedestrian ways become polluted by noxious fumes and the street becomes a convenient way to get to one's destination rather than a place to linger and browse. Kahn proposed that giving each type of traffic its own place would restore the room quality of the street, thus reinstilling the sense of community participation that is essential to the city's vitality.

In the context of this talk, Kahn's earlier viaduct concept takes on new significance. When Kahn proposed the multilayered channels for the separation of traffic in 1960, he envisioned the garages and shops on either side of the street as extensions of the street. At that time, the viaduct proposal was expressive of the street's desire to become a building. In 1971, however, he used the room as a metaphor for the building or institution. The viaduct, then, also came to support Kahn's vision of the street as a room.

Kahn stated in "The Room, the Street and Human Agreement" that the life of the city as a whole was dependent on the mutual agreement of its citizens to support a common way of life. A community is the natural result of people gathering together. If the institutions of a city are not answering the needs of the population, the city must lack a common spirit because a city is evaluated through its institutions. But as long as citizens maintain their unity of purpose, institutions will not lose their usefulness and relevance. Kahn saw urban renewal as the focusing of the desires of the citizens into a single desire, from the microcosm of the single room to the macrocosm of the city as a whole.

PRACTICE

Philadelphia was the city in which Kahn lived and based his architectural practice. Although he contributed to the development of other cities in the United States and abroad, he never ceased to use Philadelphia as a source of ideas concerning the urban environment.

Kahn's city planning work can be divided roughly into four periods of growth. The earliest can be called an unintegrated phase, during

which he was simultaneously working on small-scale residential projects and large-scale visionary schemes for Philadelphia without seeing a connection between the two. In the second, hierarchical phase (1953–1961), Kahn integrated his large- and small-scale proposals. But it was not until he began the government complex at Dacca, Bangladesh (then East Pakistan) in 1962 that he reached a complete understanding of the city's beginning inspiration. This third phase of his development can be called archetypal. Then in the 1970s he brought his deeper understanding of the city back to Philadelphia, prompting work that was metaphorical in nature.

During the 1940s, Kahn, then in partnership with Oskar Stonorov, was commissioned by the Federal Public Housing Authority to undertake several small residential projects. One of these was the Carver Court Housing Development (1941–1943) in Coatesville, Pennsylvania. The design is sensitive but not outstanding. It consists of three types of housing units arranged in a double loop that curves around the shallow rounded valley on the site. In the center of the project is an administration building containing community services and a social center.

View from interior of housing unit in Carver Court, Coatesville, Pennsylvania. The road follows the curve of the land. (*Photograph by Gottscho-Schleisner. Reproduced from the Library of Congress.*)

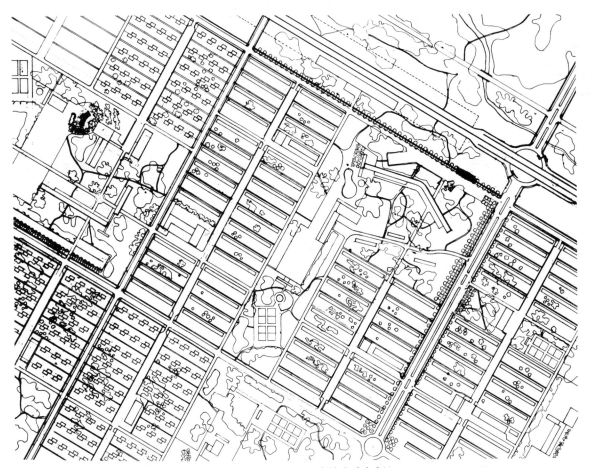

Typical residential superblock, 194X scheme for renewal of Philadelphia.

Along with this early work came ideas for the urgently needed renewal of Philadelphia's residential sections. In 1943 Kahn and Stonorov published booklets proposing shopping and recreational facilities to be built on reclaimed streets. These facilities would be centrally located in specific areas. Kahn's conception of the neighborhood grouped around a focal point clearly reflects his Carver Court scheme. Kahn also proposed making unnecessary streets into playgrounds and green areas. His projects and ideas were both practical and innovative, but he had neither developed a distinctive style nor begun to think systematically in terms of form, order, and design.

Slightly earlier, in 1939, Kahn had presented his first large-scale proposal for the renewal of Philadelphia, called the City of 194X. Kahn envisioned a system of superblocks that he superimposed over the grid pattern of existing blocks. Although 194X did take into consideration the general layout of Philadelphia streets, it was much too idealistic to have been carried out.

Another early project Kahn undertook with Stonorov, from 1945 to 1948, was the Triangle Redevelopment Plan. The Triangle Area, bordered by Market Street to City Hall, the Benjamin Franklin Parkway on the northeast, and the Schuykill River on the west, included a large empty plot of land in the center of town created by the demolition of an overhead track system called the Chinese Wall. Since the land was contained within clear-cut borders, there was no need to coordinate its proposed development with the character of the surrounding area. The Philadelphia City Planning Commission was in favor of building high-rise office towers that would drastically change Center City Philadelphia. Kahn went along with the prevailing attitude. The Triangle Area project did not challenge him to develop an approach to design that would integrate radical ideas with existing limitations.

In 1947 Kahn started an independent practice, and from 1949 to 1953, he worked on a series of traffic studies for Philadelphia. Kahn's scheme,

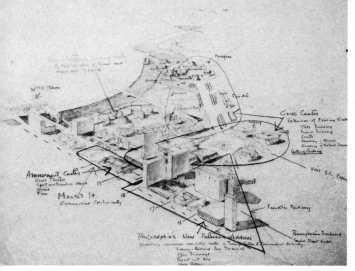

Sketch of proposed redevelopment of the Triangle Area, Philadelphia. (*Copyright The Louis I. Kahn Collection, University of Pennsylvania and the Pennsylvania Historical and Museum Commission.*)

Views east (*above*) and west (*below*) on Pennsylvania Boulevard show the proposed Penn Center in the Triangle Area plan. (*Copyright The Louis I. Kahn Collection, University of Pennsylvania and the Pennsylvania Historical and Museum Commission.*)

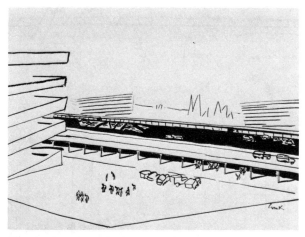

Sketch of parking facilities in the proposed Triangle Area. (*Copyright The Louis I. Kahn Collection, University of Pennsylvania and the Pennsylvania Historical and Museum Commission.*)

High-rise towers in the proposed Triangle Area. (*Copyright The Louis I. Kahn Collection, University of Pennsylvania and the Pennsylvania Historical and Museum Commission.*)

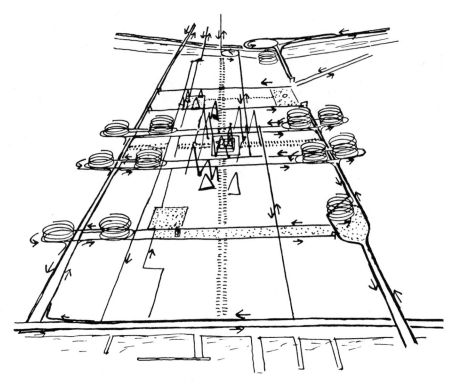

Abstract perspective of Center City, 1953. Helical coils are "wound up streets," or parking towers. (*Copyright The Louis I. Kahn Collection, University of Pennsylvania and the Pennsylvania Historical and Museum Commission.*)

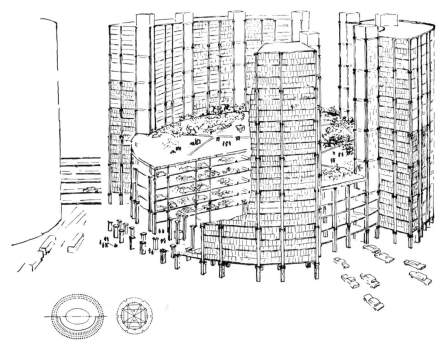

Elevation/section of parking tower for Center City.

Kahn's drawing of Chestnut Street as a pedestrian way. (*Reproduced, by permission, from Louis I. Kahn, "Toward a Plan for Midtown Philadelphia,"* **Perspecta 2: The Yale Architectural Journal,** *1953, p. 18.*)

Kahn's drawing of Market Street as a "dock." (*Reproduced, by permission, from Louis I. Kahn, "Toward a Plan for Midtown Philadelphia,"* **Perspecta 2: The Yale Architectural Journal,** *1953, p. 18.*)

an attempt to deal with the traffic problem in Center City, grew into his "order concept of movement." He pointed out that the present use of all streets by pedestrians, cars, buses, and delivery trucks was ineffectual. Retaining the existing street layout, he proposed a way to sort out traffic with respect to its speed and purpose (see diagrams, p. 104). Expressways approaching the city would lead to gigantic parking towers for motorists who intended to shop and work in the center of town. Shopping streets were to become pedestrian ways serviced by mass transportation. Major arteries would be through streets for fast-moving traffic only. These led to minor streets, which Kahn suggested be "docks" for parking and unloading. Kahn included the Triangle Area in his scheme—not as a modern oasis in the midst of antiquity, but as an integral part of the city. He saw the downtown area as a potential cultural center, nourished by the traffic proposal that encouraged access to the center of the city.

A preliminary presentation of the traffic studies in 1951 led to three commissions for residential projects from the City Planning Commission, which Kahn worked on in association with Louis E. McAllister, Kenneth Day, and Anne G. Tyng. The East Poplar and Southwest Temple schemes were planning studies that pulled together new and existing housing. Kahn, following his earlier idea of reusing unnecessary streets, suggested turning some streets into pedestrian walkways. His intent was to revive rather than to wipe out the existing community, by enhancing such traditional institutions as churches and schools with parks connected by the new pedestrian system. The third project was a prototypical study of row houses, later applied to a specific site in Northeast Philadelphia. Clusters of three, four, or five rows of houses are grouped around parking cul-de-sacs, which Kahn called "docks." This arrangement allowed for more green area and sensitivity to land contours at a density comparable to that of the traditional block of row houses.

The year 1953 was crucial in Kahn's planning experience. The row house studies were published in *Perspecta* 2, along with Kahn's movement scheme, and as the material was being collected for publication, Kahn saw the relationship between the row house cul-de-sac docks and the delivery docks he had proposed for downtown Philadelphia. Although Kahn had been developing a hierarchical traffic scheme for several years, he did not truly gain an understanding of the hierarchy of the city until he realized that his small-scale residential projects could fit into his large-scale plans. Also in 1953, Kahn developed his nature-of-the-space–order–design sequence, the prototype for his form–design theory. His initial attempts to analyze the process by which the original form idea conformed to circumstantial requirements were influenced by his work on the traffic studies and residential redevelopment projects. The fact that all these schemes worked within the existing city indicates that Kahn now had a systematic approach to design.

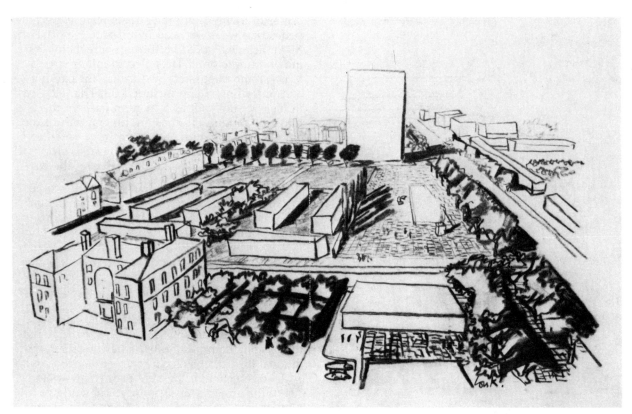

Combining new and existing housing on a residential scale, Southwest Temple area. (*Copyright The Louis I. Kahn Collection, University of Pennsylvania and the Pennsylvania Historical and Museum Commission.*)

Row house studies, showing clusters of houses grouped around parking cul-de-sacs. (*Copyright The Louis I. Kahn Collection, University of Pennsylvania and the Pennsylvania Historical and Museum Commission.*)

The Mill Creek Redevelopment Plan, which Kahn had begun in 1952 with McAllister, Day, and Tyng, was the first urban scheme in which he integrated street-by-street residential planning with a larger sense of the city's orderly movement. Because of the collapse of an old sewer culvert in West Philadelphia, many people were displaced from their homes, and to remedy the situation, Kahn designed housing that was built in two phases. The first phase provided high-density towers to house a large number of displaced families efficiently; the second phase consisted of low-rise dwellings of modest scale. The site was originally crisscrossed with noisy traffic arteries; redevelopment left only the surrounding through streets. Within the site, Kahn made unnecessary streets into green pedestrian ways, so that the remaining streets formed large superblocks. Fast traffic is restricted to the through streets around the superblocks, but cars have slower looped access to the small residential streets within the superblocks. Aspen Street, which runs directly through the site, connects new and existing schools, and low- and high-rise housing. Kahn transformed this main connecting route into one long pedestrian way. "Green fingers," other reclaimed streets, cross Aspen Street

Mill Creek housing provides both high-density towers and low-rise dwellings.
(*Reproduced by permission of Cortlandt v. d. Hubbard.*)

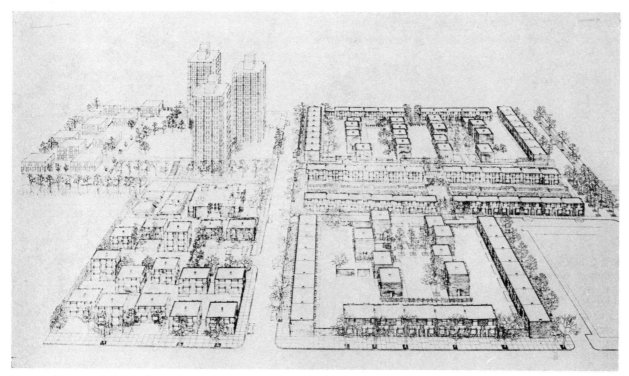

Perspective sketch for Mill Creek Housing Development, Philadelphia. Kahn
made unnecessary streets into pedestrian ways, so that the remaining streets
formed large superblocks. (*Copyright The Louis I. Kahn Collection, University of
Pennsylvania and the Pennsylvania Historical and Museum Commission.*)

Low-rise dwellings at Mill Creek consist of two- and four-family units. (*(c) John Ebstel.*)

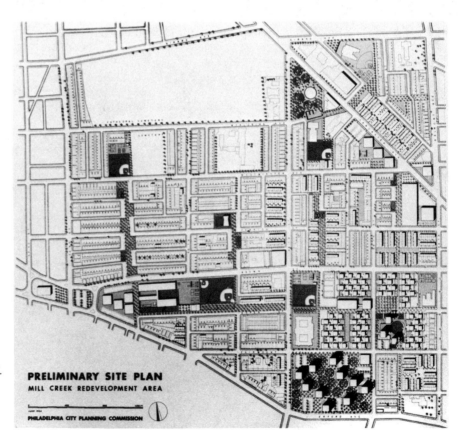

Mill Creek street plan after redevelopment. Dark areas between blocks are "green fingers." (*Copyright The Louis I. Kahn Collection, University of Pennsylvania and the Pennsylvania Historical and Museum Commission.*)

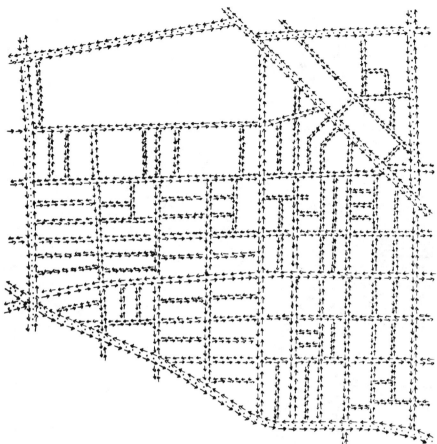

Diagram of Mill Creek street
traffic movement before
redevelopment. All streets are
two-way through streets.

at intervals. The resulting pedestrian system is
linked with the street system, but each retains its
own order indicative of its function.

After Mill Creek, Kahn received no further work
from the Philadelphia City Planning Commission. For political reasons, city officials chose
other architects to design such buildings as the

Penn Center complex, for which Kahn had laid
the groundwork. Kahn's exclusion from the on-
going development of Philadelphia was a painful
blow. Nevertheless, he continued to refine his
ideas for the revitalization of Center City. The
scarcity of work gave him time for introspection.
By 1959 he had developed the idea of form,

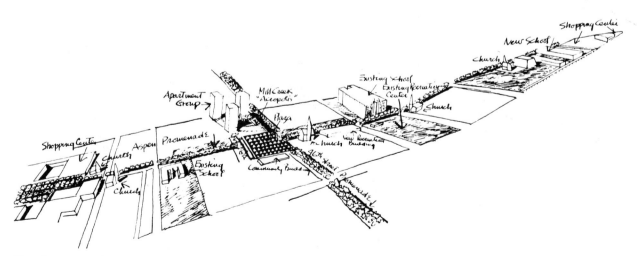

Plan for Aspen Street as a pedestrian way, Mill Creek.

Center City Philadelphia's proposed cultural center, including the city tower,
c. 1956–1957.

Viaduct scheme, looking north from Locust Street, downtown Philadelphia,
1962. The viaducts were intended to sort traffic and services under the streets,
freeing the surfaces for pedestrian traffic.

Section through Center City, showing placement of viaducts in relation to City Hall, the stadium, and expressway.

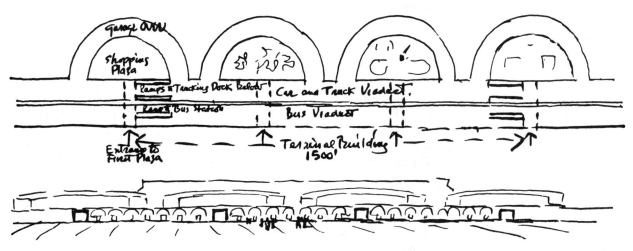

Plan (above) and elevation (below) of bus terminal. Kahn envisioned the viaduct system as a multilevel expression of the street's desire to be a building.

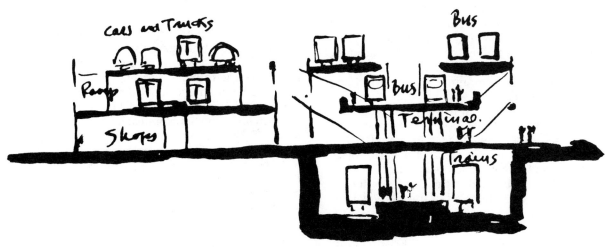

Section through bus terminal, showing above-ground parking and ground-level shops.

which gave rise to his original archetypal vision of the viaduct. In 1961 Kahn was awarded a Graham Foundation grant to continue to develop his proposals for Philadelphia. Within three years, the viaduct concept grew more specific as it was applied to the reality of existing Philadelphia streets. Form was adjusting itself to the limitations of design. Kahn's sketches of the proposed viaducts clearly show how he planned to sort traffic and services under the streets, to separate these channels from surface pedestrian traffic, and to link underground service rooms with above-ground shops and high-rise parking towers. Complex intersections in the center of the city become enclosed rooms in which each type of traffic could move without disturbing others. Kahn used the term *viaduct* as a catalyst in the translation from dream to reality. In coming to a form realization of the order of movement, Kahn focused on a word that functioned as an archetypal image. In this case, the word *viaduct* enabled him to see how the street could actually become a workable life-carrying artery.

In 1962 Kahn received a commission to design an eastern capital for Pakistan. Because of his discouraging experiences with the Philadelphia City Planning Commission, he was ready in spite of his loyalty to Philadelphia to direct his attention elsewhere. Kahn was asked by the Pakistani government to design a range of buildings—assembly, hostels for government officials, and hospital—on 840 acres of land outside Dacca. The buildings were to comprise the new legislative center of East Pakistan. This was, in a sense, the commission for which Kahn had been waiting. Although it was not a total city, Sher-e-Banglanagar was his chance to design the essential core of a city from the ground up.

Kahn literally was able to go back to the beginning of the city, when its form was not modified and obscured, and ask himself what the essences were of these institutions that he had to arrange on the site. His form realization was that the city's experience of community occurred in two different ways—spiritual and physical. New buildings that were not in the original program became part of this realization. To one side of the National Assembly complex he added a supreme court; with prayer hall and hostels, these buildings were to comprise the spiritual aspect of the city, which Kahn called the Citadel of the Assembly. On the other end of the site, near the proposed hospital, he envisioned markets, schools, a recreation center, and a living sector; these more physical expressions of urban life, he called the Citadel of the Institutions. The word *citadel* indicated to Kahn the sacred nature of each grouping. Early schemes show Kahn's indecision over how best to express the relationship between these two parts, but by 1963 the dilemma was resolved. The two citadels face each other across a park, acknowledging that their contributions to the total city form are different yet interrelated.

The Citadel of the Assembly centers around the National Assembly building itself, flanked by prayer hall and Presidential Plaza. The joining of assembly building and prayer hall was the result of Kahn's initial, powerful realization that the meaning of *assembly* attains a spiritual dimension when it is applied to community participation.[9] This religious sense of assembly, which Kahn felt was missing in most governments today, he expressed by placing the prayer hall as an entrance through which government officials would pass on their way to making decisions based on mutual agreement. Kahn also felt that, because the decision-making functions of the assembly and supreme court were different in nature, the prayer hall should be built between them hopefully to reinstill the archetypal spirit of law making and interpretation. Kahn's intuition was, to his great joy, supported by the chief justice, who felt that the prayer hall sufficiently insulated the court from the assembly.[10] His success in communicating with the government officials of East Pakistan was a triumph for Kahn, whose belief that the language of form transcended cultural differences was confirmed.

In early schemes, the Citadel of the Institutions, situated on the wider end of the site across a park, seems to bow to the shrinelike assembly while curving protectively around it. A 1963 plan shows the institutions focused around the center for physical recreation so that this building faces the National Assembly directly; thus, the plan expresses clearly the physical-spiritual dichotomy between the two citadels. In the same scheme, the recreation center is flanked by schools for art and science. Behind it are the marketplace and bazaars. Already, Kahn had realized the separate natures of the forms of university and marketplace, as he described in 1969 at The Swiss Federal Institute of Technology (ETH), Zurich. They are visually removed from each other, yet joined by the recreation center between them. Each of the institutions makes an essential contribution to the interplay of forms that comprise the citadel; Kahn believed that, without any one of its contributing parts, the citadel's form meaning would be incompletely realized.

By 1972 East Pakistan had become the independent country of Bangladesh, and Sher-e-Banglanagar was now the sole capital of the new country. As a result of the change in government, more executive offices were needed than had

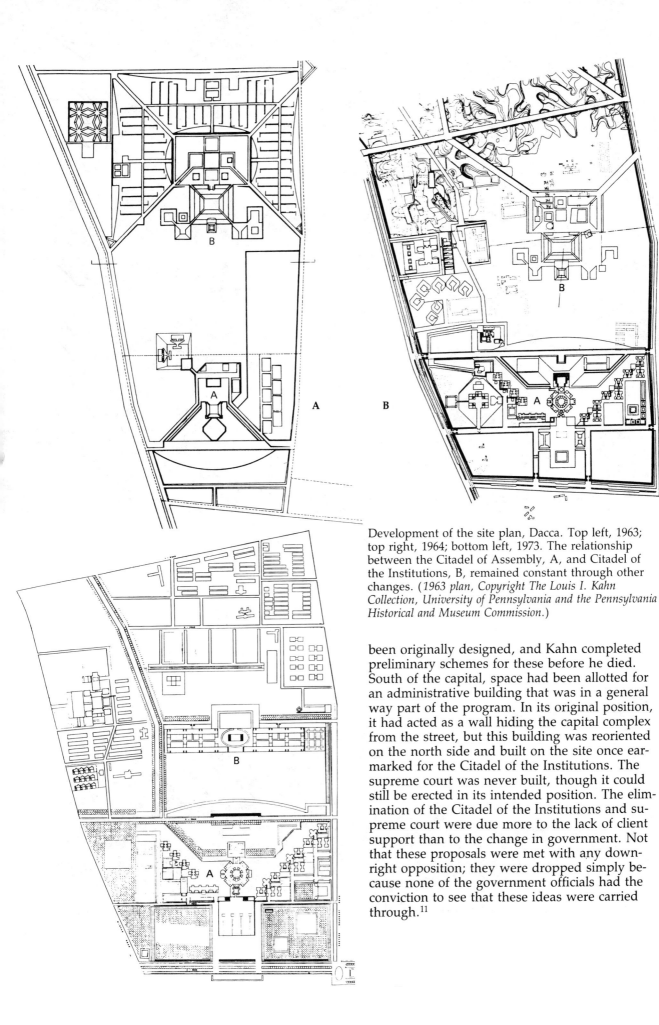

Development of the site plan, Dacca. Top left, 1963; top right, 1964; bottom left, 1973. The relationship between the Citadel of Assembly, A, and Citadel of the Institutions, B, remained constant through other changes. (*1963 plan, Copyright The Louis I. Kahn Collection, University of Pennsylvania and the Pennsylvania Historical and Museum Commission.*)

been originally designed, and Kahn completed preliminary schemes for these before he died. South of the capital, space had been allotted for an administrative building that was in a general way part of the program. In its original position, it had acted as a wall hiding the capital complex from the street, but this building was reoriented on the north side and built on the site once earmarked for the Citadel of the Institutions. The supreme court was never built, though it could still be erected in its intended position. The elimination of the Citadel of the Institutions and supreme court were due more to the lack of client support than to the change in government. Not that these proposals were met with any downright opposition; they were dropped simply because none of the government officials had the conviction to see that these ideas were carried through.[11]

The buildings of the Indian Institute of Management, Ahmedabad, are organized around the concept of meeting. (*Reprinted by permission from Louis I. Kahn, "Remarks," **Perspecta 9/10: The Yale Architectural Journal**, 1965, p. 328.*)

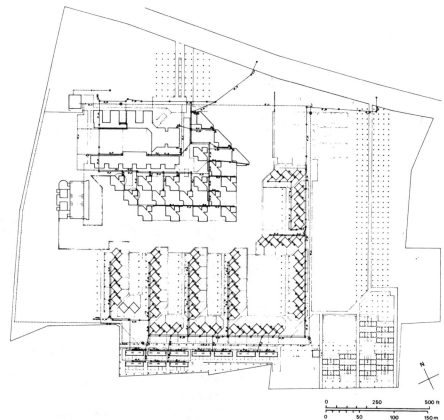

Site plan for Indian Institute of Management, Ahmedabad. Dormitories, faculty residences, and staff and married student housing radiate out from the school building (upper left).

Aerial view of construction site, Ahmedabad. Dormitories are in middle ground; school building foundations are to right. (*Copyright The Louis I. Kahn Collection, University of Pennsylvania and the Pennsylvania Historical and Museum Commission.*)

Faculty housing, Indian Institute of Management, Ahmedabad. (*Photograph by P. M. Dalwadi. (c) National Institute of Design, Ahmedabad.*)

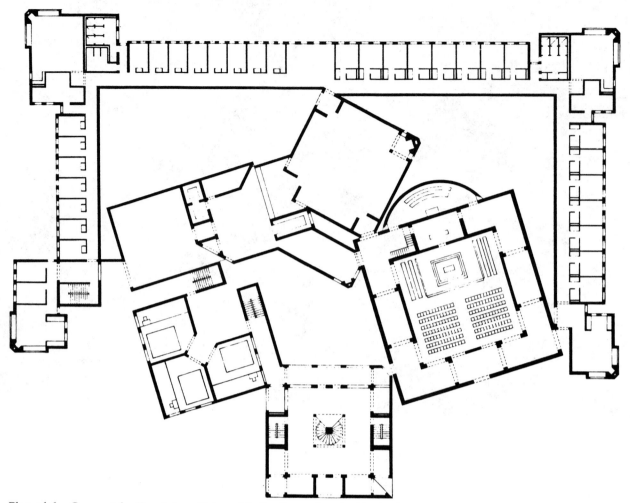

Plan of the Convent for Dominican Sisters, Media, Pennsylvania. The buildings are turned so that their corners touch, creating a connection without corridors. (*Copyright The Louis I. Kahn Collection, University of Pennsylvania and the Pennsylvania Historical and Museum Commission.*)

When Kahn gave his talk on "The Room, the Street and Human Agreement" in 1971, his work at Dacca had led him to a deeper symbolic understanding of the city and its institutions. The talk incorporates all his previous experience with urban development on a new level. Kahn's view of the street as a room based on agreement clearly evolved from his earlier viaduct concept, which combined different layers of traffic with rooms below and buildings above the street. His idea that the plan is a society of rooms[12] grew from his realization that a group of buildings that together express one nature become inseparable, so that the total entity transcends the sum of its parts. By 1971 Kahn was able to synthesize these concepts in a metaphorical description of the city.

It seems fitting that in this same year Kahn had the opportunity to express this metaphor in a design for his own city. In 1971 he began a proposal for the Bicentennial Exposition on the Delaware River, and in the following year, he was joined by a committee of other Philadelphia architects and planners. He envisioned his city as a place that could foster unlimited potential for the growth of its institutions, which he now called "availabilities." The proposed exhibition (never built) consists of one long enclosed street, which is at the same time a building and a room. It symbolizes the meeting place of all the institutions, where visitors to the exhibitions could better understand the spirit of community and thus work for a common purpose so the city would be a better place to live.

KAHN

In most urban areas, children play in the streets. . . . There are too many streets anyway. So why not make playgrounds out of unnecessary streets?[13] (1943)

Architecture is also the street. There is no order to the movement on streets. Streets look alike, reflecting little of the activities they serve—Carcassonne without walls, cities without entrances, indiscriminate movement without places to stop. The design of the street is design for movement.

Fifty years ago before the automobile and the skyscraper, this map looked the same. The open space system is substantially the street system which occupies about 30% of the site. Except for the Vine Street Expressway the streets have retained their dimensions. Yard spaces have disappeared with the growing density and coverage of buildings. Recently with the greater increase in cars, parking lots have become the new open spaces. In general parking lots and garages take over other uses now on the secondary streets between the main shopping streets. Movement through the city is difficult. A parking ban is now being tried which has increased the flow of traffic and accentuated the value of off-street parking. Those streets cleared of parking still have the conflicting *staccato* movement of buses or trolleys and the *go* intentions of the car moving in the same lanes.

It is intended by the drawings which follow to *re-define* the *use of streets* and separate one type of movement from another so that cars, buses, trolleys, trucks and pedestrians will move and stop more freely, and not get in each other's way. This system utilizes the old streets, setting aside widening and other costly improvements as untimely before a more effective use of present street area is tested. However, the widening of Lombard Street as an expressway planned by the Philadelphia City Planning Commission is important. It would accomplish the demolition of decidedly bad slums and help frame the area known as CENTER CITY.

By designating specific streets for the staccato movement of buses and trolleys, specific streets for go traffic, and others as terminal streets for stopping, the efficiency of street movement would be increased considerably. Cars may enter the areas—and not be ruled out as many of today's planners propose. Zoning would grow naturally out of the type of movement on a street. Architecture would tend to be related to the type of movement.

This system of movement is not designed for speed but for order and convenience. The present mixture of staccato, through, stop and go traffic makes all the streets equally ineffectual. The orderly discrimination of traffic of varying intentions should tend to facilitate flow and thereby encourage rather than discourage entrance of private cars into the center of town.

It is further intended by this system to stimulate more imaginative development of our shopping areas along the lines of the

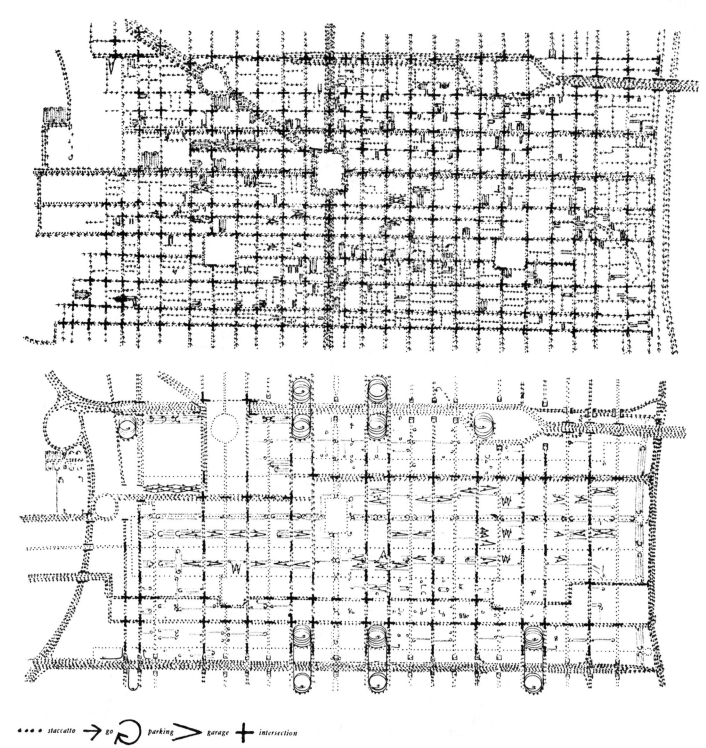

•••• *staccatto* → *go* ⟳ *parking* ⟩ *garage* ✛ *intersection*

Existing (top) and proposed traffic movement patterns for Philadelphia. Kahn's order concept of movement is based on the existing street pattern. (*Reproduced, by permission, from Louis I. Kahn, "Toward a Plan for Midtown Philadelphia," Perspecta 2: The Yale Architectural Journal, 1953, pp. 16, 17.*)

new suburban shopping centers which already provide a pattern of movement sympathetic to the pedestrian and the motor. In town, this distinction of types of movement could also give rise to new building and merchandising ideas. Chestnut Street as a pedestrian way with a single trolley line becomes virtually a 60 foot promenade. Trees could be planted or shelters built for shade, and the free zig-zag lines of the movement of people from one side of the promenade to the other would tend to free the design of shops from their present linear limitations. . . .

The harbor gateways are proposed as parking towers built at the same time as the expressway on Lombard Street and at the suggested points to be acquired by the Parking Authority on Vine Street. Each tower would house about 1500 cars. The garage buildings in the dock areas between Market and Chester, Chestnut and Walnut, are proposed as built by private enterprise aided in acquisition and standards by the Parking Authority.

The COMMERCIAL CORE is accentuated in this study for the purpose of suggesting that the contemplated development of the Chinese Wall—Pennsylvania Boulevard area (known as Penn Center) should not be isolated from the Core. The strength of the new development lies in tying it together with existing shopping and commercial patterns.

It is suggested that the address of Penn Center should be extended to include the area from 18th Street to the river, thereby tying in the Pennsylvania Station at 30th Street with its Suburban Station at 17th. Present Penn Center plans call for development from City Hall to 18th Street only. The bus station proposed at 18th Street by the City Planning Commission would serve both ends of the extended Penn Center. The NEW CITY HALL including the courts and technical buildings is located in the Triangle Area as part of our enlarged CIVIC AND CULTURAL CENTER at Logan Square. This move anticipates stimulation of developments westward and reclamation of the Schuykill River for recreation. This relatively inexpensive area would allow for the continued development of the expanding functions of our city government and would eventually reveal itself as the new Philadelphia Landmark—an impressive entrance to the center city at its rail and motor gateway.

Over part of the railroad yards of the 30th Street Station, a TRANSPORTATION GATEWAY is proposed, tying together two levels of passenger tracks, the high level freight line, a trucking level and a helicopter air connection as a transportation interchange and a freight center. This would consolidate some of the services of the Pennsylvania Railroad now spread over a large area, and serve the needs of the Post Office and the new Bulletin Building. . . .

This type of drawing made fifty years ago would show dots in all the streets—no arrows, no crosses. The symbol of staccato movement would well have applied to the delivery wagon, carriage and horse-drawn trolley. Now on the same street trolleys, buses, trucks and cars with varying speeds, purposes and destinations travel together. Uninterested traffic destined to places outside the center may choose streets at will. Motion is further restrained by loading, deliveries and parking. Frequent intersections frustrate movement.

Vine Street, widened to expressway dimensions has the same number of intersections as before. The original plans for the expressway which were not realized by the Philadelphia City Planning Commission called for a depressed cartway with entrances by ramp to cross streets.

Parking lots and garages are developing to some extent where they are most needed. Demolition of unprofitable or unfit buildings usually result in a parking lot wherever it happens. These places to stop now exist in the stream of movement. The slowest vehicle sets the pace of movement.

The added movement symbol is the wound-up street or municipal garage at the strategic gateway interchanges off the Vine and Lombard expressways. These, with the expressways of the Delaware and Schuykill frame Midtown Philadelphia. Though the number of intersections have been decreased, the gridiron pattern of the streets are intact. Staccato movement is on its system of streets separated from all go traffic. The main interior streets of Broad and Market intersecting at City Hall have been converted into linear docks. Skyscrapers, banks and department stores on these streets are thereby provided with an automobile entrance and a place for people to park. The trend indicated on the existing movement map of parking lots and garages on minor streets between main shopping streets is extended, and, these places are designed as terminals. Buses and trolleys are retained on the main shopping streets for public transportation and to keep the linear business area tied together. This plan will provide docking space for all trucks on all streets except the go streets.

The tower entrances and interchanges, wound-up parking terminals, suggest a new stimulus to unity in urban architecture, one which would find expression from the order of movement. The location and design of these entrances are an integral part of the design of the expressway financed and constructed as a unit. It is not an isolated real estate venture which could lead to compromise and the distortion of the system. At night we know these towers by their illumination in color. These yellow, red, green, blue and white towers tell us the sector we are entering, and along the approach, light is used to see by and give us direction in ideas of lighting in rhythm with our speed. From these entrances a system of canals or interior streets feed the various activities of center city life.

Shopping

Shopping streets would have no go traffic. People meet in shopping places. Promenades would induce new and revive old and even ancient merchandising ideas. Now the shopping areas are islands in a sea of traffic. They could be an interweaving of people, glass, escalators, trees, gardens and exhibits. We could walk through our Christmas decorations not only peer at them through windows.

The wares, holiday symbols intermingled with the trees, patios, music and fashion shows remind one of the seasons. Gardens finger through the shops and the exhibits which show how things are made. The scale of the architecture is in sympathy with the "path of feet and the eye" (George Howe).

Shopping is walking. Walking is also resting—in shade, at the sidewalk café, looking at the sculptor's exhibit in the garden. Shopping promenades lead to a larger area—the site of the theatres, dance hall, bowling alleys, concert hall, places for food and refreshment, and places with such fun devices as the pin ball machine, juke box and shooting galleries. Diverse entertainment now found on cheap streets—classed as "honky tonk"—are actually healthy energies—part of our blue jean era, needing the more friendly environment of the planned fun center.[14] (1953)

A street wants to be a building.

The new spaces that want to be will emerge from the designs drawn from an order of movement.

An order of movement that distinguishes staccato from go movement and includes the concept of stopping.

The zoning of streets for characteristic movement must precede the zoning of the land they serve.

Expressways are rivers that need harbors.

Streets are canals that need docks.

The architecture of stopping is equal in importance to the great walls that surrounded the medieval cities.

Carcassonne was designed from an order of defense. A modern city will renew itself from its order concept of movement which is a defense against its destruction by the automobile.

Center City is a place to go to—not to go through.

Great vehicular harbors or municipal entrance towers will surround the innermost center of the city. They will be the gateways, the landmarks, the first images that greet the visitor. Their place in this order and their strategic locations will demand of the designers meaningful form as a composite building of many uses. Its street story may be a marker, the outer ring towards the light may be used as a hotel or for offices and the inner core for storage. The main body of the tower gateways between the outer perimeter and the inner core will be the wound up street of vehicular arrival and stopping.

The spaces and buildings within the gateways must embody and strive for the fulfillment of gregarian tendencies. Only the consolidation of all centers—cultural, academic, commercial, athletic, health and civic—into one Forum will inspire renewal of a city.

Decentralization disperses and destroys the city. So-called shopping centers away from the Center are merely buying. Shopping cannot exist away from the city's core.

An arena placed outside the city for reasons of parking is isolated from its other living companions. Its existence outside is limited, unenlivened by the other places where people gather. In the Center its space will stimulate ideas for its use and strengthen other places of meeting and commerce by its presence.

The Center need not be large. It now is more complex than the village green. Consolidation and its lofty spires is contained within the scale of walking. The moving sidewalk extends the area of that scale.

The Center is the cathedral of the city.

City streets and plots are structures containing services of ever increasing complexity and importance. The building platform or plaza attempts to derive meaningful form out of the realization that a street 'wants to be' a building equally organized as to space and structure as any other piece of architecture.[15] (1957)

A modern city will renew itself from its order concept of movement. . . . Only the consolidation of all centers—cultural, academic, commercial, civic, etc.—into one forum will inspire renewal of the city. . . . In the Center its space will stimulate ideas for its use and strengthen other places of meeting and commerce by its presence.[16] (1958)

Today, building needs an atmosphere of belief for the architect to work in. Belief can come from recognizing that new institutions want to emerge and be given expression in space. New beliefs come with new institutions that need to be expressed as new spaces and new relationships. The architectural realizations sensitive to the institutions' particular form would set a new precedent, a new beginning. I do not believe that beauty can be deliberately created. Beauty evolves out of a will to be that may have its first expression in the archaic. Compare Paestum with the Parthenon. Archaic Paestum is the beginning. It is the time when the walls parted and the columns became and when Music entered architecture. Paestum inspired the Parthenon. The Parthenon is considered more beautiful, but Paestum is still more beautiful to me. It presents a beginning within which is contained all the wonder that may follow in its wake. The column as a rhythm of enclosure and opening and the feeling of entering through them to the spaces they envelop is an architectural spirit, a religion which still prevails in our architecture today.[17] (c. 1959)

The places of entrance, the galleries that radiate from them, the intimate entrances to the spaces of the institution form an independent architecture of connection. This architecture is of equal importance to the major spaces though these spaces are designed only for movement and must therefore be designed to be bathed in natural light. This Architecture of Connection cannot appear in the program of areas—it is what the architect offers the client in his search for architectural balance and direction.[18] (c. 1959)

The motor car has completely upset the form of the city. I feel that the time has come to make the distinction between the Viaduct architecture of the car and the architecture of man's activities. The tendencies of designers to combine the two architectures in a simple design has confused the direction of planning and technology. The Viaduct architecture enters the city from outlying areas. At this point it must become more carefully made and even at great expense more strategically placed with respect to the centre.

The Viaduct architecture includes the street which in the centre of the city wants to be a building, a building with rooms below for city piping services to avoid interruption to traffic when services need repair.

The Viaduct architecture would encompass an entirely new concept of street movement which distinguished the stop and go staccato movement of the bus from the 'go' movement of the car. The area framing expressways are like rivers. These rivers need harbours. The interim streets are like canals which need docks. The harbours are the gigantic gateways expressing the *architecture of stopping*. The terminals of the Viaduct architecture, they are garages in the core, hotels and department stores around the periphery and shopping centers on the street floor.

This strategic positioning around the city centre would present a logical image of protection against the destruction of the city by the motor car. In a sense the problem of the car and city is war, and the planning for the new growth of cities is not a complacent act, but an act of emergency.

The distinction between the two architectures, the architecture of the Viaduct and the architecture of the acts of man's activities, could bring about a logic of growth and a sound positioning of enterprise.

An architect from India gave an excellent talk at the University about the fine new work of Le Corbusier and about his own work. It impressed me, however, that these beautiful works he showed me were still out of context and had no position. After his lecture I was asked to remark. Somehow I was moved to go to the blackboard where I drew in the centre of the board a towering water tower, wide on top and narrow below. Like the rays of a star, I drew aqueducts radiating from the tower. This implied the coming of the trees and fertile land and a beginning of living. The buildings not yet there which would cluster around the aqueduct would have meaningful position and character.

The city would have form.[19] (1960)

In speaking of the city I like to feel that it is a realization; that there is a distinction between city and institution. Institution is a working organization of the city. A city, specifically like Philadelphia or Rome, is a symbol of that which is an undeniable focus of getting together; the feeling that man as being cannot be denied; that may take ugly forms, ugly shapes, but you can't deny it.

I wish to speak about realization in this sense and in relation to institution.

I believe that the institutions of our city are rotten to the core. If we get a program from a school board which says: Don't forget the nine-foot fence around your school, a lobby so many square feet, corridors nine feet wide, all classrooms alike—you have a red light budget that goes with it. I think nothing can come out of it in the way of what the architect is able to do.

If you were to define architecture in a few words you would say architecture is the thoughtful making of spaces. It is the duty of the architect to find what is this thoughtful realm of space, what is school—and not just take the program of the institution but try to develop something which the institution itself can realize is valid.

That is a challenge.

What is a school? It was a man sitting under a tree talking to a student who didn't know he was a student, simply talking about what occurred to him as a realization. Later of course the need for such a thing came about. Certainly the mother and child, hearing about this man, wanted to live forever. Others took on the role of teacher. Pretty soon rules were built around the teacher and pretty soon the group developed into our present institutions which have absolutely no resemblance to the existence will which generated from the man under a tree talking to a few people.

I believe it is the duty of the architect to take every institution in the city and think of it as his work, that his work is to redefine the progress brought by these institutions; not to accept programs but to think in terms of spaces—in the case of the school he may even present a large entrance space which you can't name and from there he may go to a development of spaces, spaces small, large, with light coming from above to the side, but spaces that seem to indicate a good place where learning is possible.

Every space, including the corridor itself, should not be just stuffed with lockers because it happens to be a good way of solving a problem. Quite a difference between the economic problem and the budgetary problem.

In the same way, if you were given the problem of designing a chapel for a university, certainly you would not bring out all your palette of stained glass and mosaics or devices which you know a chapel must have, but simply think of it as a place which for the moment you won't define because it is too sacred. Then you put the ambulatory around, and then you put an arcade around the ambulatory so you don't have to go into the ambulatory, and a garden around the arcade so you don't have to go into the arcade, and then a fence around the garden so you don't have to go into the garden.

Ritual is inspired, not set. I think it begins with the sense of a man who gets a criticism from a fine teacher and this instills in him a sense of dedication and he goes by the chapel and winks at it—he doesn't have to go in. He doesn't wink at the gymnasium, he winks at the chapel.

So it is not taking out your familiar tools in the development of space. It is the realization of the kind of space.

I think the city would grow great and I think the city is the true cathedral of our living. Man learns about man. He learns even how to walk graciously from man. He discovers walking by looking at another man.

Our institutions and their programs must be attacked. Architects must give great empty spaces for the institutions—those spaces must be both things of life and ways of life.

If you look at the Baths of Caracalla—the ceiling swells a hundred and fifty feet high. It was a marvelous realization on the part of the Romans to build such a space. It goes beyond function.[20] (1960)

Think in terms of light, air, the sounds that you hear, water, the green world, the animal world. If I take the last, the animal world, I see the cheetah, running at great speed; and this humiliates man. It makes him inferior to the cheetah—the cheetah you haven't got. In your mind you become conscious of this and you dream of greater locomotion. You dream of being able to move through space with speed—at the ground-speed of such as the cheetah. The cheetah is sort of an out and out jealousy of the animal. And the same is so with birds—how could you ever not think of flying if you see a bird.

The mere fact that there are things in nature that do fly, and that there are animals in creation that run faster than you, makes that part of your brain and your motivation (which are really the same thing) want to do so. Therefore, I consider the automobile, like any means of locomotion, as being something which is a definite progress, and we are just as much responsible for the design as the designer himself. It's something which belongs to man's aspirations.

Another thing, the forest wants the city and the city wants the forest. The green world isn't just simply that you like flowers, or that you like trees. Deep down in our experience we lived off such foliage. There must have been something which we deeply venerated and is still part of us. We can't divorce the city from the green world in any way. We could see urbanism completely without trees, but the trees must be made part of our living pattern because they are part of our life. You can extend it to water as being something which makes a fountain a necessity, and not just a decoration in a city—something which you must be close to. To command water, as the Romans did when they brought the water from the mountains and into the form of the fountain is something which gives you a command over that thing which is very much part of you deep down. When you see a moving stream you feel as though you have caught sight of what life really is, because you, yourself, have a record of this in you in some way—and your response to it is as something which is very much part of life and you want to make it part of your living.

And there you can make a distinction between living and life if you wish. Life is something that is. It's the nature, really, of our existence—where living is just the exercise of it. And life is the part I'm talking about. Living—like design—concerns me very little. What does concern me is that which makes design an understandable thing. And if you don't understand the sense of life, it is very hard to sense whether you are satisfying this life through living. It is the same if you stand in a square and see a number of windows. These give you the first trace of light even though you are bathed in light. You're not so much conscious of light until you see windows. You know that these windows light the interior of things.

You can't talk about the motorcar in isolation, without realizing that it is one of the items only—one of the things which we ourselves have created. And you can't even take the attitude that you can kick it around because you don't like the looks of it, or because you don't like the design of it, or because you think it destroys the city. It is a force which has to do with our life, and the living must be patterned so that you include it in what you call the force of life—of which this is an instrument of its expression. Therefore, if the car is ugly now, you must strive to make it beautiful. By beautiful, I mean that it must have no redundancies. Nothing in nature can tolerate an instrument that is full of redundancies. It's bound to be either pared down or destroyed by its own weight.

Therefore, the fight must be to make the car as efficient as it wants to be with the least materials, and the least space occupancy (and yet the largest you can make it). This is all very natural. Otherwise it would weigh too much, cost too much, take up too much room and be uneconomical to operate. So, therefore, we must strive to make it more beautiful, and that means more true to itself.

Motion—movement—is such an important part of our dreams. I don't know anybody who doesn't dream of flying through space (you've got to move your arms a little bit) and this is speed to equal any kind of speed—or to swim marvellously, without much effort at all. From this, I feel that the making of a positive architecture of movement, which I like to call a viaduct architecture—which takes into account all the aspects of movement and separates them into identities which don't inhibit—has free exercise of one characteristic or the other. So, a viaduct that requires speed cannot be mixed up with a viaduct that is designed to have frequent intervals of interchange. And it must all terminate in a kind of stopping point, because after all it is the nature of movement to stop, when it comes to the city. So, therefore, the architecture of movement.

Now the viaduct architecture in the open country is one form of architecture, with one form of material use, and one form of design, because it is moving at great speeds and also has no immediate objective but to move. This architecture is different; it doesn't require so much integration with other things. But when it reaches town, it becomes a much more respectable kind of viaduct than it was on the open road. In other words, that viaduct in the city becomes a very strategic thing. It is using valuable land and the city can't waste land. The concentration is too great. And therefore, the viaduct, when it reaches town must consider what you can use underneath the viaduct, the materials you use for the viaduct—and that it is made of a tough material, not just a fragile material so that it can withstand the relentless natural forces on it. And as it reaches the centre of town it must be strength highly used in every sense—as storage places (underneath the viaduct or associated with it), for incoming utility of sorts, and even being the centre for the control of utilities. Until it gets to the very core at the entrance to important places in the city—at which point the viaduct must terminate in service areas—service areas which are very close to the centre, and which, because they must be placed in the most strategic and expensive places must not become for one use, but for many, because the storage of a car must cost the city nothing, must cost even the building that you construct for its use, nothing—because nothing is more expensive than a car that's not moving. So therefore, this building must be large, in order to develop a value on the periphery of the building. It can itself be a hotel, or a motel, and the lower stories must be for shopping or some other service that the city needs at this point, (probably in connection with the use around it). The very core of this central shopping building, could possibly be the central air-conditioning station for the core of the city instead of having everybody scrambling for their particular air-conditioning system. Air-conditioning and the control of atmosphere could be a city function. And so you sense that an architecture can grow out of movement which can be of terrific service to the centre of the city.

When you are going on the open road no speed will satisfy the motorist. He becomes less conscious of the landscape than one might think. How much you see—what way you see isn't a question of speed. Because he is in a car, it becomes something which he has no control over. He can't go at twenty miles an hour because he's a sensitive man, against the other man who goes sixty because he's a less sensitive man. He becomes equally as insensitive. And looking at it the other way, it disregards the difference between one man and another. The motorcar has a way of demanding of you that it become a cheetah. It's completely on its own. You can't read any sentimentality into the fact. You can't make out what you think is good for another person because it's good for you. It must be thought of in that sense.

And there's no reason that you should not find the range of speeds much less as you enter the centre of the city. So one could even design roads that change accordingly. There's no sense in trying to speed when you're in the city. There's no necessity for speed when one is in the city. So therefore one can slow down. What I'm trying to say is that you can't let your car be stopped at a certain point in the city and adopt another mode of transportation to get to the centre. This I don't believe in. I believe that there can even be two or three centres that you come to instead of one. But my belief is that you cannot set an arbitrary line around the centre city unless that line is a great line. In other words that line is so great—the city is so great—that everything you touch beyond that line destroys the greatness of the city. Then you can make a man stop behind one very close line if the city itself is great.

But once the man has gone through what might be considered building landscape, and not any important part of the city—no place which is the citadel—that man will not rest until he reaches the citadel—to stop at the gates of the citadel. And so, for that reason, my belief is that the man should come as close as possible to what you'd call the centre, where everything is. And this centre must be protected from all cars and be made completely a walking place, and not have any cars in it. You can, of course, incidentally say that there's taxi service and that certain cars enter in order to have that kind of service.

But whether that is so doesn't make much difference. You have taken the major problem and solved it in terms of the cheetah. If you don't mind I'll take that analogy, because I think that is fundamentally what it is. It distinguishes you from the elephant, you see, because the elephant doesn't have any dreams of imitating the cheetah. And so, this being man, he might even destroy the city because of his dreams. But hold no reverence for the city as it is in the hope that you might save it—so as not to destroy its wonderful values. No, you must defend these values in another way—by the interjection of new forms from which a whole realm of new designs can come about and which can make the city what you never saw before—only because you recognize that man is taken as a measure, (in other words to satisfy his desires).

But I believe that many cities won't stand up against the demands of this, and that cities will actually be destroyed, (or wither away by inaction) in this light, or because the city itself cannot extend its greatness, or really capture a greatness by reason of its position—and so forth. The circumstantial demands of the car, of the parking and so forth, will eat away all the spaces that exist now, and pretty soon you have no identifying traces of what I call loyalties—the landmarks. Remember, when you think of your city, you think immediately of certain places which identify the city, as you enter it. If they're gone, your feeling for the city is lost and gone. But new landmarks can be created, new confidences, new loyalties. These need not be financial loyalties— they can be any kind of loyalties—faith in something. But in looking ahead we must sense the form which the city may take. If, because of the demands of the motorcar, we stiffen and harden the city—omitting water, omitting the green world—the city will be destroyed. Therefore the car, because of its destructive value, must start us rethinking the city in terms of the green world, in terms of the world of water, and of air, and of locomotion—and that is really the animal world.[21] (1961)

When we think of our cities for a moment, we can review again the new knowledge we have, the new sense of order we have, in relation to water, to light, to air, to movement. Just think of law and rule in this sense. If I get in front of a truck—the truck is hard; I'm soft—I'm a dead duck. I disobeyed the law. The rule is the red light and the green light. When I am driving a car, I resent the red light, the rule. I like to drive right through it. But I think of my own child, and I obey the rule.

The law is relentless; it has no feeling; but the rule has. Think of cities that have reservoirs miles away from where the water is used. Why do we have to use drinking water for air-conditioning plants, and drinking water to feed fountains that don't need filtered water? The order of movement today is based on an extension of the horse and buggy. You feel as though the manure has just been swept away. There has been no thought given to the motor car whatsoever. The same streets serve the motor car as served the horse, which was a pedestrian. The hitching post is really the garage, but the garage is a piece of real estate which should be part of the design of the street, it should be the extension of the street. The garage, therefore, is really a wound-up street, and must be made part of the design of the street. The streets must be completely redone in the center of town. Why must you rip up a street and put in a new line every time you have to repair or improve services for comfort and control of environment? We dig them up every time as though they were the Appian Way. Why isn't there a building in which a room is dedicated for piping only? The dead center of the city, where those mistakes are most unprofitable, should be completely redone. In the center of town the streets should become buildings. This should be interplayed with a sense of movement which does not tax local streets for non-local traffic. There should be a system of viaducts which encase an area which can reclaim the local streets for their own use, and it should be made so this viaduct has a ground floor of shops and useable area. A model which I did for the Graham Foundation recently . . . showed the scheme. This is finding new rules out of realizations of law.[22] (1964)

I'm scared stiff of people who look at things from the money angle. I had to meet some of them the other day at Fort Wayne in connection with an art center I'm doing there—a small Lincoln Center. The project is to locate the separate organizations. It contains a full-fledged philharmonic orchestra, (that's really remarkable for a population of 180,000), a civic center and, distinguished from it, a theatre in the round, an art school, a school of music, school of dance, dormitory, an art museum, and a historical exhibit. All this is to be in one bundle on one piece of land, and I had to say what it would cost. This is a very ticklish situation for me because I wanted them to want the project first, and then to talk about cost.

I was armed with just one fact: that the square foot areas which they required (which, of course, had nothing to do with cubage) were equal to what areas I developed in the design. This was nothing short of a miracle: most architects, not excluding me, exceed their square foot areas and have various reasons for justifying it. In this case, however, all the member organizations had written their programs individually, and they had a reasonable cushion in there for contingent areas. Such realism to begin with made it possible for me, in the composing, to equal the required area. And I was armed then with accepted area, though not the cost. Except, yes, I had the costs: I knew they exceeded very much the costs that this committee had in mind.

I presented the plans to them in as inviting a way as I possibly could, described the new philharmonic especially so that they could never refuse its existence, and did the same with the other buildings. Then, when they asked me how much it would cost, I said, "Well, gentlemen, I must first introduce the fact that the area which you have asked me to have is the same as the area on my plans." They said, "Well, all right, but how much does it cost?" I said, "Well, it will cost twenty million dollars."

They had in mind something like two and a half million dollars as the initial expenditure, but the way the buildings became inter-dependent made it seem quite impossible to begin meaningful choice with such a low amount. I waited for a reaction. I felt the quiet shock the new figure caused and one man did venture to say, "Well, Mr. Kahn, we only expected to spend two and a half million dollars. What can we get for two and a half million?" I said, "Nothing. If you had asked me six months ago what you could get for two and a half million, I'd have said you'd have gotten two and a half million dollars worth; but as you see it presented now, there is an entity present: the philharmonic is dependent upon the art school, the art school on the civic theatre, the civic theatre on the ballet, and so forth." And it is so: the plan is so made that you feel one building is dependent on the other. I said, "After all, what was the purpose of coming here? Was it to make a convenient arrangement, or was it to make something with an extra quality? I've found the extra quality," I said, "which makes the coming together more than what they are when the buildings are separated from each other. Therefore, for two and a half million dollars you would probably get the hind leg of a donkey and a tail, but you wouldn't get the donkey."

After a little bit of a wait one man asked me, "Well, suppose we simply said to you we want an art school built; it's part of other buildings which we're going to build, but now we want to build only the art school. Could you have done it without an elaborate program including all the buildings?" I said, "Yes, I could have done that, but you would have a mosquito and not a donkey." Well, they had a donkey in their minds—half a donkey, not even half a donkey—and a mosquito (a whole thing which they didn't want, of course), and that was it. Finally, one said (because they did like the entity, and they realized that there was something about the entity which was not the same as having each organization represented in its own way), "Well, I can see, Mr. Kahn, I can see spending ten million dollars, but I can't see spending twenty million." Of course, at that point I realized that I was having an easier time than I had anticipated. Then it was the time to be generous, and I said, "Well, I will try everything possible to pare down expenses and pare down costs, but you realize that you have to give up something in order to do this; and, for the moment I can't promise anything because I, myself, think that this entity is now hard to destroy."

For if you sense something which is a coming of a now-accepted thing in man's way of life, which is expressed in a realm of spaces or in a form which is different from any other form, once that happens you cannot take parts away because every part is answerable to the other. Form is of that nature. Form is that which deals with inseparable parts. If you take one thing away, you don't have the whole thing, and nothing is ever really fully answerable to that which man wants to accept as part of his way of life unless all its parts are together.

Second (Legislative) Capital, Dacca, Pakistan

I was given an extensive program of buildings: the assembly; the supreme court; hostels; schools; a stadium; the diplomatic enclave; the living sector; market; all to be placed on a thousand acres of flat land subject to flood. I kept thinking of how these buildings may be grouped and what would cause them to take their place on the land. On the night of the third day, I fell out of bed with a thought which is still the prevailing idea of the plan. This came simply from the realization that assembly is of a transcendent nature. Men come to assemble to touch the spirit of community, and I felt that this must be expressible. Observing the way of religion in the life of the Pakistani, I thought that a mosque woven into the space fabric of the assembly would reflect this feeling. It was presumptuous to assume this right. How did I know that it would fit their way of life. But this assumption took possession.

Also, the program required the design of a hotel for ministers, their secretaries, and the members of the assembly. But this requirement became in my mind a corollary to the assembly and I thought immediately that it should be transformed from the connotations of a hotel to that of studies in a garden on a lake. In my mind the Supreme Court was the test of the acts of legislation against the philosophic view of the nature of man. The three became inseparable in the thinking of the transcendent nature of assembly.

I couldn't wait until morning in my anxiety to relate these thoughts to Kafiluddin Ahmad who is in charge of this project. In the morning I was there at 9 o'clock sharp and told him about the symbolic importance of the mosque; I got no immediate response, no reaction. But he got on the phone and talked to several ministers. After he had spoken for some while, he turned to me and said, "Professor Kahn, I think you have something there." I felt enormous confidence that the plan could have form. "But," he said, "you will have a problem with the Chief Justice of the Supreme Court because he doesn't want the court next to the assembly."

We saw Chief Justice the next day, and we were greeted with the usual tea and biscuits. He said: "I know why you're here—the grapevine is very well developed in Pakistan. You're barking up the wrong tree, because I will not be a part of this assembly group. I will go to the provincial capital site near the provincial high court where the lawyers are, and I think I will feel much more at home there." I turned to him and said, "Mr. Chief Justice, is this your decision alone or is it also the decision of the judges who will follow you? Let me explain to you what I intend to compose." And I made my first sketch on paper of the assembly with the mosque on the lake. I added the hostels framing this lake. I told him how I felt about the transcendent meaning of assembly. After a moment's thought he took the pencil out of my hand and placed a mark representing the supreme court in a position where I would have placed it myself, on the other side of the mosque, and he said: "The mosque is sufficient insulation from the men of the assembly."

I was very happy that the motivations of religious thought were communicable. It was not belief, not design, not pattern, but the essence from which an institution could emerge which revealed the true receptivity of his mind.

The relationship of the assembly, mosque, supreme court and hostels in their interplay psychologically is what expresses a nature. The Institution of Assembly could lose its strength if the sympathetic parts were dispersed. The inspirations of each would also be left incompletely expressed.

In the first sketch of the mosque I indicated four minarets. The meaning of mosque with assembly was then inseparable and a necessary image; and I used the most obvious and borrowed terms. Now the question of the nature 'Mosque' related to 'Assembly' has questioned the need for minarets. At one time in design the mosque was a pyramid, the peak of which was a minaret. Now it is the Mosque Entrance to the Assembly, but the question of its form for a long time remained.

Because this is delta country buildings are placed on mounds to protect them from flood. The ground for the mounds comes from the digging of lakes and ponds. I employed the shape of the lake, too, as a discipline of location and boundary. The triangular lake was meant to encompass the hostels and the assembly and to act as a dimensional control.

The assembly, hostels, and supreme court belong to the Citadel of the Assembly and their interrelated nature suggest a completeness causing other buildings to take their distance. Whether I've even arrived at the proper expression of assembly or not I don't know, but I've also said this: the acts of assembly are the makings of the intellectual institutions of man. That made me realize that the buildings of the program other than those related to the Assembly belong to the Citadel of the Institutions which I place on axis and facing the Citadel of the Assembly.

It occurred to me in thinking about the meaning of institutions that the prime institution stems from the inspiration to live which has remained meekly expressed in the institutions of man. It is an inspiration for building I hope to sense, the form of which could lead to new explosions of programs and designs expressing the beauty of physical well-being. It would be a place of baths, exercise and meeting. It is the place where the athlete is honored and a man strives for physical perfection. I have in mind an environment of spaces far reaching in richness and delight. The responsibility of a country to its people in regard to their physical well being is certainly as important as the culture of the mind and the regulation of commerce. This institution of physical well-being is suggested as a building position harboring a stadium, the body of which will contain the rooms of meeting, baths, exercise and their gardens, and flanked by a school of science and a school of art. Also composed with these buildings is a block of satellite institutions and commercial services. This block is the anchor of the dwelling places which is being recomposed out of an old village with its mounds and depressions already established. I spoke to Mr. Steen Eiler Rasmussen about the deliberate separation of the two citadels and he has inspired me to look into this decision and sense whether the two can be brought together and have a greater meaning than the meaning of looking across the separating park at each other. I felt that their being separate was good, living on different planes of inspiration. But Mr. Rasmussen knows the beginnings of towns in their essence so beautifully that I feel that this plan needs a thorough review before I can feel confident about the belief which is in back of it.

What I'm trying to do is establish a belief out of a philosophy I can turn over to Pakistan, so that whatever they do is always answerable to it. I feel as though this plan which was made weeks after I saw the program has strength. Does it have all the ingredients? If only one is lacking it will disintegrate. This is my problem. Mr. Rasmussen described it to me with little sketches conveying the life and the beauty of the bazaar; which limited by dimensions, expresses so beautifully the power of architecture which could give self-containment to an inspired way of life: it becomes the making of a world within a world. In the same way, in this thousand acre reservation, one should feel its particular character in all the parts.

The Indian Institute of Business Management, Ahmedabad, India

The plan comes from my feelings of monastery. The idea of the seminar classroom and its meaning "to learn" extended to the dormitories comes from the Harvard Business School. The unity of the teaching building, dormitories and teachers' houses—each its own nature, yet each near the other—was the problem I gave myself. The lake between student and teacher is one way of distance with little dimension. When I found this way, the dormitories tended, psychologically, to break away from the school, though it has no appreciable distance from it. . . .

You notice I made all these buildings answerable to each other even though the scale of the house and the dormitory and the school is so different.[23] (1964)

I want first to begin by saying that architecture does not exist.

What does exist is a work of architecture. And a work is an offering to architecture in the hope that this work can become part of the treasury of architecture.

All building is not architecture.

One of the most important aids in the work I do comes from the realisation that any building belongs to some institution of man.

And I have the greatest reverence for those inspirations from which the establishment of institutions came and from the beauty of the architectural interpretations. But we solved from it. Think of one glorious expression which was inspired by Hadrian. Hadrian wanted a place where everyone could worship equally. The Pantheon was the result.

How wonderful the interpretation which gave us a circular building from which one could not derive a formalistic ritual. And how so genious was the tracing of the only opening to the sky.

I must relate to you an experience in my conduct of school recently.

The problem was a monastery.

We began by assuming that no monastery existed up to now.

I was a hermit who had the idea of socializing elements, of bringing them together into a single self-complement.

We had to forget the word monk, the word refectory, the word chapel, the cell.

For two weeks we did nothing. Then an Indian girl said: I believe the cell is the most important element of this community and that the cell gives the right for the chapel to exist, and the chapel gives the right for the refectory to exist, and the refectory gets its right from the cell, and that the retreat is also given by the cell and that the workshops are all made by the right of the cell.

Another non-Catholic, also an Indian, said I agree with Menah.

But, he said, I want to add another important realisation, and that is that the cell must be equal to the chapel, the chapel is equal to the refectory and the refectory is equal to the retreat, every part is equal to the other, one is not better than the precedent or than another.

The designs of these two Indian students, I must say, were rather inferior but the inspiration of their talk was certainly a great guide to the class.

The most brilliant student, an Englishman, produced a marvellous design in which he invented new elements. One was the necessity for a fireplace which dominated the monastery. And he also traced the refectory a half a mile away from the center and in the wake of the retreat, saying that it was such an honor for the retreat to be near the monastery, for an important arm of the monastery had to be given to it.

I am sure that if a program of requirements was given first in this problem, no such thought would come to the class.

The nucleus of the very beginning monastery was not a loss but new realisations came to it by reconsidering the spirit of the monastery.

It is for this reason my interest in this nucleus, in form realisation, form meaning, the realisation of inseparable parts of something.

It is for this reason also that I came to the realisation that in doing the Magistery Chamber of the capital of Pakistan—I had to introduce a mosque in the entrance.

It is for this same reason that when Dr. Salk came to my office and wanted to have a biological laboratory built and when he mentioned that he would like to invite Picasso there, I suddenly had the idea of having a meeting place of the unmeasurable and the science laboratory was the center of the measurable.

In the monastery which I am doing myself, which is the same monastery of which I gave the problem, I have myself discovered other things which are the contrary to discovery of the class. For instance I have a gateway building. This gateway is the transition between the inside and the outside, I mean is the center of the Ecumenical Council.

It is not in the program, it comes from the spirit and nature of the problem.

This is why I think it is so important that the architect does not follow the program but simply uses it as the point of departure of quantity, not of quality.

For the same reason that the program is not architecture—it is merely instruction, it is like a prescription by a druggist.

Because in the program there is a lobby which the architect must change to a place of entrance. Corridors must be changed to galleries. Budgets must be changed to economy and areas must be changed to spaces.

The inspirations of man are the beginning of his work.

The mind is the soul, the spirit, and the brain, the brain is purely physical.

That is why a machine will never be able to compose Bach.

The mind is really the center of the unmeasurable, the brain is the center of the measurable.

The soul is the same in all. Every mind is different. Every one is a singularity.

The inspirations come from the walks through life and through the making of man, the inspiration to live gives a life to all institutions of medicine, of sport, of those manifestations of man that come from the inspiration to live forever.

The program that you get and the translation you make architecturally must come from the spirit of man, not from the program.

The inspiration to learn is the making of all institutions of learning.

The inspiration of question is probably the center of all philosophy, and religion.

The inspiration to express, which I think is the most powerful inspiration, is the center of all art.

And art is the language of God.[24] (1967)

Going back to the university then, this was a center; it was something about the humanities that was really the university. Another part of it was that of the professions. This was the engagement of man in the various avenues of expression be he a doctor, or a lawyer, or an architect, or a bookkeeper, or a nurse, anything—it was a way of expression. You choose to be a nurse because you want to, you have something that tells you to be a nurse, or something that tells you to be an architect. And the university position has nothing to do with the marketplace. The marketplace has to do with the way that which personifies this profession is practiced by the individual; this is something the university should not be concerned with, except to inspire him in the nature of his profession, and in what way he will, in the end, be the happiest in the exercise of this expression. Problems of the marketplace really do not belong there, because no matter how much you teach it, the tendency will be for the person to find his own way, *because a man does not really learn anything that's not part of himself.* He might try very hard. He may even pass examinations, but he'll never really be a chemist, even if he studies chemistry, unless he's a chemist from the very, very start. And so, therefore, knowledge per se to me is very doubtful, you see. But knowledge taken to prime your way of expression is not; to develop a person's talent is not. Very good. Very wonderful. The place, the realm, within which the talents of people can be exercised.

So the university has nothing to do with the marketplace. It doesn't disdain it, because it gets its support from the marketplace; but it still doesn't teach it, because it's useless to teach it.[25] (1969)

I have some thoughts about the spirit of architecture. I have chosen to talk about the room, the street, and human agreement.

The room is the beginning of architecture. It is the place of the mind. You in the room with its dimensions, its structure, its light respond to its character, its spiritual aura, recognizing that whatever the human proposes and makes becomes a life. . . .

Enter your room and know how personal it is, how much you feel its life. In a small room with just another person, what you say may never have been said before, It is different when there is more than just another person. Then, in this little room, the singularity of each is so sensitive that the vectors do not resolve. The meeting becomes a performance instead of an event with everyone saying his lines, saying what has been said many times before.

Still, in a large room, the event is of commonality. Rapport would take the place of thought. This room we are in now is big, without distinction. The walls are far away. Yet I know if I were to address myself to a chosen person, the walls of the room would come together and the room would become intimate. If I were now reading, the concern would be diction.

If this room were the Baptistry of Florence, its image would have inspired thoughts in the same way as person to person, architect to architect. So sensitive is a room.

The plan is a society of rooms. The rooms relate to each other to strengthen their own unique nature. The auditorium wants to be a violin. Its envelope is the violin case. The society of rooms is the place where it is good to learn, good to work, good to live.

Open before us is the architect's plan. Next to it is a sheet of music. The architect fleetingly reads his composition as a structure of elements and spaces in their light.

The musician reads with the same overallness. His composition is a structure of inseparable elements and spaces in sound. A great musical composition is of such entity that when played it conveys the feeling that all that was heard was assembled in a cloud over us. Nothing is gone, as though time and sound have become a single image.

The corridor has no position except as a private passage. In a school, the boy walks across a hall as in his own classroom where he is his own teacher, observing others as others do. The hall asks for equal position with the library.

The society of rooms is knit together with the elements of connection which have their own characteristic.

The stair is the same for the child, the adult and the old. It is thought of as precise in its measures, particularly for the young boy who aspires to do the floors in no time flat, both up and down. It is good also to consider the stair landing as a place to sit near a window with possibly a shelf for a few books. The old man ascending with the young boy can stop here, showing his interest in a certain book, and avoid the explanations of infirmity. The landing wants to be a room.

A bay window can be the private room within a room. A closet with a window becomes a room ready to be rearranged. The lightless corridor, never a room, aspires to the hall overlooking the garden.

The library, the work court, the rooms of study, the place of meeting want to group themselves in a composition that evokes architecture. The libraries of all university schools sit well in a court entrance available to all its students as a place of invitation. The entrance courts and their libraries and the gardens and paths knitting them together form an architecture of connection. The book is an offering of the mind.

The work court of a school of architecture is an inner space encircled by workshops available to construct building experiments. The rooms of study and criticism are of a variety of dimension and spaces in their light, small for the intimate talk and work, and large for the making of full-size drawings and group work.

Rooms must suggest their use without name. To an architect, a school of architecture would be the most honored commission.

The street is a room of agreement. The street is dedicated by each house owner to the city in exchange for common services.

Dead-end streets in cities today still retain this room character. Through-streets, since the advent of the automobile, have entirely lost their room quality. I believe that city planning can start with realization of this loss by directing the drive to reinstate the street where people live, learn, shop and work as the room out of commonality.

Today, we can begin by planting trees on all existing residential streets, by redefining the order of movement which would give these streets back to more intimate use which would stimulate the feelings of well-being and inspire unique street expression.

The street is a community room.

The meeting house is a community room under a roof. It seems as though one came naturally out of the other.

A long street is a succession of rooms given their distinction, room for room, by their meeting of crossing streets. The intersecting street brings from afar its own developed nature which infiltrates any opening it meets. One block in a stream of blocks can be more preferred because of its particular life. One realizes the deadliness of uninterested movement through our streets which erases all delicacy of character and blots out its sensitive nature given to it of human agreement.

Human agreement is a sense of rapport, of commonness, of all bells ringing in unison—not needing to be understood by example but felt as an undeniable inner demand for a presence. It is an inspiration with the promise of the possible.

Dissension does not stem from need but from the mad outburst of frustration, from the hopelessness of the far-awayness of human agreement. Desire, not need, the forerunner of the new need, out of the yet not said and the yet not made seems to be the roots of hope in dissension.

How inspiring would be the time when the sense of human agreement is felt as the force which brings new images. Such images reflecting inspirations and put into being by inspired technology. Basing our challenges on present-day programming and existing technologies can only bring new facets of old work.

The city from a simple settlement became the place of the assembled institutions. The settlement was the first institution. The talents found their places. The carpenter directed building. The thoughtful man became the teacher, the strong one the leader.

When one thinks of simple beginnings which inspired our present institutions, it is evident that some drastic changes must be made which will inspire the re-creation of the meaning, *city*, as primarily an assembly of those places vested with the care to uphold the sense of a way of life.

Human agreement has always been and will always be. It does not belong to measurable qualities and is, therefore, eternal. The opportunities which present its nature depend on circumstances and on events from which human nature realizes itself.

A city is measured by the character of its institutions. The street is one of its first institutions. Today, these institutions are on trial. I believe it is so because they have lost the inspirations of their beginning. The institutions of learning must stem from the undeniable feeling in all of us of a desire to learn. I have often thought that this feeling came from the way we were made, that nature records in everything it makes how it was made. This record is also in man and it is this within us that urges us to seek its story involving the laws of the universe, the source of all material and means, and the psyche which is the source of all expression, Art.

The desire to learn made the first school room. It was of human agreement. The institution became the modus operandi. The agreement has the immediacy of rapport, the inspiring force which recognizes its commonality and that it must be part of the human way of life supported by all people.

The institution will die when its inspirations are no longer felt and when it operates as a matter of course. Human agreement, however, once it presents itself as a realization is indestructible. For the same reason a man is unable to work below his level of comprehension. To explain inspiration, I like to believe that it is the moment of possibility when what to do meets the means of doing it.

City planning must begin to be cognizant of the strength and character of our present institutions and be sensitive to the pulse of human relationship which senses the new inspirations which would bring about new and meaningful institutions. Traffic systems, sociological speculations, new materials, new technologies are servants to the pulse of human rapport which promises revelations yet not felt but in the very core of human desires.

New spaces will come only from a new sense of human agreements—new agreements which will affirm a promise of life and will reveal new availabilities and point to human support for their establishment.

I realized in India and Pakistan that a great majority of the people are without ambition because there is no way in which they are able to elevate themselves beyond living from hand to mouth, and what is worse, talents have no outlets. To express is the reason for living. The institution of learning, of work, of health, of recreation should be made available to all people. All realms of expression will be opened. Each singularity will express in his way. Availabilities to all can be the source of a tremendous release of the values locked in us of the unmeasurable in living: the art of living.

One city can distinguish itself from the other by just the inspirational qualities that exist in sensing natural agreements as the only true source of new realizations. In that sense the spaces where it is good to learn, to work and to live may remain unexpressed if their nature is not redefined. It is not just enough to solve the problem. To imbue the spaces with new-found self-quality is a different question entirely. Solution is a "how" design problem; the realization of "what" precedes it.

Now a word about inspired technology. The wall enclosed us for a long time until the man behind it, feeling a new freedom, wanted to look out. He hammered away to make an opening. The wall cried, "I have protected you." And the man said, "I appreciate your faithfulness but I feel time has brought change."

The wall was sad; the man realized something good. He visualized the opening as gracefully arched, glorifying the wall. The wall was pleased with its arch and carefully made jamb. The opening became part of the order of the wall.

The world with its many people, each one a singularity, each group of different experiences revealing the nature of the human in varied aspects, is full of the possibility of more richly sensing human agreement from which new architecture will come. The world cannot be expected to come from the exercise of present technology alone to find the realms of new expression. I believe that technology should be inspired. A good plan demands it. . . .

When the astronauts went through space, the earth presented itself as a marvelous ball, blue and rose, in space. Since I followed it and saw it that way, all knowledge left me as being unimportant. Truly, knowledge is an incomplete book outside of us. You take from it to know something, but knowing cannot be imparted to the next man. Knowing is private. It gives singularity the means for self-expression.

I believe that the greatest work of man is that part which does not belong to him alone. If he discovers a principle, only his design way of interpreting belongs to him alone. The discovery of oxygen does not belong to the discoverer.

I invented a story about Mozart. Somebody dropped a dish in his kitchen, and it made a hell of a noise. The servants jumped, and Mozart said, "Ah! Dissonance." And immediately dissonance belonged to music, and the way Mozart wrote interpreting it belonged to him.

Architects must not accept the commercial divisions of their profession into urban design, city planning and architecture as though they were three different professions. The architect can turn from the smallest house to the greatest complex, or the city. Specializing ruins the essence of the revelation of the form with its inseparable parts realized only as an entity.

A word about beauty. Beauty is an all-prevailing sense of harmony, giving rise to wonder; from it, revelation. Poetry. Is it in beauty? Is it in wonder? Is it revelation?

It is in the beginning, in first thought, in the first sense of the means of expression.

A poet is in thought of beauty and existence. Yet a poem is only an offering, which to the poet is less.

A work of architecture is but an offering to the spirit architecture and its poetic beginning.[26] (1971)

The city is essentially a meeting place. It is valued by the character of its availabilities. Our way of life is born of freedom which has inspired availabilities the like of which no nation has. The character of this freedom is so great that even a law must adjust to its unmeasurable qualities.

When I was in my early teens, I went to the Graphic Sketch Club. I walked from 7th and Poplar to 8th and Catherine. I was given an easel, paper and charcoal in the life class. All I could hear was the swishing of the strokes and the soft and privately directed voice of the critic. It was a meeting availability, a place full of offerings.

On Saturday morning I came early. No one seemed to be around. The room to the right of the entrance was open. I walked in to see the work of the masters of the school on the walls. Someday, I hoped I would be selected too. I noticed that the piano in the room was open. I had been playing at home on an ancient, large piano given to me, which was also my bed. My instrument had the sound of little bells. When I touched the keys of the school piano, angels filled the room. I sat down to play the Second Hungarian Rhapsody, not the way it was written since I could not read. When I left the room, I found several people had been listening. They asked that I play the next day at a concert which the Symphony Club was giving in this room. I tried everything to refuse but had to agree. Sunday I played the same piece but faintly as I had played it the day before. (Luckily, I was the first to play.) Mr. Fleischer offered me a scholarship to study composition (not piano). When I told the good news to J. Liberty Todd, a Quaker and Director of the School of Industrial Art, he was flabbergasted, "No, you must not accept . . . nothing but Art!", he said. My mother was heart-broken. My father agreed with him.

At Central High School, William Gray, teacher of Art, gave talks on Architecture. I was to be a painter but he touched the very core of my expressive desires. How circumstantial, but how wonderful is the light thrown upon the threshold when the door is opened.

A city should be a place where a little boy walking through its streets can sense what he someday would like to be. I have designed buildings in India, in Bangladesh. In these countries where commonality is rarely expressed in the institutions available, I might not have had such aspirations.

I have presented the idea that the Bicentennial be the "Congress of the Institutions" (Availabilities) designed to present to all visitors those beliefs that inspired our Declaration of Independence, spoke to the heart of human harmony in feeling, and inspired our people to create such richness of availabilities. Such inspiration has been so deeply woven into our way of life that citizens thought in terms of what offerings they could give to honor its beauty of conception.[27] (1973)

4
SILENCE AND LIGHT

THEORY

The concept of silence and light, Kahn's last and most abstract theory, examines the origin of creative expression within the human mind. The idea was the fusion of several threads of thought, a richly lyrical product of intellectual maturity and confidence, which continued to develop until Kahn's death in 1974. Within the context of this idea, Kahn saw light as the means or tool of expression given by nature, and silence as the desire for expression welling up from the collective unconscious. At the point of their meeting occurs the inspiration that leads to the creation of a work of art.

The relationship that Kahn saw between silence and light is an enlargement of his earlier theory that the human urge to express acting with nature's laws makes inspiration possible. Kahn's interest in the laws of nature developed early in his career. In 1959, as he solidified his form-design idea, he began to give much thought to nature's role in the process of inspiration. According to Kahn, nature is material, objective reality. It produces its infinite variations with no consciousness of what it does. The laws of nature are eternal and unyielding. They work in a harmonic interplay that Kahn called order, and yet nature has no awareness of its own harmony because it is part of that scientific reality that exists in total disregard for the subjectivity of human perception.

On the other end of the spectrum from nature, Kahn placed the intuitively felt collective soul found in humans as well as in all other living forms. Kahn called this soul the "psyche," using the word in a context different from the one popularized by C. G. Jung. Kahn's use of the word *psyche* more closely resembles Jung's description of the collective unconscious.[1] Whereas Jung distinguished the collective unconscious from the conscious state of waking life, Kahn saw the soul as "conscious" not because he disagreed with Jung but because he believed it possessed a life of its own, a striving toward expression that nature lacked. He envisioned the psyche as having two components: the "spirit of life," pure consciousness with no will, which was common to all life forms; and the "existence will," which differentiated each life form from the next, making a tree want to be a tree and a human being strive toward humanness.

In 1959 Kahn began to refer to the collective spirit of the psyche by the lower-case letter *i*, to distinguish it from ego, which is commonly represented by a capital *I*. He soon decided that *i* was not enough of a word and lengthened it to *ina*,[2] possibly a contraction of "in all life." Kahn's one attempt to invent a word did not endure, because *ina* had no history of meaning and therefore its sound evoked no image. He continued to speak in terms of the psyche however, because, like the words *form* and *order*, *psyche* had phonetic and historical associations that appealed profoundly to him.

The psyche in its desire to express demands the collaboration of nature's physical instrument of expression in order to realize beauty, just as the

Rose *elements ⎧ina - common ⎫ Man*
of the ⎨ ⎬
psyche ⎩inee - different⎭

ι = ina spirit of life
(not ego I)
/ = Existence will

Kahn's drawing of the psyche, 1960. (*Reprinted from the April 1961 issue of* **Progressive Architecture,** *copyright 1961, Reinhold Publishing.*)

architect with a driving sense of inspiration must also have pencils and paper to execute a masterpiece. How does the creative individual integrate the tangible and intangible aspects of expression? People, because they are products of nature, like the rest of the universe, are themselves creative instruments. And because nature never makes the same snowflake or the same brain twice, each person is physiologically unique. However, Kahn always made a distinction between the brain and the mind: the mind is dependent on the physical structure of the brain for its existence, but from the point of view of inner experience, the mind is capable of reaching far beyond the brain's boundaries. Kahn believed that the mind could achieve a perspective from which each individual could communicate with other individuals through a shared symbolic language, just as people of diverse cultures use the same archetypal images in art, myth, and dreams. When this level of understanding is achieved, the objectivity of nature's physiological instrument works together with the psyche's vital, instinctual urges and creativity is sparked.

Kahn's idea that both measurable and unmeasurable aspects contribute to creativity harks back even further, to his 1953 description of the roles of thought and feeling in the design process (see p. 64). In the 1960s, as Kahn pondered the relationship between nature and the psyche, he was also refining and articulating the two complementary ingredients of creativity that he had originally identified as thought and feeling. Al-

though Kahn consistently spoke of the dichotomy between the desire for expression and the means of expression, after 1967 he ceased to represent these components as things—thought and feeling, nature and the psyche—and began to refer to the more abstract "auras" of silence and light.

A major source for the theory of silence and light is Kahn's reverence for the spiritual quality of light. This reverence developed gradually over a period of several decades. In 1954 he spoke of light's relation to structure purely in terms of mechanical needs. But by 1960 he had articulated the intriguing thought that the structure of a room is defined by its light. This thought marked the beginning of a more metaphorical approach to light. (A year earlier he had solidified the archetypal concept of form.) When rooms illuminated by natural light are arranged together as a plan, Kahn saw the result as a musical composition in which the harmony is formed by notes of light.[3] At the same time, he was beginning to write and speak about the magical effect sunlight has as it touches the surface of a building. Light washes over the walls, differentiates the faces of a three-dimensional solid, and fills interior spaces through openings. Structure and light are inseparable. Kahn saw architectural elements, such as the column, arch, dome, and vault, in terms of their various ways of molding light and shadow, and thereby of figuring in design. By 1967 Kahn's fascination with light had given rise to his observation that structure actually makes or molds light by taming it into a workable state.[4]

Natural light, to Kahn, was the only true light. He considered the window the most significant part of the room, the part that gave character and vitality to the space. Kahn was intrigued by the nuances of mood created by the time of day, the weather, and the seasons. Scorning the static artificiality of electric light, he would often sit at his desk between the tall windows of his office, waiting until the daylight was completely gone from the room before deigning to reach for the light switch. He believed that the changeable quality of daylight gave life to architecture because one's relationship to a building changed according to the light surrounding and penetrating it. For this reason, no space was truly a space unless it received the life-giving touch of natural light.

The different aspects of light are usually perceived as colors. The bluish light of a cloudy day might represent sobriety and depression. The build-up of tension before the drama of an approaching storm is symbolized in the angry and

Architecture comes from The Making of a Room

The Plan— A society of rooms is a place good to live. Louis Kahn

A great American Poet once asked The Architect 'What slice of the sun does your building have, what light enters your Room' as if to say the sun never knew how great it is until it struck the side of a building.

The Room

Is The place of the mind. In a small room one does not say what one would in a large room. In a room with only one other person could be generative. The vectors of each meet. A room is not a room without natural light. natural light gives the time of day and the mood of The seasons to enter.

The structure of a room is defined by its light.

threatening qualities of purple light. The sun breaking through the clouds afterward has the subtle luminosity of silver. Colors encourage the play of the imagination. As they occur in nature, they are the sources of inspiration for the architect who composes a variety of spaces, each with its own mood and purpose. Without color, there is only white light, and Kahn believed there was no such thing as white light. Light's ability to give life to architecture is dependent on its own life, its changeability.

Kahn sensed a magical quality in the interaction of light and architecture. Although light is a part of nature and not in itself a conscious force, it gives a kind of consciousness to architecture as it comes into contact with a building. Kahn believed that light possessed an awesome power. He saw it as the ultimate inspiring force; literally, as the Divine Light. Kahn's notion of light as the giver of life to architecture draws its meaning from both the religious and evolutionary roles of light in the beginning of life.

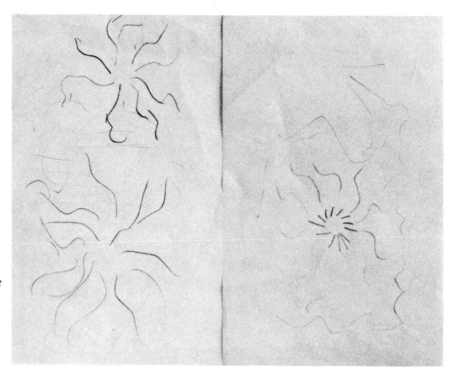

Light as the source of life; preliminary sketches for silence and light drawing, c. 1971. (*Copyright The Louis I. Kahn Collection, University of Pennsylvania and the Pennsylvania Historical and Museum Commission.*)

In 1967 Kahn first expressed a relationship between light and a new term, *silence*. Together, he explained, silence and light produced inspiration. Silence was difficult for him to describe because it was a process in motion rather than a fixed phenomenon. He never used the word in the conventional sense to mean "quiet." In 1967, at a lecture given at the New England Conservatory, Kahn stated that silence was not an already existing desire but a desire that grew toward existence. A year later, he elaborated on this explanation in an essay for *Via*, a University of Pennsylvania publication. The essay is a series of vividly poetic passages that imply rather than define silence. The first two paragraphs describe the garden of the Mexican architect Luis Barragan. Kahn stresses the primordial darkness of the water flowing from the stream into the garden, recognizing its unawakened potential, its striving toward consciousness; one senses from his description that silence springs from a state of complete introversion or oneness with the inner self. These implications were clarified in 1969 at the Swiss Federal Institute of Technology (ETH), Zurich, when Kahn described silence as neither light nor dark, but an urge to become that exists somewhere deep inside all living things.

In later conversations, Kahn indicated that he saw silence as a great void beyond the confines of time and space, a void without life of any kind. Yet out of such "emptiness" came the galaxies, the stars, the planets—and life. Thus silence, although it is ostensibly a void, must contain the potential for life. Kahn was really looking for the moment of beginning, then looking beyond it to the moment before the beginning. How can something come out of nothing? What existed before the spark of creation which caused that spark? Can a vast realm of silence contain the potential of something about to become? In posing these questions, Kahn was showing the same inquisitiveness he expressed in the desire to read "Volume Zero" of English history. He realized, however, that the closer one gets to unraveling the mystery of the beginning, the farther the knowledge recedes from one's grasp.

Kahn's use of light in relation to silence was an extension of his sense of light as the source of life. Light became complementary to silence. Whereas silence is primordial and immaterial with a desire for conscious expression, light on the other hand contains the potential for becoming material, but it is unruly and untamed because it is without conscious purpose. Kahn extended this concept further by saying that the physical features of the world are composed of light that has spent itself in their creation. Light, then, is the means of expression that is present in nature and that has been tamed and utilized to create what already exists.

Silence, the desire to express, and light, the means of expression, join at an infinitely thin, constantly changing threshold. At this threshold, inspiration occurs. The meeting point of silence and light is different for every individual and for every type of expression. Kahn often used the contrasting examples of the poet and the scientist to show the different possible routes that inspiration could take through silence and light. The poet, who is comfortable in the realm of feeling and intuition, will follow his urge to express for as long as possible before finding the means of expression that would put his images into concrete words. On the other hand, the scientist, who is at home in the rational world, might stay as long as he could in the realm of light, collecting facts and figures to prove his hypothesis before acknowledging its connection with wonder and mystery.

When Kahn developed the idea of silence and light, he was unaware of its resemblance to the ancient Chinese yin–yang dichotomy. The yin–yang symbol is a circle divided into light and dark hemispheres rotating around a central axis. It signifies a whole consisting of two opposite but interdependent natures. Within each nature is the seed of the other, because neither yin nor yang exists in a pure or static state. Yin, the feminine principle, represents the intuitive and instinctual qualities of the soul. Yin also refers to darkness and primeval waters. It is significant that in one of Kahn's first attempts to describe silence he spoke of silence as coming from the water in the darkness of the forest. Yang, on the other hand, is the masculine principle. It is rational and unyielding like the laws of nature, but not necessarily material, because it is an energy rather than a concrete presence. Yang represents all that is spiritual and light, just as Kahn recognized the spiritual quality of light. In relation to each other, the yin "symbolizes primordial darkness before the yang light of creation."[5] The masculine–feminine implication is missing from Kahn's theory, maybe because he has gone a step further in his understanding of creativity; nonetheless, his view of the interaction of silence and light is remarkably like the yin–yang relationship.

Psychologist and philosopher Carl Jung recognized the yin and yang as significant archetypes.[6] In the psychological makeup of the male, the yang qualities are dominant and the yin qualities are recessive. The man's internal yin nature contains his potential for emotions, moods, and relationships. It represents his subjectivity and his capacity for intuition and fantasy. It is the womb of nature in which originates the urge to give birth, to strive for creation. Whereas Kahn

Kahn's idea of silence and light resembles the ancient Chinese dichotomy between Yin and Yang.

called these recessive yin qualities the sense of silence, Jung called them the man's feminine soul, or *anima*. In the woman, the yin nature is dominant and the yang nature is recessive. The woman's unconscious yang stands for reason, judgment, and objective understanding. It represents her capacity for action and aggression. These qualities, which Kahn described as light or the means of creation, Jung saw as the woman's masculine soul, or *animus*. According to Jung, then, the desire for expression is conscious in the woman and unconscious in the man, whereas the means of expression is conscious in the man and unconscious in the woman.

Jung's observation that the recessive characteristic of each sex remains in the unconscious does not imply that one remains unaware of its existence. Neither does Jung's theory imply that the unconscious yin or yang should be brought into consciousness. Jung saw psychological growth as dependent on the establishment of a dialogue with this recessive contrasexual aspect of oneself. The source of creativity is always in the unconscious yin or yang, and this source must always remain in communication with the more conscious aspect of the personality in order for one's creative potential to be fully realized. Consider for example the man who has utilized his dominant yang—his capacity for logical reason, control, and responsibility—with professional success. In a desire to establish communication with his repressed yin, he begins to develop his latent artistic talent; however, his expectation of instant success turns his work into slick, superficial formulas. His art never reaches its full expressive potential because he brings it into the realm of his conscious yang rather than using it as an opening to continued dialogue with his anima. There is also the example of the woman whose talent is profound but lost in obscurity because she remains out of touch with her unconscious yang capacity for action, for "selling herself" in the competitive market. Or she may be an artist who drowns her work in emotional excess bordering on sentimentality because she does not maintain a dialogue with her own internal capacity for objective judgment.

Just as Jung described the human need for communication between the yin and yang components of the personality, Kahn believed that silence (the desire for expression) and light (the means of expression) must work together before creative realization occurs. Although Kahn was aware of Jung's theories since the early 1960s, he never read Jung thoroughly, so his appreciation of Jung stemmed from an intuitive sense of kinship rather than from a systematic knowledge of Jung's work. It would be unrealistic to assume that Kahn's thoughts were influenced by Jung's animus and anima archetypes, because Kahn totally avoided the sexual differentiation that is such an integral part of Jung's archetypes. Moreover, by the time Kahn developed his silence and light theory, he was too advanced in his thinking to borrow so fundamentally from existing symbolism. More likely, he was reaching for the same archetypes in himself that produced Jung's theory of the animus and anima and the yin–yang symbol in Chinese culture.

George Cruikshank, "Mr. Bumble and Mrs. Corney taking tea," *Oliver Twist*, 1860. Kahn's conception of light as the contrast between the whiteness of the paper and the darkness of the lines drawn on it was inspired by the luminosity that Cruikshank achieved in his illustrations. (*Reprinted from George William Reid,* **A Descriptive Catalogue of the Works of George Cruikshank**, *Vol. 3, Bell and Daldy, London, 1871.*)

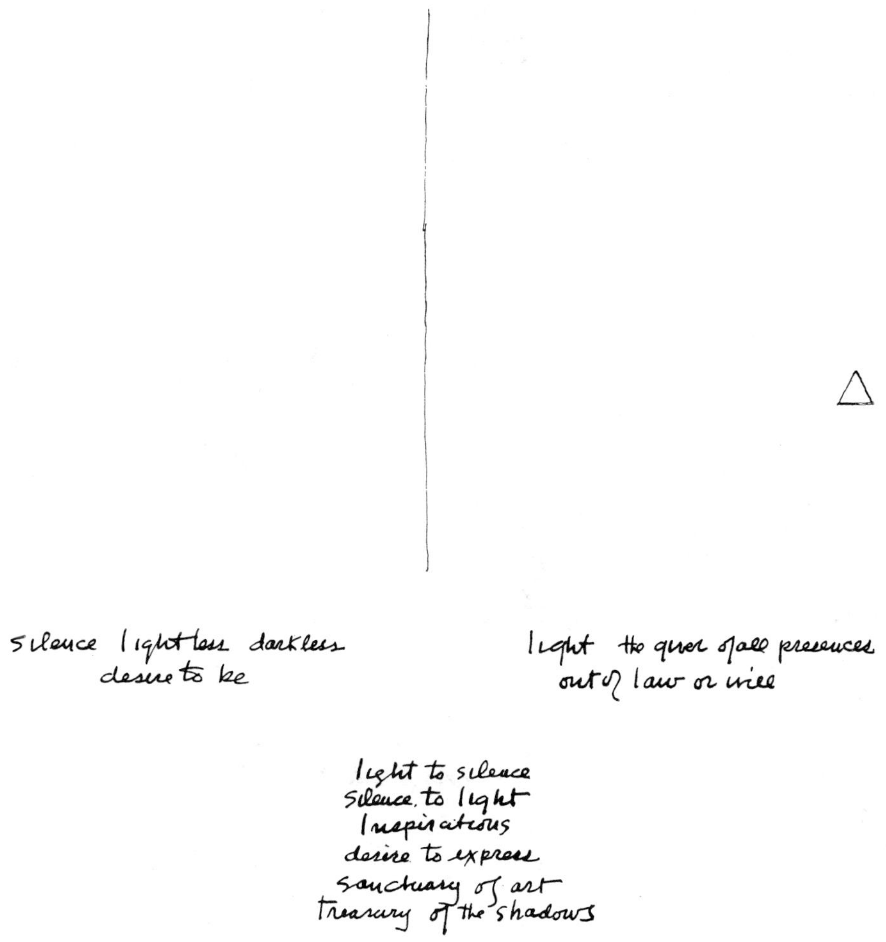

silence lightless darkless
desire to be

light the giver of all presences
out of law or will

light to silence
silence to light
Inspirations
desire to express
sanctuary of art
treasury of the shadows

In this 1968 diagram, silence and light are separated by a clear boundary line. (*Graduate School of Fine Arts, University of Pennsylvania.*)

Silence to Light
Light to Silence

The desire to express crosses at a common wall
The Threshold
The Inspirations
The Sanctuary of Art
The Treasury of The Shadows

In a 1972 diagram, the boundary between silence and light is a vague area with many possible crossings. (*Copyright The Louis I. Kahn Collection, University of Pennsylvania and the Pennsylvania Historical and Museum Commission.*)

As the concept of silence and light reached its final evolution, Kahn's thoughts became increasingly abstract. Gradually, he pared down his descriptions from longer, more flowing passages to a few choice words that he felt evoked especially powerful images. He began to avoid the use of punctuation and traditional sentence structure, and at the same time, his drawings became less representational. Whereas his 1968 sketch uses a pyramid to represent a creation of spent light, by 1973 light is shown as the contrast between the whiteness of the paper and the darkness of the lines drawn on it—an abstracted reference to the luminosity that Cruikshank achieved in his illustrations. Silence in this later sketch is a series of horizontal lines signifying the unarticulated quality of potential expression. The 1968 diagram shows silence and light separated by a clear boundary line, but in 1971 the line is dotted, and by 1972 the threshold is drawn as a vague area with many possible crossings.

The ambiguity of this boundary as shown in later sketches illustrates Kahn's belief that silence and

Kahn saw eternity in terms of
two aspects, or two brothers,
that were really one, c. 1972.
(*Copyright The Louis I. Kahn
Collection, University of
Pennsylvania and the
Pennsylvania Historical and
Museum Commission.*)

light never existed in differentiated states. He separated them only for the convenience of discussion. After having described the idea of silence and light many times over a period of several years, Kahn attempted to portray more accurately the lack of differentiation between these two components of creativity. The difficulty of doing so in ordinary prose may have spurred the development of a more cryptic style in which questions are deliberately left unanswered. By 1972 he often avoided speaking in terms of two separate words, *silence* and *light*, and instead described light as "two brothers." The first brother, "the desire to be to express," was the absence of luminosity; and the second brother, whom he called either "to be to be" or "to be to make," was luminosity with as yet no definite presence, a glow that had not quite become focused into light.[7] The first brother had the qualities Kahn otherwise attributed to silence, and the second brother had the qualities he usually assigned to light. Kahn stressed that these two brothers were *actually one*, exemplifying his own mental separation of the whole into components in order to make understanding of the whole easier.

His description of the interaction of the two brothers who are really one penetrated beyond his previous descriptions of the convergence of silence and light. In these later more powerfully visionary images, Kahn emphasized that both the luminous and nonluminous forerunners of light are two aspects of eternity and that their "fiery dance" takes place before eternity becomes finite reality and light subsides into crumpled pieces of material or "spent light."

Kahn's vision sounds uncannily like a description of the formation and structure of the universe. As astronomers penetrate deeper into space, they are actually seeing further and further back in time; theoretically, if they could look far enough into space, they would visually reach the beginning of time. The "big bang" origin of the universe is usually imagined as an outward explosion, but since by looking in all directions at once one would eventually have to see the same beginning, the birth of the universe may actually be an explosion "inward"—into the measurable realm of space–time from a greater reality. Scientists may see the universe as expanding only because human perception is limited by the boundaries of time and space; the true shape and motion of the universe eludes human understanding. Scientists can, however, project backward in time to a point at which matter solidified from untamed light energy, and before—or beyond—that to a point at which the laws of measurable space–time become useless. Kahn, in

tracing the path forward from the eternal void to the emergence of light and finally to the spending of light into matter, seems to sense intuitively these mysterious beginnings.

Kahn's words are also reminiscent of the Biblical story of creation. In the Christian and Judaic traditions, as well as in other religions, God is seen as creating night and day from an undifferentiated state of chaos; similarly, Kahn perceived silence as a "lightless, darkless" void out of which came the luminous and nonluminous auras. He tentatively explored a realm that has mystified human beings for centuries and has led them to countless systems of religion and philosophy. In his concept of silence and light, Kahn was fusing the scientific and religious contemplations of the beginning of life, just as he fused light and silence by instinctively penetrating backward in time to an eternity beyond time's boundaries. In essence, he invented his own version of the myth of creation.

PRACTICE

To work with light is to tame its fierceness while utilizing its changeability. It involves both practical considerations and a sense of light's symbolic meaning. Kahn's understanding of light began on a practical level, and, as he gained experience in dealing with light's role in design, he began to generalize this experience into theory. The first written evidence of Kahn's fascination with light is contemporary with his clarification of the meaning of form in 1959. However, his architecture since the late 1940s indicates that he was struggling with the consideration of light for at least 12 years before it figured in his philosophy. The Weiss house of 1948–1949 has an entire wall of five double-hung windows. Four of these have one pane of plywood, the other of glass, the positions of which can be switched. Kahn's intent, like Le Corbusier's contemporary efforts, was to provide on the south side of the house a device that would control, according to the angle of the sun, the amount of light reaching the interior. In the following year, Kahn adapted his idea for use in his occupational therapy building for the Philadelphia Psychiatric Hospital, where windows similar to those in the Weiss house can be adjusted to accommodate a need for different degrees of light and privacy. In another wing of the hospital, he used sunshades made of ceramic chimney pots, which create an interesting pattern of light on the window surfaces.

Although Kahn had a particular interest in the effects of sunlight even at this early date, his correspondence with Anne Tyng during 1953–

South side of the Weiss house, Norristown, Pennsylvania. The window wall of double-hung panes of glass and plywood is a device for controlling the amount of light reaching the interior. [(c) John Ebstel.]

Philadelphia Psychiatric Hospital, Radbill Wing. [(c) John Ebstel.]

The geometric structures of the Yale Art Gallery (top) and the AFL-CIO Building (bottom) are independent of plate glass exteriors. [*Yale Art Gallery photograph, Lionel Freedman; AFL-CIO Building photograph* (c) *John Ebstel.*]

Richards Building, University of Pennsylvania. Panes of blue glass did not filter out injurious rays as intended. (*Photograph by Alexandra Tyng.*)

1955 shows that his consideration of light in relation to architecture remained on a purely practical level. Kahn was, in essence, experimenting with light. While he was curious, his curiosity was not consistent. Plate glass curtain walls are applied to the exteriors of both the Yale Art Gallery and the AFL–CIO Medical Service Plan Building in Philadelphia, Pennsylvania (1954–1956, now demolished) according to the ethic of the International Style. The flat sheaths of windows give no indication of the bold structural systems within and show no concern for the control of light. In the Richards Medical Research Building (1957–1961), however, Kahn grappled with the problem of glare by specifying solar screening, which was eliminated because of cost and replaced by blue glass windows. These were guaranteed by the manufacturers to filter out glare and harmful rays, but they did not serve their intended purpose. As a result, scientists performing light-sensitive experiments have been forced to install makeshift devices for the control of sunlight. At the Salk Institute laboratory buildings (1959–1965), the projecting windows of the studies are oriented toward the Pacific Ocean for the view and shaded from the western sun by wooden shutters. Still, the sun is dealt with by an applied device rather than by the structure itself. The experimental attitude Kahn had toward problems of glare at this time can best be attributed to a lack of consistent philosophical principles governing light. Architects must first achieve control over their medium before structural concerns become second nature and they are able to express their deepest convictions in their work.

From 1958 to 1960 Kahn began work on the commissions that would influence his initial thoughts concerning light's metaphysical effect on architecture. In the Tribune Review Publishing Company Building, the First Unitarian Church, the project for the U.S. Consulate in Luanda, Portuguese Angola; and the Bryn Mawr dormitories, Kahn paid consistent attention to letting the appropriate quantity of light into the building. More important, he also took into account the quality of light, thus shifting the emphasis of his work to a more theoretical plane. At the same time, his thoughts on the subject matured, became more poetic, more personal. By 1960 he was speaking of the unpredictability of natural light as opposed to the static quality of artificial light. He described the magical role of daylight in transforming the room. Most significant in terms of his architecture, he began to consider the life-giving relationship between structure and light.

Windows of the Salk Institute studies face the Pacific Ocean and are shielded from the western sun by shutters. (*Photographs by Alexandra Tyng.*)

The central room in the First
Unitarian Church, Rochester, is
lit indirectly by overhead light
wells. ((c) John Ebstel.)

To understand the experience behind Kahn's
new way of thinking about light, it is necessary
to examine thoroughly the projects he began
during these three years. One line of development involved his growing interest in indirect
lighting. The First Unitarian Church in Rochester
(1959–1961) consists of schoolrooms and offices
enclosing a great central room that is the church
itself. The peripheral spaces receive light filtered
indirectly through bays in the exterior walls. The
high central room is lit by four overhead light
wells, one in each corner. Sunlight entering
through these openings strikes the walls and
diffuses through the room, eliminating the glare
that would have been caused by contrast between brightness outside and dimness within.

Again in the Bryn Mawr dormitories (1960–1965),
Kahn used the combination of large skylit central
spaces surrounded by smaller bedrooms receiving light through square bay windows in the
sides of the building. Sunlight is a friend, slant-
ing sideways into a bedroom or illuminating the
dining hall with an overall glow. In both these
buildings, Kahn was learning to control light as
he used it to define the nature and mood of a
space.

Meanwhile, experimentation with the window
was progressing. Kahn's scheme for the Tribune
Review Building involved windows that would
give maximum usable wall space. These are composed of two sections: above, a large, wide pane;

Aerial view of Erdman Hall Dormitories, Bryn Mawr. Clerestory windows light central spaces. (*Copyright the Louis I. Kahn Collection, University of Pennsylvania and the Pennsylvania Historical and Museum Commission.*)

Diffuse light illuminates dining room of the Bryn Mawr dormitories. (*Photograph by Alexandra Tyng.*)

Experiments with the "keyhole window," Tribune Review Building, Greensburg, Pennsylvania. (*Photograph by James Cook. Copyright The Louis I. Kahn Collection, University of Pennsylvania and the Pennsylvania Historical and Museum Commission.*)

Newsroom of the Tribune Review Building. The windows have two sections: a large pane at the top to admit light and a vertical slit below to provide maximum wall space. (*Copyright The Louis I. Kahn Collection, University of Pennsylvania and the Pennsylvania Historical and Museum Commission.*)

below, at human height, a vertical slit. Identical windows appear in the Esherick house, in Philadelphia (1959–1961), and a variation of this distinctively shaped opening, with an arched upper section, was used in the Fleisher house in Elkins Park, Pennsylvania (1959).

In this same year, the "keyhole window" was adapted for use as a free-standing device for screening the sun's glare. This device was invented by Kahn after he traveled to Africa with the intention of designing the U.S. Consulate in Luanda. During his stay, he observed that the light, although necessary for life, became an enemy because it was so glaring. He decided that every window should face a wall that would take the sun's direct rays and reflect them into the interior spaces. An isometric diagram of the consulate exterior illustrates Kahn's intention. The outer walls with their keyhole-shaped openings were intended to protect the inner recessed glass from the sun's full force. Because these outer panes would be separate from the wall behind them, Kahn was reminded of ruins in which gaping window frames revealed emptiness behind, and he began to think of the consulate design as a ruin wrapped around a building. Although the consulate was never built, Kahn was inspired by the glare-shielding walls he had

invented for it. He used the idea as the basis for early schemes for the Salk Institute lecture halls, the part of the project on which he had begun work in 1959. Here the "ruins" become self-supporting: square shells wrapped around circular buildings, and vice versa. The openings in these shells are again of the keyhole shape.

Kahn often spoke of the Greek column in terms of light. As early as 1954, he had the idea that the column could be hollowed out so that its periphery became the filter for light entering the column (see p. 66). By 1960 this concept was finally applied to the Salk Institute lecture halls. Here the concept of wrapping a building in a free-standing shell can also be seen as an enlargement of the hollow column to the scale of the building itself. In 1961 Kahn began the Mikveh Israel Synagogue project in Philadelphia. Here he inserted hollow columns into the exterior walls at intervals. These nonstructural cylinders act as diffusion chambers. Daylight shines through their exterior openings, ricochets around the inside of the columns, and filters subtly through openings into the synagogue. Similar light wells were used in the Ahmedabad classroom building and the Fort Wayne Fine Arts Center. Kahn was beginning to use the hollow column as a sophisticated light-regulating device.

The Esherick house, Philadelphia, PA. has the same two-section windows as the Tribune Review Building. (*Photograph by Alexandra Tyng.*)

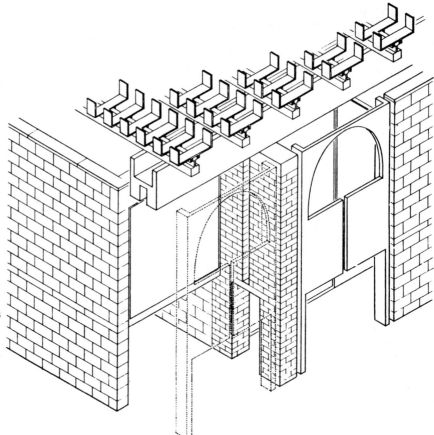

Isometric drawing of sunshades for U.S. Consulate, Luanda, Portugese Angola. The outer walls with their keyhole-shaped openings were intended to screen the sun's glare. (*Reproduced, by permission, from "Louis Kahn," Perspecta 7: The Yale Architectural Journal, 1961, p. 22.*)

Kahn realized in 1964 that the hollow column that was large enough to be a room actually used light to enhance its structure, because its walls could have windows that gave definition and life to the spaces inside. At this time, work had been under way for two years on the government complex at Dacca, and Kahn's efforts were focused on achieving the proper form expression of the assembly complex. The National Assembly building is a cylinder divided above by a structural system of radial sections somewhat like a cut pie. Each section is pierced by circular openings that let light enter from the exterior and filter it through into adjacent sections. Essentially, the building is a hollow column with perforated walls, but it is also a solid column in the sense that its mass overrides its translucence. Kahn also used the column as a light-regulating structural member in other parts of the assembly complex. Three-quarter cylinders at each corner of the prayer hall subdue the light entering the interior. And the residences for legislators are in themselves hollow columns pierced by arcs and entrance archways.

A second line of development arose simultaneously from the consulate project for Luanda.

The "ruins" that were intended to shield the walls from glare became in Kahn's subsequent schemes an integral part of the structure. Kahn himself pointed out that his solution for filtering light into the buildings at Ahmedabad (begun 1962) was far superior to that for Luanda. He set the windows of the Ahmedabad school building back away from the facade in long niches that he called "reverse bay windows"[8]—similar to the Mikveh Israel columns—so that there is no need for sunshades, blinds, polarized glass, or any other applied device. With similar intentions, the dormitory windows are sunken into hollows behind arches so as to create cool pockets of shade. At Dacca, also, Kahn incorporated the shielding elements into the structure itself by designing "anti-glare porches"[9] for the hostels, beyond which direct sunlight does not pass.

A synthesis of the two offshoots of the Luanda project—the hollow column and the "ruin"—can be found in the Suhrawardy Central Hospital at Dacca, designed in 1963. The hospital's brick arcade, which stretches across the low facade, protects the inner spaces from glare and is firmly bonded into the structure by a three-dimensional system of arches. The space created within this

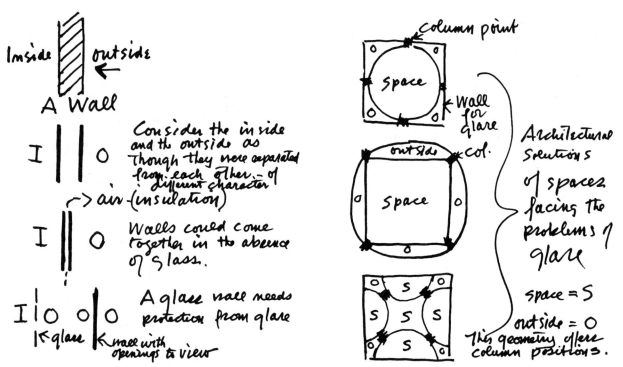

Inside | outside
←
A Wall

I ‖ O — Consider the inside and the outside as though they were separated from each other — of different character

→ air (insulation)

I ‖ O — Walls could come together in the absence of glass.

I | O O | O — A glass wall needs protection from glare

←glare ←wall with openings to view

column point

space — Wall for glare

outside — col.

space

S S S S S — Architectural solutions of spaces facing the problems of glare

space = S
outside = O
This geometry offers column positions.

Kahn's ideas for glare-shielding walls, 1960. (*Reprinted from the April 1961 issue of* **Progressive Architecture,** *copyright 1961, Reinhold Publishing.*)

Model of Salk Institute lecture halls surrounded by three-dimensional "ruins."
(*George Pohl.*)

system forms an arcade that catches the sunlight and shelters a second inner hallway from glare. The difference in the amount and quality of light that reaches the outer and inner hallways is remarkable. Like the Salk lecture halls, the hospital is essentially a building for living, surrounded by a building for the sun.[10]

As Kahn's ability to work with light grew more sophisticated, he found himself putting into words the feelings he was exploring through design. In the mid-1960s, he was involved in projects in which he paid consistent attention to light's interaction with space. He spoke of introducing a light-giving structural element into the assembly building at Dacca; at the same time, he observed how such ancient buildings as the Greek temple and such contemporary works as Le Corbusier's Ronchamp let light into the interior spaces. By 1967 Kahn had integrated his

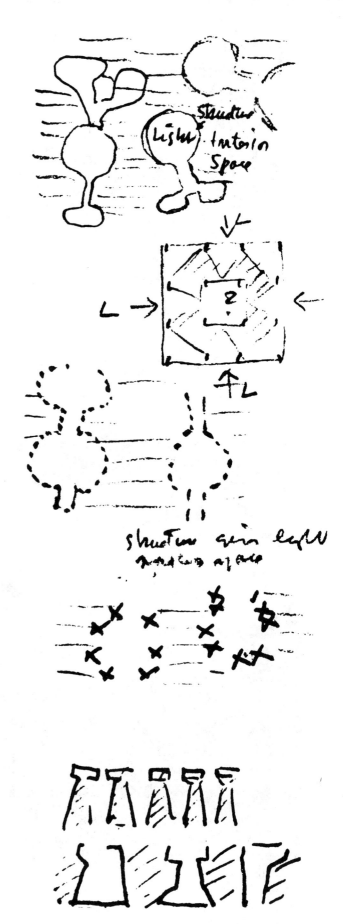

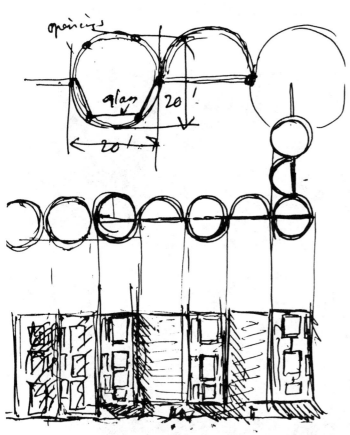

Study of hollow column in exterior walls of Mikveh Israel Synagogue, Philadelphia.

Kahn's ideas for the changing role of the column to a "giver of light," c. 1961. (*Reproduced, by permission, from Louis I. Kahn, "Remarks,"* **Perspecta 9/10: The Yale Architectural Journal,** *1965, p. 310, ill. 7.*)

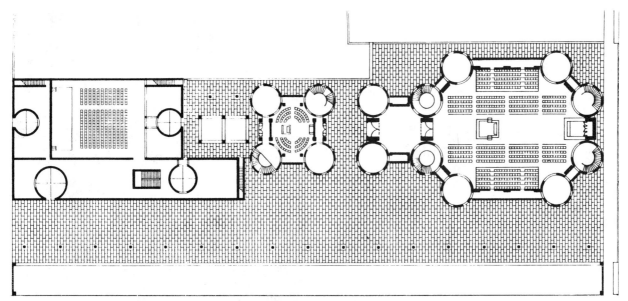

Plan for Mikveh Israel Synagogue, showing how the system of hollow columns
creates an ambulatory around central space.

Model of Mikveh Israel Synagogue. (*Copyright The Louis I. Kahn Collection,
University of Pennsylvania and the Pennsylvania Historical and Museum Commission.*)

Kahn's conception of the Mikveh Israel interior.
(*Reproduced, by permission, from Louis I. Kahn,
"Remarks,"* **Perspecta 9/10: The Yale Architectural
Journal,** *1965, p. 321, ill. 27.*)

The light that reaches the Mikveh Israel interior is
diffused within hollow columns. (*Copyright The Louis I.
Kahn Collection, University of Pennsylvania and the
Pennsylvania Historical and Museum Commission.*)

observations and experiences into words. Establishing the interdependency of light and structure, he explained that light defines the space while the space enlivens the light within it. He was attempting to describe the spiritual quality of light, something that he was already describing figuratively in such buildings as the Mikveh Israel Synagogue, the Suhrawardy Central Hospital and National Assembly at Dacca, and the Indian Institute of Management at Ahmedabad.

By the time he received the commission to design the Kimbell Museum in 1966, Kahn was purposely setting out to create spaces whose light would speak metaphysically. The Kimbell Museum, more than any other of Kahn's buildings, has spaces that evoke a sense of the magi-

cal quality of light. The structure is composed of six parallel cycloid vaults. Down the length of each vault runs a narrow slit through which direct sunlight enters the building. A reflecting device consisting of a double curve of perforated metal, installed in 10-foot lengths below the slit, spreads the natural light evenly over the sides of the vault so that it washes down the walls into the room. This device also filters out rays that would be harmful to works of art.

With the realization that colors are created by the changeable play of sunlight, Kahn designed the museum to include open-air courts, anticipating for each a special hue and intensity of light depending on such factors as dimensions, degree of enclosure or openness to the sky, and reflec-

Model of National Assembly building, Dacca, Bangladesh. The building is a cylinder divided above by a system of radial sections. (*George Pohl.*)

Interior of National Assembly building. Above is clerestory that reflects light onto the walls. (*Reproduced by permission of Henry Wilcots.*)

Plan of classroom building, Indian Institute of Management, Ahmedabad. "Reverse bay windows" are set back from the facade in long niches. (*Copyright The Louis I. Kahn Collection, University of Pennsylvania and the Pennsylvania Historical and Museum Commission.*)

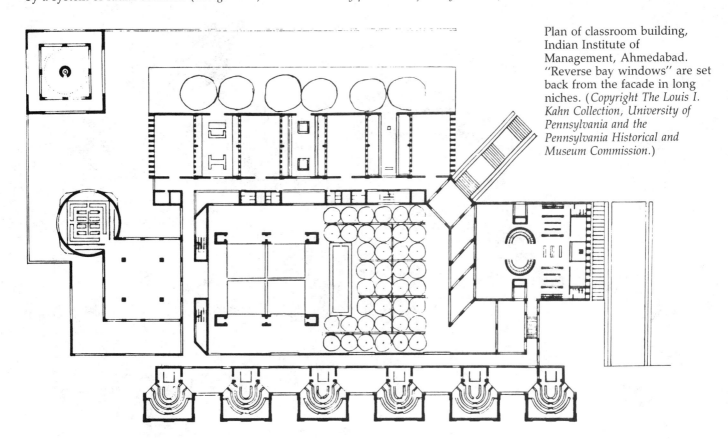

Detail of dormitory windows, Indian Institute of Management. Windows are sunken into hollows behind arches to create pockets of shade. (*Copyright The Louis I. Kahn Collection, University of Pennsylvania and the Pennsylvania Historical and Museum Commission.*)

Outpatients Department, Suhrawardy Central Hospital, Dacca. The space created within the three-dimensional system of arches forms an arcade that catches the sunlight and shelters an inner hallway from glare. (*Photograph by Anwar Hosain. Copyright The Louis I. Kahn Collection, University of Pennsylvania and the Pennsylvania Historical and Museum Commission.*)

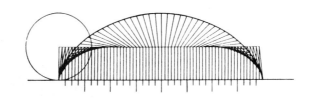

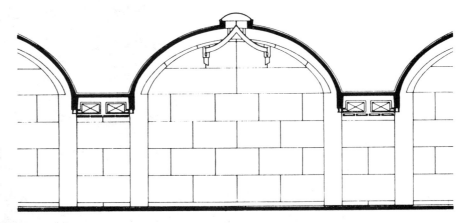

Section of vault with "natural light fixture," Kimbell Museum, Fort Worth, Texas. (*Copyright The Louis I. Kahn Collection, University of Pennsylvania and the Pennsylvania Historical and Museum Commission.*)

(*Below*) Interior of the Kimbell Museum, before and after the reflecting device was installed along vaults. (*Photographs by Marshall D. Meyers, © 1971, 1972.*)

An open-air court at the Kimbell Museum. Kahn intended each court to have its own special hue and intensity of light. (*Photograph by Alexandra Tyng.*)

View through dining area to large sculpture court, Kimbell Museum. (*Photograph by Marshall D. Meyers, © 1972.*)

tion of the sky on water, concrete, or travertine. The results are not literal translations of Kahn's intent; thus, the unpredictability of sunlight had its say in the design. Yet each court has its own atmosphere of intimacy or spaciousness, warmth or coolness. The quality of the sunlight is mellow, harsh, indirect, or reflected, creating a definite sensor of color. Kahn's exclusive use of natural light throughout the Kimbell Museum stemmed from his conviction that works of art would reveal new characteristics with every mood of light in which they are viewed. According to Kahn, the room that offered this choice of mood was expressive of the form Museum. Some would consider this a radical concept; to Kahn it was merely a rediscovery of the spirit that instigated the first museum.

Kahn's understanding and appreciation of light's mutability eventually led him to a point at which he used it as a medium of creativity like brick or concrete. He was literally creating designs in light, as was his spoken intention. When in the last years of his life he spoke of the sun's awareness of wonder as it came into contact with architecture, he had been consciously evoking a sense of wonder in his buildings for almost a decade. During the late 1960s and early 1970s, his thought and work achieved a state of tightly knit interaction. In 1967 Kahn invented the concept of silence and light, which incorporated light in its most metaphysical sense.

One year after he began thinking in terms of silence and light, Kahn began preliminary studies for the Hurva Synagogue in Jerusalem. Hurva rose out of his continued attempts to use light almost like a building material in controlling its quality and intensity. Its ground plan consists of a square within a square—an outer stone building surrounding an inner concrete structure. Sixteen pylons, four on each side, soften the sun's glare. Their interior faces are hollowed into niches, places for reflection that also function in the candle service, in itself a small-scale tribute to the divine connotations of natural light. Within the pylons, a concrete structure supports the roof, defines the inner sanctuary, and creates an ambulatory in the hollow spaces of its own construction. The form realization is reminiscent of that of the First Unitarian Church, and yet Hurva's conception is much more like the Exeter Library in that intermediate space between the inner and outer "doughnuts" is found within the structure itself. Also similar to Exeter, Hurva's external walls are intended to be made of a material that acknowledges the history of its surroundings.

But the intent to build the Hurva Synagogue with the stone from Jerusalem's West Wall is more than an historical homage. When Kahn was asked to design a new synagogue on the site of the old one that had been destroyed in 1948, he decided to let the ruins remain and build the

(*Above and p. 156*) Exterior and interior views of Hurva Synagogue model. Sixteen stone pylons shield the inner concrete structure from the sun's glare. Their interior faces are hollowed into niches. (*George Pohl.*)

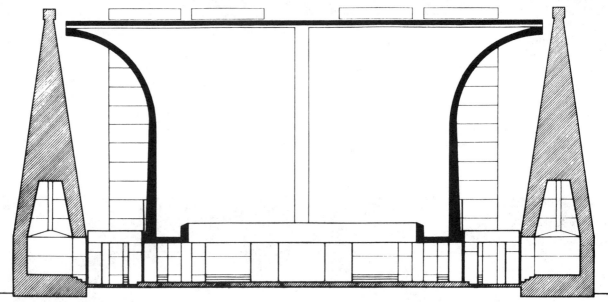

Section of Hurva Synagogue. Outer stone building is tied to inner concrete structure.

new temple beside them. Its name, Hurva, is the Hebrew word for ruin. Kahn had used the concept of the ruin in connection with light as early as 1959, when he described his design for the consulate in Luanda as surrounding a building with a ruin. In the Salk Institute lecture halls, these "ruins" are free standing. They become fused into the structure in the Suhrawardy Central Hospital at Dacca. It was not until 1964, five years after he first used the "ruin" in his archi-

tecture, that Kahn asked himself what the ruin meant in the life of a building: freedom from the servitude of performing the practical function for which it was designed, freedom to fully express its spirit or form essence. Kahn's conception of the Hurva Synagogue came out of his new consciousness of the ruin's meaning. Structurally, Hurva is a "ruin" all the way through to its core because its glare-shielding element is part of its fabric.

As a result of his experience with the Hurva Synagogue, Kahn linked the ruin with silence—the word he used to describe the eternal quality in a great work of art that is recognized by all human beings. When one sees the remains of a great building—Kahn especially liked the example of the pyramids—one feels a sense of silence, because when the building is a ruin its spirit is again free to emerge. The significance of the Hurva Synagogue is that it, more than any other building by Kahn, evokes this feeling of silence. Although it was never built, the model shows that the simple geometry of its rough textured walls has a timelessness that links the structure to the fallen fragments that surround it. By juxtaposing old and new, Kahn was saying that the significance of the ruin is not its age, but the sense of silence that it evokes.

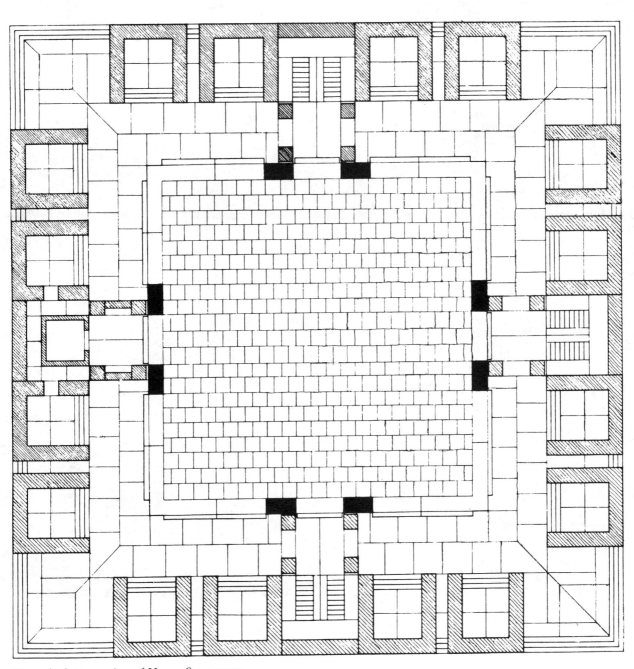

Plan of a later version of Hurva Synagogue.

Hurva synagogue site from north, Jerusalem. (*Copyright The Louis I. Kahn Collection, University of Pennsylvania and the Pennsylvania Historical and Museum Commission.*)

Hurva Synagogue site model. (*George Pohl.*)

Kahn

You will recognize that I was not satisfied with 'wing ga bird' because the 'will' was suspended when I forgot consciousness. THE most wonderful sense unreasonable and unmaterial. Also I did not like the word consciousness. It sounds like a cheap perfume. So I invented INA. Another reason is that there can be no consciousness without will but there can be no will without consciousness. So INA is pure consciousness with out will. [so far it makes no sense to me either].

The wing ga bird
will
will
a will a will
a will to fly
a will to fly
to fly
to fly
fly — fly — fly ...
so The wing ga bird.

Existence will — Is it not an element of the Psyche.?
I must insert an other element of the Psyche the 'Ina' a name I choose like to give to what I though symbolizes primordial consciousness i.

INA
The beginning of all conscious existance

INA and WILL
The beginning of form and of feeling,
The entrance of will — conscious direction

This is the beginning of the odyssey of
conscious existence.

A rose wants to be a rose.
Ina is the same for all living things
The character of will is different
This make a rose different from a man.
There is no will in rocks there is no consciousness
There is conscious existence and non conscious existence
Feeling is the book of the odyssey of the ina and will
This book is our richest inheritance It is a book with only intuition no facts.

The beginning of feeling — the experience of INA and conscious direction
The beginning of thought. The experience conscious direction.
[This may be said another way — Feeling is the record of consciousness and will experienced
during the evolution]
(must work on this part ↑)

From all this I intend to develope the idea of
Realization.
So far I sense our own feeling and our
own thought must reach out to the
Realm of Feeling and the Realm of Thought
which is as much as to say the recognition of
Thought and the recognition of Feeling,
Realization cannot come to us except
thru the introspection in the Thoughts and Feelings
of others.
Realization is the sensing of a harmony
of systems. It is the sense of Order, or one may
say that Order is the name given to a harmony
of systems.
The Scientist works from Realization
The Artist works from Realization
The scientist senses Realization to (a division) search for the elements of Form, in Nature. He is not concerned with the making of Form itself
the artist thru his realizations turns to form.

from which form may come.

non of this is properly developed

The wing of a bird
   will
   will
   a will a will
   a will to fly
a will to fly
   to fly
   to fly
    fly—fly—fly . . .
is the wing of a bird

You will recognize that I was not satisfied with "wing of a bird" because the "will" was suspended when I forgot consciousness THE most wonderful sense unmeasurable and unmaterial. Also I did not like the word consciousness. It sounds like a cheap perfume. So I invented INA. Now the reason is that there can be consciousness without will but there can be no will without consciousness. So INA is pure consciousness without will. (so far it makes no sense to me either).

Existence will—is it not an element of the Psyche?

I must insert another element of the Psyche the 'Ina' a name I should like to give to what I thought symbolizes primordial consciousness i.

INA
The beginning of all conscious existence
INA and WILL
The beginning of form and of feeling.
The entrance of will—conscious direction

This is the beginning of the odyssey of conscious existence.

A rose wants to be a rose.
Ina is the same for all living things
The character of will is different
This makes a rose different from a man.
There is no will in rock there is no consciousness
There is conscious existence and nonconscious existence
Feeling is the book of the odyssey of the ina and will

This book is our richest inheritence. It is a book with only intuition no facts.

The beginning of feeling—The experience of INA and conscious direction

The beginning of thought. The experience conscious direction.

(This may be said another way—Feeling is the record of consciousness and will experienced in our evolution.)

(must work on this part)

From all this I intend to develop the idea of *Realization.*

So far I sense our own feeling and our own thought must reach out to the Realm of Feeling and the Realm of Thought which is as much as to say the recognition of Thought with the recognition of Feeling.

Realization cannot come to us except thru its introspection in the Thoughts and Feelings of others.

Realization is the sensing of a harmony of systems. It is the sense of order, or one may say that order is the name given to a harmony of systems.

The Scientist works from Realization.

The Artist works from Realization.

The scientist leaves Realizations to search (or discover) for the elements in Nature from which form may come. He is not concerned with the making of form itself.

The artist thru his realizations turns to form.

none of this is properly developed[11] (1959)

Man makes rules which are of the laws of nature and of the spirit. Physical nature is of law. The laws of nature work in harmony with each other. Order is this harmony. Without a knowledge of the law, without a feeling for the law, nothing can be made. Nature is the maker of all things, the psyche desires things and challenges nature to make that which expresses the inexpressible, that which cannot be defined, that which has no measure, that which has no substance. . . . love, hate, nobility. Still the psyche wants to express just that and cannot without an instrument. Law is the maker of instruments. The violin . . . beautiful out of the law, how the upper and lower diaphragm of the violin lends itself to the stresses of a bow, and the vertical strip dividing the two membranes are in a sense a continuous column. Even the sound holes in the upper diaphragm are cut so that little of the continuity of the beam is lost. Laws lead to rules. A rule is subject to change, being man-made.

Nature makes its designs through the tenets of order.
Nature does not know how beautiful the sunset is.
Nature is of non-conscious existence.
Living things are of conscious existence.
Rule is conscious. Law is non-conscious.[12] (c. 1960)

A space can never reach its place in architecture without natural light. Artificial light is the light of night expressed in positioned chandeliers not to be compared with the unpredictable play of natural light. . . . The structure is a design in light. The vault, the dome, the arch, the column are structures related to the character of light. Natural light gives mood to space by the nuances of light in the time of the day and the seasons of the year as it enters and modifies the space.[13] (c. 1960)

To the musician a sheet of music is seeing from what he hears. A plan of a building should read like a harmony of spaces in light.

Even a space intended to be dark should have just enough light from some mysterious opening to tell us how dark it really is. Each space must be defined by its structure and the character of its natural light. Of course I am not speaking about minor areas which serve the major spaces. An architectural space must reveal the evidence of its making by the space itself. It cannot be a space when carved out of a greater structure meant for a greater space because the choice of a structure is synonymous with the light and which gives image to that space. Artificial light is a single tiny static moment in light and is the light of night and never can equal the nuances of mood created by the time of day and the wonder of the seasons. . . .

I am doing a building in Africa, which is very close to the equator. The glare is killing, everybody looks black against the sunlight. Light is a needed thing, but still an enemy. The relentless sun above, the siesta comes over you like thunder.

I saw many huts that the natives made.

There were no architects there.

I came back with multiple impressions of how clever was the man who solved the problems of sun, rain and wind.

I came to the realization that every window should have a free wall to face. This wall receiving the light of day would have bold opening to the sky. The glare is modified by the lighted wall and the view is not shut off. In this way the contrast made by separated patterns of glare which skylight grilles close to the window make is avoided.[14] (1960)

American Consulate, Luanda, Portuguese Angola

One doesn't feel like having the view cut away, so I thought of placing openings in the wall; the wall then becomes part of the window. When that wall got the light—even the direct sunlight—it would modify the glare. So therefore I thought of the beauty of ruins . . . the absence of frames . . . of things which nothing lives behind . . . and so I thought of wrapping ruins around buildings; you might say encasing a building in a ruin so that you look through the wall which had its apertures by accident. But, in this case you'd want to formalize these openings and I felt this would be an answer to the glare problem. I wanted to incorporate this into the architecture instead of it being a device placed next to a window. . . . I should say, desire for light, but still an active fighting of the glare.[15] (1961)

Life to me is existence with a psyche; and earh is existence without the psyche; but both are existence. I think of the psyche as being a kind of prevalence—not a single soul in each of us—but rather a prevalence from which each one of us always borrows a part. This applies to every living thing, be it a flower, be it a microbe, or be it a man or an animal. Every living thing. And I feel that this psyche is made of immeasurable aura, and that physical nature is made of that which lends itself to the measurement. I think that the psyche prevails over the entire universe. It demands an instrument of expression which it cannot hope to have in some other area of the universe. . . .

The instrument is made by nature—physical nature, a harmony of systems in which the laws do not act in an isolated way, but act in a kind of interplay which we know as order. Man isolates the law and makes every good use of it. But it must not be assumed that the law, when gotten by the tail this way, is very happy except when it is in relation to other laws where its real life actually exists.

When I hear a scientist speak in categorical terms of what he has discovered, I feel that as he grows older, he will change his categorical term into something which is not quite so sure. He discovers that the law is in a degree unchangeable, whereas rule is changeable; you check it off and say, "one down, and so many to go." It isn't quite as simple as that in my mind. Now we are made out of what nature makes of the demand of the psyche for an instrument to play the wonderful song which will never actually be finished. We must take pot-luck from nature, because nature has no consciousness whatsoever. Nature is not conscious of the sunset; nature is not conscious that the sunset is beautiful. As a matter of fact, if a painter were to faithfully duplicate the sunset, the sunset would laugh at him and say, "I'll make a better one tomorrow." But if man paints a sunset as a reaction and his product says to the young man, "I'll have a good time tonight," and to the older man, "I haven't got long to live," then nature is very jealous, because it cannot do this. Nature is unconscious, but the psyche is conscious, demands life, and gives life. Nature makes the instruments which make life possible. It will not make the instrument unless the desire for life is there.

Wonder is in us—you might say—a record of the way we were made. It is a well, which is completely full of all the things you will ever learn; because nature, in making things, records every step of its making. It is, one may call it, a seed. But it's understood much more if you realize that in wonder lies the source of all that we'll ever learn or feel. Knowledge which is derived from wonder is unhappy unless it relates itself to other knowledge. And this relation of knowledge to knowledge is what you might call, a sense of order; a sense of the position of this knowledge in relation to other things around. When we get a sense of order—not just knowledge or information—then we are very happy. We wink at wonder and say, "How am I doing, wonder?" Because wonder is activated by this knowledge and better still, by this sense of order. And wonder becomes more reachable, more full of that of which we were made.

From wonder we can also derive the position of that which is intangible; because you cannot measure love; you cannot measure hate; you cannot measure nobility; they're completely unmeasurable things. We may, though, come to points where we know the nature of man sufficiently to know there is a commonness in all of man, because man is man, all over. I don't believe that if you can think of a soul belonging to one man, it is different from another soul. I think all souls are alike, because they are first of all, unmeasurable; and secondly, they are gathered from all of earth. But what is different is the instrument. Nature, being an unconscious thing, cannot make the same instrument again, as we do in factories. Nature cannot, because the moment, at another moment in time, is a different thing entirely to nature. Nature is the interplay of these laws; any one time is not the same as any other. It's a kind of readjustment of equilibrium. When you come about, when you are born, you are not the same person as any other—you are a singularity, as an instrument, but not as a soul.

Nature is the instrument maker. Nothing can be made without nature. In fact, you might say that nature is the workshop of God. With a sense of order, and with the greatest moment in feeling—the feeling of religion in general, combined with the high moment in thought, which is philosophy—you get the area of realization; you realize something. This realization is very true somehow, but still you cannot describe it. This is a great moment for the scientist as well as the artist. . . .

In the Salk project again, I am developing walls around buildings to take care of the glare. I do not think that venetian blinds and curtains and all kinds of window devices are architectural. They are department store stuff and don't belong to architecture. The architect must find an architecture out of the glare, out of the wind, from which these shapes and dimensions are derived. And these glare walls are based on a very simple principle, which I got out of observation when I was in Africa, where the glare is very startling. There the people worked with their backs against the sun, and they got the light off walls near where they worked. Their buildings are close together, and their windows look into walls. They modify the glare, by looking at something that is in light. These walls I'm developing for the Salk Center in San Diego are in recognition of this discovery of the law of light, from which I have made a rule for myself in the design of the building.[16] (1964)

Sunday 15 Sept.

The quiet ruin reveals again the spirit out of which it once stood as a proud structure. Now it is free of its bonds

To of this spirit is a building being built now more wonderful than when it will be completed. Its spirit is young and anxious to become. It say it too is free and need not answer.

The building standing complete has its spaces locked in unbending structure. Its bonds are the duties of use. The spirit is engaged and must answer.

The quiet ruin now freed from use welcomes wild growth to play joyously around it and is like a father who delights in the little one tugging at its clothes

The ancient building still vigorous in use has the light of eternity.

The quiet ruin reveals again the spirit out of which it once stood as a proud structure. Now it is free of its bonds.

To of this spirit is a building being built now more wonderful than when it will be completed. Its spirit is young and anxious to become itself. It too is free and need not answer.

The building standing complete has its spaces locked in unbending structure. Its bonds are the duties of use. The spirit is engaged and must answer.

The quiet ruin now freed from use welcomes wild growth to play joyously around it and is like a father who delights in the little one tugging at its clothes.

The ancient building still vigorous in use has the light of eternity.[17] (1964)

And at this point it would be well to speak about the difference between the eternal and the universal. That which is universal is really just what deals with the physical. But that which is eternal is a kind of completely new essence that nonconscious nature does not understand or know about, whereas man is the conscious desire that exists in nature. And I believe that because of this dichotomy, nature will change because of the presence of man, because man is of dream, and what nature gives him as instrument is not enough. He wants much more.

Architecture is what nature cannot make. Nature cannot make anything that man makes. Man takes nature—the means of making a thing—and isolates its laws. Nature does not do this because nature works in harmony of laws, which we call order. It never works in isolation. But man works with this isolation, so whatever he makes is really quite minor, you might say, compared to what is really wanting to be expressed by the desire and the spirit of man. Man is always greater than his works. He could never, with his instrumentation, bring out that which is completely full.

Second (Legislative) Capital, Dacca, Pakistan

In the assembly I have introduced a light giving element to the interior of the plan. If you see a series of columns you can say that the choice of columns is a choice in light. The columns as solids frame the spaces of light. Now think of it just in reverse and think that the columns are hollow and much bigger and that their walls can themselves give light, then the voids are rooms, and the column is the maker of light and can take on complex shapes and be the supporter of spaces and give light to spaces. I am working to develop the element to such an extent that it becomes a poetic entity which has its own beauty outside of its place in the composition. In this way it becomes analogous to the solid column I mentioned above as the giver of light. The problem of an element in a composition appears again in the making of the anti-glare porches for the hostels. In this element it is recognized that the light be on the inside of the porch as well as the outside. If you have light (not necessarily sunlight) on the interior, the contrast between the darkness of the solids and the brightness of the openings is not great and, therefore, you do not feel the glare. The staggering of porches as the building rises offers the chance to get light into the porch, but a sliver of light is needed to give the presence of light to the interior. The sun is unwelcome. So far I have only half solved the problem. I am stating it, but I have not solved it. The various explorations I have made of possible openings, some reminiscent of the past, are not really concrete forms although I think some of them are much more so than others.

Mikveh Israel Synagogue, Philadelphia

The spaces are enclosed by window rooms 20 feet in diameter connected by walled passages. These window room elements have glazed openings on one exterior side and larger unglazed arched openings facing the interior. These rooms of light surrounding the synagogue chamber serve as an ambulatory and are the high places for women. These window rooms prevail in the composition of the entrance chamber and the chapel across the way. In the community building, light is given to the interior by exterior roofless rooms born out of the same idea which, incidentally, gave rise to the plans at Dacca.

The windows on the outside do not support the building; what supports the building, as you can see on the plan, are the spaces between the windows. The windows could never be a support because of their shape. I chose to support the roof between the windows where a clear definition can be made between a column, a beam and a wall. A column means a beam; a wall says a multitude of beams or a slab. They're different things.

In the model, the open spaces which make the window rooms independent of the structure are made too wide; but they are important to give light to the round shapes. The light from the exterior captured in the interior room of the window is seen from the synagogue chamber as free of glare. The whole idea comes from realizing that contrast of walls in darkness against openings in light renders interior shapes illegible and turns the eyes away.

soul. But I feel that if all living plants and creatures were to disappear, the sun would still shine and the rain still fall. We need Nature, but Nature doesn't need us. . . .

I feel fusion of the senses. To hear a sound is to see its space. Space has tonality, and I imagine myself composing a space lofty, vaulted, or under a dome, attributing it to a sound character alternating with the tones of a space, narrow and high, with graduating silver, light to darkness. The spaces of architecture in their light make me want to compose a kind of music, imagining a truth from the sense of a fusion of the disciplines and their orders. No space, architecturally, is a space unless it has natural light. Natural light has varied mood of the time of the day and the season of the year. A room in architecture, a space in architecture, needs that life-giving light—light from which we were made. So the silver light and the gold light and the green light and the yellow light are qualities of changeable scale or rule. This quality must inspire music.

I am designing an art museum in Texas. Here I felt that the light in the rooms structured in concrete will have the luminosity of silver. I know that rooms for the paintings and objects that fade should only most modestly be given natural light. The scheme of enclosure of the museum is a succession of cycloid vaults each of a single span 150' long and 20' wide, each forming the rooms with a narrow slit to the sky, with a mirrored glass shaped to spread natural light on the side of the vault. This light will give a glow of silver to the room without touching the objects directly, yet give the comforting feeling of knowing the time of day. Added to the sky light from the slit over the exhibit rooms, I cut across the vaults, at a right angle, a counterpoint of courts, open to the sky, of calculated dimensions and character, marking them Green Court, Yellow Court, Blue Court, named for the kind of light that I anticipate their proportions, their foliation, or their sky reflections on surfaces, or on water will give.

A student of mine came to my room, which is, by the way, everybody's room, and asked me a question: "How would you describe this area?" I was terribly interested. Reflecting, I said to him, "What is the shadow of white light?" Repeating and reflecting on what I said, "White light white light, the shadow of white light" (he whispered), I don't know." I answered, "It's black. But really there is no such thing as white light, black shadow. I was brought up, of course, when light was 'yellow' and shadow was 'blue'. White light is a way of saying that even the sun is on trial, and certainly all our institutions are on trial."

I feel that in the present revolt against our institutions and ways, that there is no Wonder. Without Wonder the revolt looks only to equality. Wonder motivates Desire toward Need. Demands for equality of means can rise only to the trade of old lamps for new without the genii. I feel when Wonder is, the light will become a brighter yellow and the shadow a brighter blue.[20] (1967)

Architecture has no presence. A work is an offering to the Sanctuary.

The paths of living reveal nature Man evoking in the singular the powers of anticipation renewing the desire to be to express.

A work is made in the urging sounds of industry and when the dust settles the pyramid echoing silence gives the sun its shadow.

1. In his house, a great window looks out to a garden that has the feeling of a fragment of natural landscape captured out of context by a high wall which itself is completely covered with green. Only a narrow clearing laid with recento, a rhinoceros-hide-looking stone, adjoining this window is paved. No paths, no flowers, just wild wind-blown grass. In the clearing is a very large bowl carved out of the same dark hard stone filled to over-flowing with water. A source tipped with a rotted splinter of wood breaks the flow of water, and each drop falls like a silver tear spreading rings of silver over the sides of the great bowl extending their wetness to the paved place. The black stone is the alchemist.

Out of the Odyssey in nature of the stream from the tiniest mountain sources, through the varied grooves of its path in light and shade, he selected the darkest place of its dance on the rocks to sense silver of water in a dark bowl and brought it home to contribute to the sense of silence which, as even in the song, prevails in all his house.

2. Later in the day we all gathered. Barragan asked me, "What is tradition?" I answered, "My mind goes to the Globe Theater in London. Shakespeare's 'Much Ado' was being performed. As the first actor attempted a movement, he collapsed in a heap of dust and bones under his costume. This befell all actors and onlookers in succession. I realize that the course of happening can never return. The circumstances of their making is but a vehicle. Man's way through life and what he makes in his quest for expression reveals his nature, which falls as a golden dust eternal. Those who feel their desires through this dust gain the powers of anticipation, which is the inheritance of tradition."

3. I asked Barragan to come to La Jolla and help me in the choice of the planting for the garden to the Studies of the Salk Laboratory. When he entered the space he went to the concrete walls and touched them and expressed his love for them, and then said as he looked across the space and towards the sea, "I would not put a tree or blade of grass in this space. This should be a plaza of stone, not a garden." I looked at Dr. Salk and he at me and we both felt this was deeply right. Feeling our approval, he added joyously, "If you make this a plaza, you will gain a facade—a facade to the sky."

4. Once we had breakfast in Mexico City. We talked about a commission he was just offered to design a religious place in the heart of a large city in Texas. He explained how happy it made him to be offered such a trust, but also how let down he was when he saw the site surrounded by uninspired buildings. "I cannot," said he, "find a beginning. I am afraid that I must refuse." I reminded him of Independence Square which gained its significance from all structures around by simply being four feet

above the level of the street and then asked, "If you were able to tear down the buildings on one side, revealing to the religious place a mountain range in the distance, would their silence inspire in you a beginning?"[21] (1968)

To me, when I see a plan I must see the plan as though it were a symphony, of the realm of spaces in the construction and light. I sort of care less, you see, for the moment whether it works or not. Just so I know that the principles are respected which somehow are eternal about the plan. As soon as I see a plan which tries to sell me spaces without light, I simply reject it with such ease because I know that it is wrong. And so, false prophets, like schools that have no natural light, are definitely un-architectural. Those are what I like to call—belong to the marketplace of architecture but not to architecture itself.

So I must put on the board something which I thought of only recently which could be a key to my point of view in regard to all works of art including architecture.

And so, I put this on the board: Silence and Light. Silence is not very, very quiet. It is something which you may say is lightless; darkless. These are all invented words. Darkless—there is no such a word. But why not? Lightless; Darkless. Desire to be; to express. Some can say this is the ambient soul—if you go back beyond and think of something in which light and silence were together, and maybe are still together, and separated only for the convenience of argument.

I turn to light, the giver of all Presences; by will; by law. You can say the light, the giver of all presences, is the maker of a material, and the material was made to cast a shadow, and the shadow belongs to the light.

I did not say things yet made here, desire being that quality, that force, unmeasurable force, everything here stems from the unmeasurable. Everything here promises the measurable. Is there a threshold where they meet? Can a threshold be thin enough to be called a threshold in the light of these forces; these phenomena? Everything you make is already too thick. I would even think that a thought is also too thick. But one can say, light to silence, silence to light, has to be a kind of ambient threshold and when this is realized, sensed, there is Inspiration.

Inspiration must already have something of a promise of being able to express that which is only a desire to express, because the evidence of the material making of light gives already a feeling of inspiration. In this inspiration, beside inspiration, there is a place, the Sanctuary of Art, Art being the language of man before French, you know, or German. It says the language of man is art. It stems from something which grows out of the needing, of the desire to be, to express, and the evidence of the promise of the material to do it. The means somehow are there. The Sanctuary of art—sort of the ambience of a man's expressiveness—has an outlet, you might say. It is my belief that we live to express. The whole motivation of presence is to express. And what nature gives us is the instrument of expression which we all know as ourselves, which is like giving the instrument upon which the song of the soul can be played. The sanctuary of art . . . is the treasury of the shadows.

I'm sure there is no such separation. I'm sure that everything began at the same time. . . . And I would say the desire to be, to express, exists in the flowers, in the tree, in the microbe, in the crocodile, in man. Only we don't know how to fathom the consciousness of a rose. Maybe the consciousness of a tree is its feeling of its bending before the wind. I don't know. But I have definite trust that everything that's living has a consciousness of some kind, be it as primitive. I only wish that the first really worthwhile discovery of science would be that it recognizes that the unmeasurable, you see, is what they're really fighting to understand, and the measurable is only a servant of the unmeasurable; that everything that man makes must be fundamentally unmeasurable.

. . . . A man motivated not by profit of any kind—just a sense of offering—he writes a book, hoping that it will be published. He's trying to—he's motivated by the sense that he has somewhere in there, whether it is deep, deep in the silence, or whether it is already on the threshold of inspiration. He must be there to write it, and what he draws from here, and what he draws from there, somehow, he motivates his writing a book. And he gets it also from another, beautiful source, and that is through the experience or the Odyssey of a life that goes through the circumstances of living and what falls as important are not the dates or what happened, but in what way he discovered man through the circumstance. It's a golden dust that falls which, if you can put your fingers through, you have the powers of anticipation. The artist feels this when he makes something. He knows that he does it now, but he knows also that it has eternal value. He's not taking circumstances as it happens. He's extracting circumstances from whatever fell which revealed man to him. Tradition is just mounds of these circumstances, you see, the record of which also is a golden dust from which you can extract the nature of man, which is tremendously important if you can anticipate in your work that which will last—that which has the sense of commonness about it. And by commonness, I mean really, the essence of silence is commonness. That's the essence of it. When you see the pyramids now, what you feel is silence. As though the original inspiration of it may have been whatever it is, but the motivation that started that which made the pyramids, is nothing but simply remarkable. To have thought of this shape personifying a kind of perfection, the shape of which is not in nature at all, and striving with all this effort, beating people, slaves, to the point of death to make this thing. We see it now with all the circumstances gone, and we see that when the dust is cleared, we see really silence again. So it is with a great work. I see a Giotto painting also with a feeling of silence—as though it came from here, you see—as though it didn't come from any sense of the marketplace. Like, I will make a painting that's worth so much money, you see, or anything of that nature. It came from there.

. . . . I cannot speak enough about light because light is so important, because, actually structure is the maker of light. When you decide on the structure, you're deciding on light. In the old buildings, the columns were an expression of light, no light, light, no light, light, no light, light, you see. The module is also light–no light. The vault stems from it. The dome stems from it, and the same realization that you are releasing light.[22] (1969)

The structure of the room must be evident in the room itself. Structure, I believe, is the giver of light. A square room asks for its own light to read the square. It would expect the light either from above or from its four sides as windows or entrances.

Sensitive is the Pantheon. This nondirectional room dedicated to all religions has its light only from the oculus above, placed to invest the room with inspired ritual without favoritism. The entrance door is its only impurity. So powerful was this realization of appropriate space that even now the room seems to ask for its release to its original freedom.

Of the elements of a room, the window is the most marvelous. The great American poet Wallace Stevens prodded the architect, asking, "What slice of the sun does your building have?" To paraphrase: What slice of the sun enters your room? What range of mood does the light offer from morning to night, from day to day, from season to season and all through the years?

Gratifying and unpredictable are the permissions that the architect has given to the chosen opening on which patches of sunlight play on the jamb and sill and that enter, move and disappear.

Stevens seemed to tell us that the sun was not aware of its wonder until it struck the side of a building. . . .

A word about silence and light. A building being built is not yet in servitude. It is so anxious to be that no grass can grow under its feet, so high is the spirit of wanting to be. When it is in service and finished, the building wants to say, "Look, I want to tell you about the way I was made." Nobody listens. Everybody is busy going from room to room.

But when the building is a ruin and free of servitude, the spirit emerges telling of the marvel that a building was made.

When we think of great buildings of the past that had no precedent, we always refer to the Parthenon. We say that it is a building that grew out of the wall with opening. We can say that in the Parthenon light is the space between the columns—a rhythm of light, no-light, light, no-light which tells the tremendous story of light in architecture that came from the opening in a wall.

We are simply extending what happened long ago; the beginning may be considered the most marvelous: without precedent, yet its making was as sure as life.

Light is material life. The mountains, the streams, the atmosphere are spent light.

Material, nonconscious, moving to desire; desire to express, conscious, moving to light meet at an aura threshold where the will senses the possible. The first feeling was of beauty, the first sense was of harmony, of man undefinable, unmeasurable and measurable material, the maker of all things.

At the threshold, the crossing of silence and light, lies the sanctuary of art, the only language of man. It is the treasury of the shadows. Whatever is made of light casts a shadow. Our work is of shadow; it belongs to light.[23] (1971)

Kimbell Museum of Art, Fort Worth, Texas

By the nature of the vault-like structure, you have the play of lofty rooms with a space between each vault which has a ceiling at the level of the spring of the vault. The lower space does not have natural light, but gets it from the larger chamber. In the loftier rooms, how the room is made is manifest; the dimension of its light from above is manifest without partitions, because the vaults defy division. Even when partitioned, the room remains a room. You might say that the nature of a room is that it always has the character of completeness.

Indian Institute of Management, Ahmedabad, India

Shade. Closeness. Buildings hugging buildings. It's all a recognition of the seeking after shade. So the system is fundamentally that of porches. The exterior is given to the sun, and the interior is where you live and work and study. The avoidance of devices like brises-soliel brought about the deep porch which has in it the cool shadow.

Hurva Synagogue, Jerusalem, Israel

I sensed the light of a candle plays an important part in Judaism. The pylons belong to the candle service and have niches facing the chamber. I felt this was an extension of the source of religion as well as an extension of the practice of Judaism.

Exeter Library, Exeter, New Hampshire

Exeter began with the periphery, where light is. I felt the reading room would be where a person is alone near a window, and I felt that would be a private carrel, a kind of discovered place in the folds of construction. I made the outer depth of the building like a brick doughnut, independent of the books. I made the inner depth of the building like a concrete doughnut, where the books are stored away from the light. The center area is a result of these two contiguous doughnuts; it's just the entrance where books are visible all around you through the big circular openings. So you feel the building has the invitation of books.[24] (1971)

The will to be to learn, to be to express is expressed by silence. By silence I don't mean quiet—but in the sense that Malraux calls his book "Silence"—I think it's *The Halls of Silence*—he means only the feeling you get when you pass the pyramids, you feel that they want to tell you. . . . Not *how* they were made, but what made them *be*, which means what was the force that caused them to be made. . . . These are the voices of silence. . . .

And I believe that all material is spent light. I say, "Light to Silence, Silence to Light." It is the desire to express, meeting the means to express. . . .

At this point of meeting (which to everyone is a different threshold—to some, silence is so great, and it can go a great distance before it meets the means to express, and to some it goes a short distance to find the means to express, so in each form there is a different kind, which I don't explain anywhere)—and this is the inspirations, at the point where . . . the threshold where the urges to express meet the possible. . . .

Here's the Fort Worth Museum, and here's a natural light fixture—all the light here is natural. It's a lighting fixture which takes the light from the garden and spreads it over the entire museum—no unnatural light. . . . And the whole thing is done with this lunette—the light source is here, the light fixture is here, which spreads the light over these cycloids, and the injurious rays are filtered at this point. So the amount of light you get inside is no more injurious to whatever is there than electric light is. . . .

So this is a kind of invention that comes out of the desire to have natural light. Because it is the light the *painter* used to paint his painting. And artificial light is a static light—you see?—where natural light is a light of mood. And sometimes the room gets dark—why not?—and sometimes you must get close to look at it, and come another day, you see, to see it in another mood—a different time, you see, to see the mood natural light gives, or the seasons of the year, which have other moods.

And the painting must reveal itself in different aspects if the moods of light are included in its viewing, in its *seeing*. This is another example of what one sets in his mind as being a *nature* of something. I think that's the nature, really, of a place where you see paintings. And research would *never* have given it to me, because all I could find was ways of doing it completely contrary to the ways I think a museum might be. So it must be derived out of your own sense of its nature, of its service, of the *nature* of a school, of the *rooms* of a school, or the rooms of a museum.[25] (1972)

The travel from the desire to express to the means to express, which is in all nature, varies in each individual. The scientist would hold back his sense of desire and allow nature to come to it. By holding it back, he holds back the movement of what may be any poetic thought to avoid that which may make what he is searching for have too much singularity, or better still, too much of the undefinable or unmeasurable limits because he is looking for the measurable. And he looks for every means to get the measurable pure of what may be his other senses, and that is of desire itself.

When the poet marches toward the means and marches for a long, long time, hoping the means is never necessary—but he finds the means is necessary because he has to print things—he has to say something; you can't just leave out all words, which is his real intention. And so nature is held back, that is, the maker, the means; and he is able to send forth that which has the greatest power of transcendence in his poetry.

Everyone has this balance of the measurable and unmeasurable in him; but a man like Einstein would be one like the poet who resists knowledge because he knows that if he were to talk about what he knows, he knows that it is only a miniscule part of what is yet to be known. Therefore, he does not trust knowledge but looks for that which can be order itself. He travels like the poet, the great distance, resisting knowledge; and then when he does get a smidgen of knowledge, already he reconstructs the universe. . . .

When I speak about silence and light or the desire to express and the means, I say that all material is spent light. Light that has become exhausted. Creation makes me think of two brothers who were really not two brothers. One had the desire to be, to express; the other had the desire to be something that becomes tangible, something which makes the instrument upon which the spirit of man can express itself. If the will to be is to become something of the predominance or the prevalence of the luminous, then the luminous will turn into a wild dance of flame, spending itself into material. And this material, this little lump, this crumpled lump, made the mountains, the streams, the atmosphere—and ourselves.

We come from spent light.

I see a drawing of the section around Siena by Leonardo da Vinci. Doesn't it look like a crumpled kind of thing which looks like spent light? He's such a marvelous artist. I'm sure he didn't think of this particular theory, but in him I'm positive that he had a sense of wonder enough to make such a drawing. I'm sure it's an inaccurate map; but one that's better than a map. He tells you somehow that this is the product of light. . . .

Isn't it a miracle that a man, with no examples around him, can make such a thing manifest as a column which grows out of the wall and makes its own window by the rhythm of the lightless, light, lightless, light?

In drawing, it's the same thing. You can say that drawing is made by the stroke of a pen where the light is not.

Look at a drawing.

Look at the sources of light.

How it marches with the light, and then disappears where the light cannot reach, into places where it goes into reverse because the direction of light is lost.

The stroke of the pen is where the light is not.[26] (c. 1973)

I love beginnings. I marvel at beginnings. I think it is beginning that confirms continuation. If it did not—nothing could be or would be. I revere learning because it is a fundamental inspiration. It isn't just something which has to do with duty; it is born into us. The will to learn, the desire to learn, is one of the greatest inspirations. I am not that impressed by education. Learning, yes; education is something which is always on trial because no system can ever capture the real meaning of learning.

In my own search for beginnings a thought has recurred—generated by many influences—out of the realization that material is spent light. I likened the emergence of light to a manifestation of two brothers, knowing quite well that there are no two brothers, not even One. But I saw that one is the embodiment of the desire *to be/to express*; and one (not saying "the other") is *to be/to be*. The latter is non-luminous; and "One" (prevailing) is luminous, and this prevailing luminous source can be visualized as becoming a wild dance of flame which settles and spends itself into material. Material, I believe, is spent light. The mountains, the earth, the streams, the air, and we ourselves are spent light. This is the center of our desires. The desire *to be/to express* is the real motivation for living. I believe there is no other.

I began by putting up a diagram calling the desire *to be/to express* silence; the other, light. And the movement of silence to light, light to silence, has many thresholds; many, many thresholds; and each threshold is actually a singularity. Each one of us has a threshold at which the meeting of light and silence lodges. And this threshold, this point of meeting, is the position (or the aura) of inspirations. Inspiration is where the desire *to be/to express* meets the possible. It is the maker of presences. Here also is the sanctuary of art, the center of the expressive urges and the means to expression.

When I first made this diagram, I made it to read from left to right; and here it is in mirror-writing (to mystify and evoke an even greater source than itself) and so as to put nothing in front of you that is really thoroughly readable; by this means you can strive to find something that even goes beyond this realization. Again, I am always looking for a source, a beginning. I know it's in my character to want to discover beginnings. I like English history, I have volumes of it, but I never read anything but the first volume, and even at that, only the first three or four chapters. And of course my only real purpose is to read Volume 0 (zero), you see, which has yet not been written. And it's a strange kind of mind that causes one to look for this kind of thing.[27] (1973)

The Pyramids seem to want to tell
us of its motivations and its meeting
with Nature in order to be

I sense   Silence as the aura of the 'desire to be to express'
           Light as the aura 'to be to be'
           Material as 'Spent Light'
(The mountains the streams the atmosphere
and we are of spent light.)

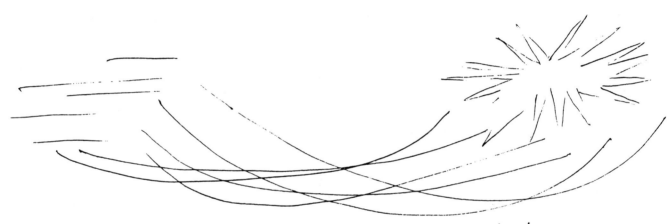

Silence to Light
Light to Silence
     The Threshold of their crossing
        is the Singularity
        is Inspiration
(where the desire to express meets the possible)
        is the Sanctuary of Art
        is the Treasury of the Shadows
(Material casts shadows shadows belongs to light —)

I wanted to illustrate Silence and Light.
Silence I felt —— this way about.

Light? — how could I do better than
accept the white area of the paper itself?
Looking at an illustration of the Waverly Tales
by Cruickshank I noticed his lines followed
the direction of the source of light. I realized that
the stroke of the pen was where the light was not.

This was the clue to the illusion
My remark that structure is the giver of light
is here by recalled. The column in the Greek Temple
is where the light is not.

Louis Kahn June 15'73 [28]

EPILOGUE

There are poets in all professions, and they each seek beginnings in their own ways. The physicist looks outward toward the mysteries of deep space, while the psychologist and the philosopher delve inward beyond the temporal regions of conscious thought. But whether the search takes a person outside himself or within his own mind, it is the same search. Because the very atoms that make up all living things are part of the same "cosmic dust" that was formed at the origin of the universe, it is natural that the symbolic language of the innermost mind is actually the genetic memory of events that occurred as space–time was created from a greater spaceless, timeless realm. Kahn intuitively sensed that these inner and outer eternities were really one eternity. Perhaps because of his shunning of systematic knowledge, he freed himself to make connections that the scientist can only begin to make after years of rigorous adherence to fact.

If eternity is within and around man, then the human body is an insignificant bit of material between these infinities. Kahn believed that a person is born out of a common soul, and after a brief existence as a conscious individual, he will return again to the realm from which he emerged. In the same way, a building begins as a form archetype and goes through the limiting process of becoming tangible, only to regain more and more of its original timeless quality as it falls into ruin. Kahn saw the human brain as a mere instrument through which the eternal spirit is sensed, and thus architecture was merely his chosen vehicle for expressing what was basically inexpressible. But to Kahn, architecture was an important, perhaps essential, vehicle. Through the several decades of his career, his philosophy became less confined to the context of his profession, and yet he produced his most brilliant work when his thought was most transcendent. Although Louis Kahn was often frustrated by the limitations of words, paper, and building materials, he was also fascinated and challenged by them. In his words, "Man is always greater than his works," but "to live and make nothing is intolerable."

Architecture

silence and light

~~the reflection~~ → material (spent light)

16 The ~~beauty~~ beauty

THE ETERNITY   THE ETERNITY   NARDALAN
OF THE SPIRIT   OF THE UNIVERB   FULLER
THE WILL (THE WISH) — DEMANDS ~~SCIENCE~~   invisible
expressed in the silent   reality
voices of an great work   manifest ~~in~~ the feelings
reflecting the beauty   of beauty in the material
of soul.   presence.

ART. (UNMEASURABLE   (MEASURABLE REALITY)
       REALITY

DESIRE   NEED   ← HIDDEN POTENTIALS →

TROTH (the reality of   Form
        the existing)   elements   state
a sense of the nature man   design.   hall
The golden dust.   the orders
                                             building.
                                         the orders the
        How we were made.   City
        the records of light

All architecture serves the way of life   Dacca
even a house architecturally is not strictly
personal. It must be so good in the expression
of its nature as to be transferable to the next families
        TO-DAY
The school   The University   libraries   bazaar
   the architecture of connection   courts   +
                                     gardens   America
                                     plaza.
NEW INSTITUTIONS OF THE CITY   place of happening   grosnoros of
~~THE GREAT INSTITUTIONS OF THE CITY~~ (city Hall)   shopping
CENTER OF AUDITORIA   POLITICAL - TALENTS   Center
THE CENTER OF WELL BEING   TO HONOR THE BODY
THE UNIVERSITY.   ~~TO HONOR THE MIND~~   Mellon
THE CENTER OF LEARNING FREE OF THE MARKET PLACE   Center
        U. —   THE FORUM. — MARKET PLACE
                  PLANNING
        Schools of Talents.
                Knowledge —
laboratories
factory   ~~Theatre~~ Auditorium Theatre.
school   The VIOLIN.

the making of a room   the assembly of rooms

good to learn life

toward Civilization
(Toward a way of life)

nomadic people   the way of life
settlement
village   privacity, of
Town   living
City

THE CITY is like a goal
in aspiration to
make your into unfulfilled
the natural talents of a
CITY —
MAN

O of water
light
wind
spaces (sound)
structure (acting)
constructions
Civil

Baltimore   my impressions

the modern plan
VILLAGE

Library

THE STREET (the first agreement)
THE AGREEMENT
a national center of the
institutions of man (WAY OF LIFE)
living
learning
working and Talent
health   ← religion
recreation

TOWN. — reflects the national
agreement of . . . . .

the school
the mosque
the clinic
water - sanitation

what should it be now in the light of
toward civilization.
The house parties and varied living places   near a River
The national places   sea a
what the nation gives   a mountains
to the village.   a climatic phenomena
                       path.
                       the water
                       the sanitation
                       the school
                       the clinic.

Tradition — (Technology)
                 (the golden dust.)
a sense of validity
in the nature man worth   orientation to new
expressions of Truth.   (as against old habits
                      or out moded methods
                      or expressions).

NOTES AND CREDITS

CHAPTER 1

1. There is some controversy over the year of Kahn's birth. His birth certificate says 1901, but Kahn claimed he was actually born in 1902.
2. According to Esther I. Kahn, Leopold was a craftsman in the art of reverse painting on glass. However, Kahn himself and other family members recall that Leopold was said to have worked in stained glass. It is possible that he may have been skilled in both crafts.
3. The Mendelssohn connection has not been proven genealogically.
4. This description of Kahn's maternal grandmother is extracted from the memories of Harriet Pattison and Rosella Sherman. Esther I. Kahn believes this information is not correct.
5. Reprinted by permission from "A Statement by Louis I. Kahn; A Paper Delivered at the International Design Conference, Aspen, Colorado," *Arts & Architecture*, May 1964, p. 19.
6. Reprinted by permission of Westview Press from *Louis I. Kahn: Complete Works 1935–1974*, edited by Heinz Ronner, Sharad Jhaveri, and Alessandro Vasella. Copyright © 1977 by The Swiss Federal Institute of Technology, Zurich Institute for the History and Theory of Architecture.
7. Reyner Banham, *Theory and Design in the First Machine Age* (New York: Reinhold, 1960), p. 14.
8. Conversation with Norman N. Rice, September 17, 1981.
9. Paul Cret, "Modern Architecture," in *The Significance of the Fine Arts*, ed., The Committee on Education of the American Institute of Architects, (Boston: Marshall Jones, 1923), pp. 183–242.
10. Conversation with Norman N. Rice, September 17, 1981.
11. Vincent Scully, Jr., *Louis I. Kahn* (New York: Braziller, 1962), p. 13.
12. "Letter from Paris," *The Builder*, August 3, 1901, p. 98.
13. *The Random House Dictionary of the English Language; The Unabridged Edition*, s.v. "functionalism."
14. Scully implies in his 1962 edition of *Louis I. Kahn* that Kahn read Le Corbusier's writings in 1928. In reality, he did not do so until 1947–1950.
15. Reprinted, by permission, from Louis I. Kahn, "Remarks," *Perspecta 9/10: The Yale Architectural Journal*, 1965, p. 331.
16. Reprinted from Talbot Hamlin, *Forms and Functions of Twentieth Century Architecture* (New York: Columbia University Press, 1952), vol. 6, pp. 7–8.
17. Reprinted by permission of Westview Press from *Louis I. Kahn: Complete Works 1935–1974*, edited by Heinz Ronner, Sharad Jhaveri, and Allessandro Vasella. Copyright © 1977 by The Swiss Federal Institute of Technology, Zurich Institute for the History and Theory of Architecture.
18. Kahn first used this word in the late 1950s to mean something that could not be measured. At that time, it was not listed in the dictionary.
19. *AIA Journal*, (c) American Institute of Architects.
20. Reprinted from Talbot Hamlin, *Forms and Functions of Twentieth Century Architecture* (New York: Columbia University Press, 1952), vol. 6, p. 5.
21. Reprinted, by permission, from Louis I. Kahn, Letter to Anne G. Tyng, June 6, 1954, and June 13, 1954, p. 4.
22. Reprinted, by permission, from Louis I. Kahn, Letter to Anne G. Tyng, April 25, 1954, p. 4.
23. Reprinted, by permission, from Louis I. Kahn, Letter to Anne G. Tyng, July 21, 1954.
24. J. M. Dixon, "Another Kind of Castle," *Architectural Forum*, November 1965, p. 60.
25. Conversation with Esther I. Kahn, February 15, 1982.
26. Excerpted with permission from an interview with Patricia McLaughlin that appeared in the December, 1972, issue of *The Pennsylvania Gazette*, alumni magazine of the University of Pennsylvania. Copyright (c) 1972 by *The Pennsylvania Gazette*.
27. This observation was corroborated by Denise Scott Brown, in a conversation on January 2, 1975.
28. *The Architectural Review*, London, December 1955.
29. *The Architectural Review*, London, December 1955. Italics are the author's.
30. Reprinted, by permission, from Richard Saul Wurman and Eugene

Feldman, eds., *The Notebooks and Drawings of Louis I. Kahn*, (Philadelphia: Falcon Press, 1962).
31. Excerpted with permission from an interview with Patricia McLaughlin that appeared in the December, 1972, issue of *The Pennsylvania Gazette*, alumni magazine of the University of Pennsylvania. Copyright (c) 1972 by *The Pennsylvania Gazette*.

CHAPTER 2

1. Louis I. Kahn, Letter to Anne G. Tyng, December 18, 1953, p. 4.
2. Kahn, Letter to Tyng, December 18, 1953, pp. 1–3.
3. Louis I. Kahn, "Order and Form," *Perspecta* 3 (1955): 59.
4. Kahn, "Order and Form," p. 59.
5. Compare Kahn's poem on order in *Perspecta* 3 with his definitions of form and design in his lecture "Structure and Form," the Voice of America *Forum Lectures*, in *Louis I. Kahn*, Vincent Scully, Jr. (New York: Braziller, 1962), p. 115.
6. For a discussion of archetypes, see Carl Gustav Jung, *The Collected Works of C. G. Jung*, trans. R. F. C. Hull, 2nd ed. (Princeton: Princeton University Press, 1971), vol. 9, pt. 1.
7. Kahn, "Order and Form," pp. 45–47.
8. Conversation with Anne G. Tyng, February 21, 1975.
9. Alluded to in Kahn's letter to Richard Saul Wurman and Eugene Feldman, June 15, 1973, in Richard Saul Wurman and Eugene Feldman, eds., *The Notebooks and Drawings of Louis I. Kahn*, 2nd ed. (Cambridge, Mass.: M.I.T. Press, 1973).
10. Louis I. Kahn, "Structure and Form," in *Louis I. Kahn*, Scully, pp. 119–120.
11. Reprinted from Louis I. Kahn, "Monumentality," in *New Architecture and City Planning*, ed. P. Zucker (New York: F. Hubner, 1944), pp. 577–578.
12. Reprinted, by permission, from Louis I. Kahn, "Toward a Plan for Midtown Philadelphia," *Perspecta 2: The Yale Architectural Journal*, 1953, pp. 23, 26.
13. Reprinted, by permission, from Louis I. Kahn, Letter to Anne G. Tyng, December 18, 1953, pp. 1–4.
14. Reprinted, by permission, from Louis I. Kahn, Letter to Anne G. Tyng, April 25, 1954, p. 5.
15. Reprinted, by permission, from Louis I. Kahn, "Order and Form," *Perspecta 3: The Yale Architectural Journal*, 1955, p. 59.
16. Reprinted from Walter McQuade, "Architect Louis Kahn and His Strong-Boned Structures," *Architectural Forum*, October 1957, pp. 139, 142.
17. Reprinted, by permission, from Richard Saul Wurman and Eugene Feldman, eds., *The Notebooks and Drawings of Louis I. Kahn* (Philadelphia: Falcon Press, 1962).
18. Reprinted, by permission, from Richard Saul Wurman and Eugene Feldman, eds., *The Notebooks and Drawings of Louis I. Kahn* (Philadelphia: Falcon Press, 1962).
19. Reprinted, by permission, from Richard Saul Wurman and Eugene Feldman, eds., *The Notebooks and Drawings of Louis I. Kahn* (Philadelphia: Falcon Press, 1962).
20. *AIA Journal*, (c) American Institute of Architects.
21. Permission granted by George Braziller, Inc., *Louis I. Kahn*, by Vincent Scully, (c) 1962; originally appeared in the Voice of America *Forum Lectures*, a series on Modern American Architecture in 1960.
22. Reprinted, by permission, from "A Statement by Louis I. Kahn," *Arts & Architecture*, May 1964, pp. 19, 33.
23. Reprinted, by permission, from Louis I. Kahn, "Remarks," *Perspecta 9/10: The Yale Architectural Journal*, 1965, pp. 332–333.
24. *L'Architecture d'Aujourd'hui*.
25. Reprinted by permission of Westview Press from *Louis I. Kahn: Complete Works 1935–1974*, edited by Heinz Ronner, Sharad Jhaveri, and Allessandro Vasella. Copyright (c) by The Swiss Federal Institute of Technology, Zurich Institute for the History and Theory of Architecture.
26. Reprinted, by permission, from "Louis Kahn Silence and Light," *A + U Journal*, January 1973, p. 27.
27. Excerpted with permission from an interview with Patricia McLaughlin that appeared in the December, 1972, issue of *The Pennsylvania Gazette*, alumni magazine of the University of Pennsylvania. Copyright (c) 1972 by *The Pennsylvania Gazette*.

CHAPTER 3

1. Louis I. Kahn, "Toward a Plan for Midtown Philadelphia," *Perspecta* 2 (1953): 11.
2. Kahn, "Toward a Plan"; also in, "Order in Architecture," *Perspecta* 4 (1957): 61; and in "Louis Kahn and the Living City," *Architectural Forum*, March 1958, p. 108.
3. Kahn, "Toward a Plan," p. 11.
4. Kahn, "Order in Architecture," pp. 61–62.
5. Louis I. Kahn, "Structure and Form," Voice of America *Forum Lectures*, in *Louis I. Kahn*, Vincent Scully, Jr. (New York: Braziller, 1962), p. 116.
6. Louis I. Kahn, "The Room, the Street and Human Agreement," *AIA Journal*, September 1971, pp. 33–34.
7. Kahn, "The Room, the Street;" also in Richard Saul Wurman and Eugene Feldman, eds., *The Notebooks and Drawings of Louis I. Kahn* (Philadelphia: Falcon Press, 1962).
8. Wurman and Feldman, eds., *Notebooks and Drawings*; also in Louis I. Kahn, "Silence and Light—Louis Kahn at ETH," in *Louis I. Kahn Complete Works 1935–74*, ed. Heinz Ronner et al. (Boulder, Col.: Westview Press, 1977), p. 449.
9. Louis I. Kahn, "Remarks," *Perspecta* 9/10 (1965): 306.
10. Kahn, "Remarks," pp. 306–307.
11. Conversation with David Wisdom, November 12, 1981.
12. Kahn, "The Room, the Street," p. 33.
13. Reprinted from Louis I. Kahn and Oskar Stonorov, "Why City Planning Is Your Responsibility," *Revere's Part in Better Living*, 1943, pp. 6–7.
14. Reprinted, by permission, from Louis I. Kahn, "Toward a Plan for Midtown Philadelphia," *Perspecta 2: The Yale Architectural Journal*, 1953, pp. 11–18.
15. Reprinted, by permission, from Louis I. Kahn, "Order in Architecture," *Perspecta 4: The Yale Architectural Journal*, 1957, pp. 61–62.
16. Reprinted from "Louis Kahn and the Living City," *Architectural Forum*, March 1958, p. 118.
17. Reprinted, by permission, from Richard Saul Wurman and Eugene Feldman, eds., *The Notebooks and Drawings of Louis I. Kahn* (Philadelphia: Falcon Press, 1962).
18. Reprinted, by permission, from Richard Saul Wurman and Eugene Feldman, eds., *The Notebooks and Drawings of Louis I. Kahn* (Philadelphia: Falcon Press, 1962).
19. Permission granted by George Braziller, Inc., *Louis I. Kahn*, by Vincent Scully, (c) 1962; originally appeared in the Voice of America *Forum Lectures*, a series on Modern American Architecture in 1960.
20. *AIA Journal*, (c) American Institute of Architects.
21. This article first appeared in *Canadian Art*, January/February 1962.
22. Reprinted, by permission, from "A Statement by Louis I. Kahn; A Paper Delivered at the International Design Conference, Aspen, Colorado," *Arts & Architecture*, May 1964, p. 19.
23. Reprinted, by permission, from Louis I. Kahn, "Remarks," *Perspecta 9/10: The Yale Architectural Journal*, 1965, pp. 304, 306–307, 310, 322, 327.
24. Reprinted from "Louis Kahn: Statements on Architecture," *Zodiac* 17(1967): 55–57. Minimal editing by author.
25. Reprinted by permission of Westview Press from *Louis I. Kahn: Complete Works 1935–1974*, edited by Heinz Ronner, Sharad Jhaveri, and Allessandro Vasella. Copyright (c)

by The Swiss Federal Institute of Technology, Zurich Institute for the History and Theory of Architecture.

26. *AIA Journal*, (c) American Institute of Architects.

27. Reprinted courtesy Philadelphia Museum of Art.

CHAPTER 4

1. For a thorough discussion of the collective unconscious, see Carl Gustav Jung, *The Collected Works of C. G. Jung*, trans. R. F. C. Hull, (Princeton: Princeton University Press, 1971), vol. 9, pt. 1.

2. According to Harriet Pattison.

3. Louis I. Kahn, "Structure and Form," the Voice of America *Forum Lectures*, in *Louis I. Kahn*, Vincent Scully, Jr. (New York: Braziller, 1962), p. 118.

4. Louis I. Kahn, "Space and the Inspirations," *L'Architecture d'Aujourd'hui* 142 (February/March 1969): 13.

5. J. C. Cooper, *An Illustrated Encyclopaedia of Traditional Symbols* (London: Thames and Hudson, 1978), p. 197.

6. For a more complete explanation of the animus and anima archetypes, see Jung, *Collected Works*; and Emma Jung, *Animus and Anima* (New York: The Analytical Psychology Club, 1957).

7. Louis I. Kahn, "Architecture and Human Agreement," in *The Art of Design Management*, 2nd ed. (New York: Tiffany, 1975), pp. 22–23; and Kahn, "I Love Beginnings," in *Louis I. Kahn*, (Tokyo: A + U Publishing, 1975), pp. 279–286.

8. Louis I. Kahn, "Remarks," *Perspecta* 9/10 (1965): 324.

9. Kahn, "Remarks," p. 311.

10. J. Bailey, "Louis Kahn in India: An Old Order at a New Scale," *Architectural Forum*, July 1966, p. 46. Kahn used similar words to describe this system in relation to Ahmedabad.

11. Reproduced, by permission, from Louis I. Kahn, Letter to Harriet Pattison, December 29, 1959.

12. Reprinted, by permission, from Richard Saul Wurman and Eugene Feldman, eds., *The Notebooks and Drawings of Louis I. Kahn* (Philadelphia: Falcon Press, 1962).

13. Reprinted, by permission, from Richard Saul Wurman and Eugene Feldman, eds., *The Notebooks and Drawings of Louis I. Kahn* (Philadelphia: Falcon Press, 1962).

14. Permission granted by George Braziller, Inc., *Louis I. Kahn*, by Vincent Scully, (c) 1962; originally appeared in the Voice of America *Forum Lectures*, a series on Modern American Architecture in 1960.

15. Reprinted, by permission, from "Louis Kahn," *Perspecta 7: The Yale Architectural Journal*, 1961, p. 9.

16. Reprinted, by permission, from "A Statement by Louis I. Kahn; A Paper Delivered at the International Design Conference, Aspen, Colorado," *Arts & Architecture*, May 1964, pp. 18–19, 33.

17. Reproduced, by permission, from Louis I. Kahn, Letter to Harriet Pattison, September 15, 1964.

18. Reprinted, by permission, from Louis I. Kahn, "Remarks," *Perspecta 9/10: The Yale Architectural Journal*, 1965, pp. 305, 311, 320, 324, 330–331.

19. Reprinted from "Louis Kahn: Statements on Architecture," *Zodiac* 17 (1967): 57. Minimal editing by author.

20. *L'Architecture d'Aujourd'hui.*

21. Graduate School of Fine Arts, University of Pennsylvania.

22. Reprinted by permission of Westview Press from *Louis I. Kahn: Complete Works 1935–1974*, edited by Heinz Ronner, Sharad Jhaveri, and Allessandro Vasella, Copyright (c) 1977 by The Swiss Federal Institute of Technology, Zurich Institute for the History and Theory of Architecture.

23. *AIA Journal*, (c) American Institute of Architects.

24. Reprinted from "The Mind of Louis Kahn," *Architectural Forum*, July/August 1972, pp. 59, 66, 69, 77.

25. Excerpted with permission from an interview with Patricia McLaughlin that appeared in the December, 1972, issue of *The Pennsylvania Gazette*, alumni magazine of the University of Pennsylvania. Copyright (c) 1972 by *The Pennsylvania Gazette*.

26. Tiffany & Co.

27. Reprinted, by permission, from Louis I. Kahn, "I Love Beginnings," in *Louis I. Kahn* (Tokyo: A + U Publishing, 1975), pp. 279–286.

28. Richard Saul Wurman and Eugene Feldman, eds., *The Notebooks and Drawings of Louis I. Kahn*, 2nd ed., The M.I.T. Press, 1973.

BIBLIOGRAPHY

PRIMARY SOURCES

Unpublished Material

Kahn, Louis I. Letters to Harriet Pattison. 1959, 1964.

——. Letters to Anne G. Tyng. 1953–1954.

——. Personal notebooks. c. 1955–1973.

Published Versions of Kahn's Speeches and Writings

"Clearing: Interviews with Louis I. Kahn." *Via* 2 (1973): 158–161.

Deichler, J. deB. "Louis Kahn from Silence and Light." *Yarrowstalks*, April/May 1973, pp. 7–9.

"'How'm I Doing, Corbusier?' An Interview With Louis Kahn." *Pennsylvania Gazette*, December 1972, pp. 18–26.

Kahn, Louis I. "Architecture and Human Agreement." In *The Art of Design Management*, pp. 17–30. 2nd ed. New York: Tiffany, 1975.

——. "Design with the Automobile: The Animal World." *Canadian Art*, January/February 1962, pp. 50–51.

——. "I Love Beginnings." In *Louis I. Kahn*, pp. 279–286. Tokyo: A + U Publishing, 1975.

——. Letter to Fleischer Art Memorial. *Bulletin*, Philadelphia Museum of Art, Spring 1974, pp. 56–57.

——. Letter to Richard Saul Wurman and Eugene Feldman. In *The Notebooks and Drawings of Louis I. Kahn*, edited by Richard Saul Wurman and Eugene Feldman. 2nd ed. Cambridge, Mass.: The M.I.T. Press, 1973.

——. "Monumentality." In *New Architecture and City Planning*, edited by Paul Zucker, pp. 577–578. New York: F. Hubner, 1944.

——. "Order in Architecture." *Perspecta* 4 (1957); 61–62.

——. "Poetics." *Journal of Architectural Education*, February 1974, p. 10.

——. "Remarks." *Perspecta* 9/10 (1965): 304–305.

——. "The Room, the Street and Human Agreement." *AIA Journal*, September 1971, pp. 33–34.

——. "Silence." *Via* 1 (1968): 88–89.

——. "Silence and Light—Louis Kahn at ETH." In *Louis I. Kahn Complete Works 1935–74*, edited by Heinz Ronner et al., pp. 447–449. Boulder, Col.: Westview Press, 1977.

——. "Space and the Inspirations." *L'Architecture d'Aujourd'hui*, February/March 1969, pp. 13–16.

——. "Structure and Form." The Voice of America Forum Lectures, a series on Modern American Architecture in 1960. In *Louis I. Kahn*, Vincent Scully, Jr., pp. 114–121. New York: Braziller, 1962.

——. "Toward a Plan for Midtown Philadelphia." *Perspecta* 2 (1953): 10–27.

Kahn, Louis I., and Stonorov, Oskar. "Why City Planning is Your Responsibility." *Revere's Part in Better Living*, 1943, pp. 3–14.

"Louis Kahn." *Perspecta* 7 (1961): 9–28.

"Louis Kahn and the Living City." *Architectural Forum*, March 1958, pp. 114–119.

"Louis Kahn Silence and Light." *A + U Journal*, January 1973, entire issue.

"Louis Kahn: Statements on Architecture, From a Talk Given at the Politecnico di Milano in January, 1967." *Zodiac* 17 (1967): 55–57.

"Marin City Redevelopment." *Progressive Architecture*, November 1960, pp. 149–153.

"The Mind of Louis Kahn." *Architectural Forum*, July/August 1972, pp. 47–85.

"Not for the Faint-Hearted." *AIA Journal*, June 1971, pp. 25–31.

"On Philosophical Horizons." *AIA Journal*, June 1960, pp. 99–100.

"Order and Form." *Perspecta* 3 (1955): 59.

Philadelphia City Planning Commission. *Mill Creek Redevelopment Area Plan*. Philadelphia, 1954.

"A Statement by Louis I. Kahn." *Arts & Architecture*, February 1961, p. 14.

"A Statement by Louis I. Kahn; A Paper Delivered at the International Design Conference, Aspen, Colorado." *Arts & Architecture*, May 1964, pp. 18–19, 33.

Wurman, Richard Saul, and Feldman, Eugene, eds. *The Notebooks and Drawings of Louis I. Kahn*. Philadelphia: Falcon Press, 1962.

SECONDARY SOURCES

Conversations

Kahn, Alan. Several during 1980–1982.

Kahn, Esther I. February 15, 1982; May 8, 1982.

Kahn, Nathaniel. Several during 1981–1982.

Kahn, Sue Ann. Several during 1975–1982.

Kantor, Rhoda. Several during 1980–1982.

Meyers, Marshall D. November 12, 1981.

Pattison, Harriet. Several during 1981–1982.

Rice, Norman N. September 17, 1981.

Sherman, Rosella. Several during 1981–1982.

Tyng, Anne G. Several during 1974–1982.

Venturi, Robert, and Brown, Denise Scott. Jaunary 2, 1975.

Wisdom, David. November 12, 1981.

Articles

"An Appreciation of Louis Kahn." *DVMI Newsletter*, February 1975, p. 1.

"Architects in the News: Elder Named at B. C.; Kahn, Stone, Saarinen Honored." *Architectural Record*, May 1962, p. 58.

"Architecture Fitting and Befitting." *Architectural Forum*, June 1961, p. 88.

"Art Serves Science." *Architectural Record*, August 1960, pp. 149–156.

Bailey, J. "Louis Kahn in India; an Old Order at a New Scale." *Architectural Forum*, July 1966, pp. 39–47.

Banham, Reyner. "The New Brutalism." *Architectural Review*, December 1955, pp. 335–361.

Bottero, Maria. "Louis Kahn e l'Incontro fra Morfologica Organica e Razionale." *Zodiac* 17 (1967): 47–53.

———. "Opera Recenti di Louis Kahn." *Comunita*, June 1967, pp. 30–43.

———. "Viaggio in India: Da Le Corbusier a Kahn." *Zodiac* 16 (1966): 120–135.

"Building with Spent Light." *Time*, January 15, 1973, pp. 60–65.

"Carver Court." *Architectural Forum*, December 1944, pp. 114–119.

"Conference Center for Venice." *Architectural Record*, March 1969, p. 40.

"Criticism by William H. Jordy." *Architectural Review*, June 1974, pp. 330–335.

"Developmental Drawings." *Architectural Review*, February 1965, pp. 147–148.

Dixon, J. M. "Another Kind of Castle." *Architectural Forum*, November 1965, pp. 58–65.

Fitch, J. M. "A Building of Rugged Fundamentals." *Architectural Forum*, July 1960, p. 82.

Giurgola, Romaldo. "Louis I. Kahn, 1901–1974." *Progressive Architecture*, May 1974, pp. 4–5.

Hitchcock, Henry-Russell. "Notes of a Traveller: Wright and Kahn." *Zodiac* 6 (1960): 14–21.

"House in Melrose Park, Penn." *Architectural Forum*, August 1945, pp. 132–134.

"Indian Kahn." *Architectural Review*, November 1966, pp. 315–316.

"INTERAMA Explosion Hailed as 'Full-Scale Experiment in Urban Design'." *Architectural Record*, March 1967, pp. 40–41.

Jordy, William H. "Medical Research Building for Pennsylvania University, Philadelphia." *Architectural Review*, February 1961, pp. 98–106.

———. "The Span of Kahn." *Architectural Review*, June 1974, pp. 119–120.

"Kahn Enshrined." *Architectural Forum*, June 1966, p. 30.

"Kahn Honored." *AIA Journal*, July 1962, p. 20.

"Kahn in Venice." *Architectural Review*, April 1969, p. 304.

"Kahn: Kimbell." *Architectural Review*, June 1974, pp. 321–329.

"Kahn Newspaper Shop." *Architectural Forum*, April 1962, pp. 82–85.

"Kahn: Phillips Exeter." *Architectural Review*, June 1974, pp. 336–342.

"Kahn's Medical Science Building Dedicated at U of P: Exciting Structure Makes Use of Precast Concrete." *Progressive Architecture*, June 1960, p. 61.

"The Kimbell Art Museum." *Architectural Record*, November 1972, p. 43.

Komendant, August. "Komendant on Concrete." *Progressive Architecture*, October 1966, pp. 208–214.

"Labs Slab." *Architectural Review*, March 1968, pp. 173–174.

Le Ricolais, Robert. "Introduction to the Notion of Form." Unpublished paper. Philadelphia: University of Pennsylvania, n. d.

"Letter From Paris." *The Builder*, August 3, 1901, p. 98.

"Logic and Art in Precast Concrete." *Architectural Record*, September 1959, pp. 232–238.

"Louis I. Kahn Honored by Danish Architects." *Architectural Record*. December 1965, p. 36.

"Louis I. Kahn Oeuvres 1963–1969." *L'Architecture d'Aujourd'hui*, February/March 1969, pp. 1–100.

"Louis Kahn and the Living City." *Architectural Forum*, March 1958, pp. 114–119.

"Louis Kahn Doctor Mirabilis." *Perspecta* 7 (1961): 73–76.

"Louis Kahn Honored." *Architectural Record*, May 1960, p. 25.

"Louis Kahn to Receive RIBA Gold Medal." *Progressive Architecture*, April 1972, p. 35.

McQuade, Walter. "Architect Louis Kahn and His Strong-Boned Structures." *Architectural Forum*, October 1957, pp. 134–143.

"Medical Research Buildings—Louis Kahn." *Arts & Architecture*, July 1961, p. 14.

"Mellon Art Center at Yale." *Interiors*, April 1972, p. 30.

"Mental Hospital." *Architectural Forum*, September 1951, pp. 198–200.

"The Mind of Louis Kahn." *Architectural Forum*, July/August 1972, pp. 42–91.

"Modern Space Framed with Traditional Artistry." *Architectural Forum*, September 1950, pp. 100–105.

Monk, J. "The First Unitarian Church, Rochester, N.Y.: by Louis I. Kahn, 1900–." *RIBA Journal*, July 1964, pp. 315–316.

"More Than Just a Volume." *Architectural Forum*, April 1971, pp. 20–25.

"On the Responsibility of the Architect." *Perspecta* 2 (1953): 45–47.

"Order and Form." *Perspecta* 3 (1955): 46–58.

"Palace of Congress for Venice." *Progressive Architecture*, April 1969, pp. 42–43.

"The Paul Mellon Center for British Art." *Architectural Record*, July 1972, p. 41.

"Romaldo Giurgola on Louis Kahn." *Zodiac* 17 (1967): 119.

Rowan, Jan C. "Wanting to Be: The Philadelphia School." *Progressive Architecture*, April 1961, pp. 130–149.

Scully, Vincent, Jr. "Form, Design, and the Human City." *Show*, May 1965, pp. 22–27.

———. "Light, Form, and Power; New Work of Louis Kahn." *Architectural Forum*, August/September 1964, pp. 162–170.

"Shapes of Tomorrow." *Interiors*, July 1961, p. 41.

"3 Projects," *Architectural Review*, May 1971, pp. 318–319.

"Visionary Architecture and a One-Man Show at Museum of Modern Art." *Progressive Architecture*, July 1961, p. 48.

Winter, John. "Louis Kahn." *RIBA Journal*, February 1972, pp. 61–62.

"Within the Folds of Construction." *Architectural Forum*, October 1973, pp. 26–35.

Books

Banham, Reyner. *The New Brutalism: Ethic or Aesthetic?* New York: Reinhold, 1966.

———. *Theory and Design in the First Machine Age.* New York: Praeger, 1960.

Cooper, J. C. *An Illustrated Encyclopaedia of Traditional Symbols.* London: Thames and Hudson, 1978.

Cret, Paul. "Modern Architecture." In *The Significance of the Fine Arts*, edited by the Committee on Education of the American Institute of Architects, pp. 183–242. Boston: Marshall Jones, 1923.

Cruden, Stewart. *The Scottish Castle.* Edinburgh: Thomas Nelson, 1960.

French, A. P., ed. *Einstein: A Centennary Volume.* Cambridge, Mass.: Harvard University Press, 1979.

Giedion, Sigfried. *Space, Time, and Architecture: The Growth of a New Tradition.* 5th ed. Cambridge, Mass.: Harvard University Press, 1967.

———. *Walter Gropius: Work and Teamwork.* New York: Reinhold, 1954.

Gropius, Walter. *The New Architecture and the Bauhaus.* Translated by P. Morton Shand. London: Faber and Faber, 1935.

Hamlin, Talbot. *Forms and Functions of Twentieth Century Architecture.* Vol. 6. New York: Columbia University Press, 1952.

Harbeson, John F. *The Study of Architectural Design.* New York: Pencil Points Press, 1927.

Hitchcock, Henry-Russell. *Architecture: Nineteenth and Twentieth Centuries.* The Pelican History of Art Series, edited by Nikolaus Pevsner. Baltimore: Penguin Books, 1971.

Johnson, Philip, and Hitchcock, Henry-Russell. "The International Style." In *Roots of Contemporary American Architecture*, edited by Lewis Mumford, pp. 382–395. New York: Dover Publications, 1972.

Jordy, William H. *The Impact of European Modernism on the Mid-Twentieth Century.* American Buildings and Their Architects, vol. 4. New York: Doubleday, 1972.

———. *Progressive and Academic Ideals at the Turn of the Twentieth Century.* American Buildings and Their Architects, vol. 3. New York: Doubleday, 1972.

Jung, Carl Gustav. *The Collected Works of C. G. Jung.* Vol. 9, pt. 1. 2nd ed. Translated by R. F. C. Hull. Princeton: Princeton University Press, 1971.

———. *The Collected Works of C. G. Jung*, Vol. 6. Translated by H. G. Baynes. Princeton: Princeton University Press, 1971.

Jung, Emma. *Animus and Anima.* New York: The Analytical Psychology Club, 1957.

Le Corbusier. *Towards a New Architecture.* Translated from the 13th French ed. by Frederick Etchells. New York: Doubleday, 1953.

Neumann, Erich. *Art and the Creative Unconscious.* Translated by Ralph Manheim. New York: Pantheon Books, 1959.

Pevsner, Nikolaus. *Pioneers of Modern Design.* Revised ed. Baltimore: Penguin Books, 1960.

Reid, George William. *A Descriptive Catalogue of the Works of George Cruikshank.* Vol. 3. London: Bell and Daldy, 1871.

Scully, Vincent, Jr. *Louis I. Kahn.* New York: George Braziller, 1962.

INDEX